Law, Society, Policy

Series Editor: **Rosie Harding**,
University of Birmingham

Law, Society, Policy offers an outlet for high-quality, socio-legal research monographs and edited collections with the potential for policy impact.

Also available in the series:

Vulnerability Theory and the Trinity Lectures
by **Martha Albertson Fineman**

Future Directions in Surrogacy Law
by **Kirsty Horsey**, **Zaina Mahmoud** and **Katherine Wade**

Adult Social Care Law and Policy
by **Jean McHale** and **Laura Noszlopy**

Mental Capacity Law, Sexual Relationships, and Intimacy
edited by **Beverley Clough** and **Laura Pritchard-Jones**

Children's Voices, Family Disputes and Child-Inclusive Mediation
by **Anne Barlow** and **Jan Ewing**

Observing Justice
by **Judith Townend** and **Lucy Welsh**

Egalitarian Digital Privacy
by **Tsachi Keren-Paz**

Fragile Rights
by **Anne Revillard**

Polygamy, Policy and Postcolonialism in English Marriage Law
by **Zainab Naqvi**

Intersex Embodiment
by **Fae Garland** and **Mitchell Travis**

Unsettling Apologies
edited by **Melanie Judge** and **Dee Smythe**

Death, Family and the Law
by **Edward Kirton-Darling**

Find out more at:

bristoluniversitypress.co.uk/
law-society-policy

Law, Society, Policy

Series Editor: **Rosie Harding**,
University of Birmingham

Find out more at:

bristoluniversitypress.co.uk/
law-society-policy

QUEERING UK REFUGEE LAW

Sexual Diversity and Asylum Administration

Alex Powell

BRISTOL
UNIVERSITY
PRESS

First published in Great Britain in 2026 by

Bristol University Press
University of Bristol
1–9 Old Park Hill
Bristol
BS2 8BB
UK
t: +44 (0)117 374 6645
e: bup-info@bristol.ac.uk

Details of international sales and distribution partners are available at bristoluniversitypress.co.uk

DOI: 10.51952/9781529242591

British Library Cataloguing in Publication Data
A catalogue record for this book is available from the British Library

ISBN 978-1-5292-4257-7 hardcover
ISBN 978-1-5292-4258-4 ePub
ISBN 978-1-5292-4259-1 ePdf

Cover design: Andrew Corbett
Front cover image: iStock/Mario De Moya
Bristol University Press uses environmentally responsible print partners.
Printed and bound in Great Britain by CPI Group (UK) Ltd, Croydon, CR0 4YY

Bristol University Press' authorised representative in the European Union is:
Easy Access System Europe, Mustamäe tee 50, 10621 Tallinn, Estonia,
Email: gpsr.requests@easproject.com

FSC
www.fsc.org
MIX
Paper | Supporting responsible forestry
FSC® C013604

To the thousands of lives lost in the seas of normative ideology. In the hope that a better world may be possible.

Contents

Series Editor's Preface

The Law, Society, Policy series publishes high-quality, socio-legal research monographs and edited collections with the potential for policy impact.

Cutting across the traditional divides of legal scholarship, Law, Society, Policy offers an interdisciplinary, policy-engaged approach to socio-legal research which explores law in its social and political contexts with a particular focus on the place of law in everyday life.

The series seeks to take an explicitly society-first view of socio-legal studies, with a focus on the ways that law shapes social life, and the constitutive nature of law and society. International in scope, engaging with domestic, international and global legal and regulatory frameworks, texts in the Law, Society, Policy series engage with the full range of socio-legal topics and themes.

Acknowledgements

This book is the product of seven years of research, many sleepless nights and far too many missed social obligations. Thanks are due to many people for their support, inspiration and influence on my own thinking. Particular thanks are due to Dr Nora Honkala, without whom I would not be an academic. From indulging my undergraduate interests and lending me books, to encouraging me to submit a PhD application and believing in me. Your kindness and the respect for others which you place so centrally in all that you do have had a lasting impact on me and I hope you can see them echoed in these pages. I also owe heartfelt thanks to Dr Tawhida Ahmed, Dr Griejtje Baars, Dr Mazen Mazri and Dr Mara Malagodi for their support, encouragement and just generally being the most amazing doctoral supervision team anyone could hope for.

Thanks are also due to the City Law School and Oxford Brookes University, both of whom have provided funding, support and intellectual homes without which this work could not have been completed. I only hope that the current state of higher education will not mean that the next generation of scholars is shut out from the kind of institutional fostering from which I, at times feeling like I have arrived at the party at five minutes to midnight, have benefited.

I am enormously grateful to the legal representatives and third sector staff who gave up their time to speak to me and share their experiences, despite the busy and high pressured environments in which they work. Though your names are not included here, to protect confidentiality, you know who you are.

Thank you also to Grace Carroll, Helen Davis, Professor Rosie Harding and everyone at Bristol University Press for your patience, encouragement and support. Sorry for the number of extension requests!

Finally, thank you to Max Morris, my intellectual companion, partner and best friend. It feels particularly on brand that we ended up submitting our book manuscripts in the same week. Thank you for inspiring me, challenging me and just generally putting up with my nonsense. So many of the ideas and arguments in this book have arisen from our conversations, arguments and mutual doom-scrolling at the world in which we have found ourselves.

1

Introduction

From France to Germany and the United States, nationalist and nativist forces have increasingly colonized the political mainstream. In Germany, the Alternative for Germany secured 20.8 per cent of the vote in the February 2025 elections, becoming the second largest party in the Bundestag on a platform that explicitly endorses a policy it calls 'remigration', effectively the large-scale removal of foreign-born people from Germany (Parker, 2025). In France, the National Rally, an openly far-right party, secured 33.2 per cent of the first-round votes in the 2024 election, securing 142 seats in the French Parliament on a platform which included the ending of family reunification rights and an end to birthright citizenship for the children of non-French nationals (Kirby, 2024). While in the United States, one of Donald Trump's first acts following his re-election as president was to attempt to introduce executive orders to similarly end birthright citizenship,[1] an action which has subsequently been followed up by the deportation of American citizens and refusals to comply with judicial orders in matters relating to migration and asylum.[2]

As this shows, within a diverse range of countries within the conceptual grouping often referred to as 'the west',[3] migration and seeking asylum has become a highly salient political issue – often sitting alongside a backlash against LGBTIQA+ rights in general and trans rights in particular – forming a part of a broader conservative and nationalist renaissance, often associated to the alt-right movement (Winter, 2019), which has catapulted political parties and figures commonly regarded as far right into the political mainstream

1 Executive Order, Protecting the Meaning and Value of American Citizenship (20 January 2025).

2 *Kristi Noem, Secretary Department of Homeland Security, Et Al v Kilmar Armando Abrego Garcia, Et Al* 604 USC (10 April 2025).

3 Note should be taken here that this is not a geographical concept, but rather a political concept that ties together a disparate range of characteristics with the most salient perhaps being associations with whiteness.

(Brown et al, 2021). It is commonly argued that in the UK the first-past-the-post electoral system functions to stop extreme parties from being able to access power.[4] However, as I have argued elsewhere, the UK has also departed from several fundamental norms underlying the international refugee protection framework in the years since 2020 (Powell, 2024b). Even following the change of government in July 2024, several actions of the new UK government, such as the decision to change the good character requirement associated with citizenship in order to exclude refugees from access to recognition as citizens or the use of filmed deportations, can be seen as an example of this broader nationalist trend continuing under the leadership of a purportedly social-democratic government (Ali, 2025). On a similar footing, one of the early acts of the new Labour government was to make permanent a ban on the prescription of puberty blockers to under 18s, save for those on a restrictive trial.[5] This, again, speaks to how the ideas of the new political right have come to govern UK politics even if the parties have not yet done so. Put in simple terms, extreme parties may not have succeeded in the same electoral terms as in other nations, but extreme politics has been given a place within the political mainstream through the transformation of 'mainstream' political parties.

On 26 September 2023, Suella Braverman, then Secretary of State for the Home Department, gave a striking example of how this shift has impacted UK politics in a speech in Washington, DC. In that speech, she asserted that 'illegal migrants' were claiming to be LGBTIQA+ in order to subvert the UK immigration system. She argued that the UK 'will not be able to sustain an asylum system if in effect, simply being gay, or a woman, and fearful of discrimination in your country of origin is sufficient to qualify for protection'.[6] Putting aside, for now at least, the legal inaccuracy of her statement, it would be easy to dismiss this as just another push of a culture war button within the broader political context. A quick nod to reassert her position on the right of the British political mainstream and posit her as one of the few people who would *do something* to address 'illegal migration'. However, we should not be either so quick, nor so ready, to dismiss her claims. There is a need to recognize the salience of these remarks as a part of

4 The idea of first-past-the-post as a moderating force has attracted the status of a truism within the context of arguments around its continuation.

5 The Medicines (Gonadotrophin-Releasing Hormone Analogues) (Restrictions on Private Sales and Supplies) Order 2024.

6 Suella Braverman, Keynote Address by UK Home Secretary Suella Braverman, 'UK-US security priorities for the 21st century' (American Enterprise Institute, 26 September 2023), transcript available at: https://www.aei.org/wp-content/uploads/2023/09/230926-Keynote-Address-by-UK-Home-Secretary-Suella-Braverman-Transcript.pdf?x91208 (accessed 9 February 2024).

two interconnected moral panics around both the rights of asylum seekers and people who do not fit into normative conceptions of gender and sexuality (Cohen, 2011). These two phenomena form a part of a wider parcel of socio-cultural narratives which have commonly been called a 'culture war' (Anthony, 2021).

These moral panics are directed at those who do not fit into traditional conceptions of British society, those who undermine or otherwise challenge the fantasy of British identity produced through nationalist cultural and political structures. Indeed, as Rubin has argued, moral panics of sexuality and gender often arise at moments where hegemony is being established or challenged, offering new arrangements of morality that become building blocks of new normative agendas, of the kind you might find within a shift in political rationales (Rubin, 2006). It is my argument that the current political dynamics we are seeing across the examples explored here are a prime example of this kind of new hegemony being established.

Often, the forms of persecution faced by sexually diverse people take mundane, everyday and fundamentally normative shapes. For example, Dean Spade has argued that some of the most salient issues that trans people face relate to bureaucratic tasks like matching the gender markers on identification to the way that one's gender is socially perceived (2015). The use of mundane is not to say that this is not hugely individually salient, but rather that the persecution experienced by sexual and gender diverse people is not experienced by society more broadly as a crisis. As such, these forms of persecution and victimization do not easily correspond to the emerging logics of forced migration in the UK across the years 2022–2024 (Powell, 2024b). The marginalization of those who are sexually diverse fits as a part of long-standing practices of 'othering' that seek to contrast an imagined, highly racialized (and restrictively sexed) conceptualization of a people with some kind of external threat. Namely, migrants and those whose performances of diversity do not conform to the narrow space of assimilationist conformity within which sexual difference is permitted (see Adler, 2018). As argued across this book, both groups, LGBTIQA+ people and migrants, are subjected to a kind of performative cruelty perpetuated in order to consolidate the idea of the in-group as requiring protection from the dangerous other.

The processes of othering associated with the construction of those outside of a tightly policed conceptualization of the normal is far from new. Constructions of race, nation, sex (both in terms of the act and the biological assignation) have always been fundamental to establishing nationalisms and 'in-groups' to which politicians can appeal (Clarke, 2024). It was in this sense that Carl Schmitt once argued that politics is the distinction between friends and enemies (Schmitt, 2008). In this register, the creation of new in- and out-groups becomes the modus operandi of political organization.

The creation of an in-group, a 'people' who are unified against an external threat, represented by the other. Considered from a Foucauldian perspective where, in conditions of modernity, and indeed post-modernity, the nature of power has shifted to a focus on fostering life or disavowing it to the point of death, the state is not focused on directly destroying the other (Foucault, 2019). But rather, the other is the one who must be exiled in order to permit 'the people' to flourish. This again identifies a situation where the drawing of an imagined us, contrasted against an imagined them, is central to the formulation of subjectivities. In this sense, bordering becomes a practice of not just imagining the physical geographies around the state, but also of conceptualizing the cleavages and occlusions through which 'a people' is constituted.

Taken in this register, Braverman's remarks are neither throwaway nor simply a gesture towards her own politics. Rather, they speak to the very apparatus (Agamben, 2009: 3) through which personhood is conceptualized. As I have argued elsewhere, the changes made to the UK asylum system across 2022–2025 constitute a fundamental shift away from the liberal refugee concept, which sees an individual fleeing a country and seeking protection due to factors which affect them as a person, and instead towards a far narrower conceptualization of safe and unsafe countries (Powell, 2024b). This can be spoken of in terms of a movement from the universal right to asylum and towards bespoke (Lenegan, 2022; Tomlinson, 2022; Sigona and Benson, 2024) regimes of protection such as those provided to people fleeing the conflict in Ukraine[7] or the imposition of a new National Security Law in Hong Kong.[8] However, there is a need to go further, to recognize how the logics deployed in these moral panics speak to who is viewed as the subject of human rights protections and concomitantly who is viewed merely as a threat or danger to that 'human' population. Think here of the difference between framing those crossing the English Channel in small boats as refugees (that is, people in need of protection) or as foreign national offenders (playing on racialized imaginaries of violence and danger). In this sense, while refugee status confers a form of epistemic legitimacy (Ferreira, 2022) – signifying its recipient as deserving of respect and protection – contemporary discourses mark forced migrants as something to be feared, a threat to the norms, values and people of the UK (see Butler, 2009).

When facing questions over who the human of human rights is, asylum claims based on sexual or gender diversity represent a uniquely interesting

---

7 UK Visas and Immigration, *Homes for Ukraine: Sponsor Guidelines*, available at: https://apply-to-offer-homes-for-ukraine.service.gov.uk/ (accessed 6 September 2023).

8 UK Visas and Immigration, *British National (Overseas) Visa*, available at: https://www.gov.uk/british-national-overseas-bno-visa (accessed 6 September 2023).

site of analysis. Not only are these claims fundamental to individuals' rights, but they also represent one of the few frameworks within which legal reasoning is called to determine who is – and by implication who is not – a sexually diverse person. In recent years, this question has been fairly conclusively determined to be operated on the basis of identity rather than behaviour (Bruce-Jones, 2015; Ferreira, 2022). So, in this realm, we see a need for decision-makers to determine what forms of sexual diversity are legitimate, what performances register as recognizable, and through these means, who should be granted protection. While this book is focused on issues of sexual diversity, these are not easily separable from issues of gender and, indeed, in some cultures the line between sex, sexuality and gender is far less defined than in the UK. As such, decision-makers not only need to consider what performances of sexual diversity are recognizable, but also the extent to which sexual diversity relates to gendered behaviours, identities and presentations.

To that end, this book draws on twenty-six semi-structured interviews with people who have lived experience of the UK asylum system, and, in particular, sexual diversity claims within that system. Eight of these interviews, with people who had claimed asylum in the UK on the basis of their sexual diversity, were undertaken between 2018 and 2020. The other eighteen, with legal representatives and people working within the third sector, all of whom directly work with sexually diverse refugees and asylum seekers, were undertaken between 2022 and 2023. As such, these twenty-six interviews bring together some of the key stakeholders of the UK system to chart it at a moment of fundamental change, allowing us access to the street-level logics operating within the system during this period of reform (Lipsky, 2010). During the period where these interviews were undertaken, we have seen three landmark legislative enactments.[9] As well as a Memorandum of Understanding with Rwanda.[10] This was followed up by a treaty with Rwanda and an associated act of parliament in the form of the Safety of Rwanda (Immigration and Asylum) Act 2024 and, as I am finishing this book, the Border Security (Asylum and Immigration) Bill is currently also making its way through parliament.

The Treaty and Safety of Rwanda Act are perhaps particularly notable as they were specifically enacted in order to reverse the findings of the UK

[9] The Nationality and Borders Act 2022; The Illegal Migration Act 2023; The Safety of Rwanda (Asylum and Immigration) Act 2024.

[10] Home Office, 'Memorandum of understanding between the government of the United Kingdom of Great Britain and Northern Ireland and the government of the Republic of Rwanda for the provision of an asylum partnership arrangement' (updated 6 April 2023), available at: http://www.gov.uk/government/publications/memorandum-of-understanding-mou-between-the-uk-and-rwanda (accessed 15 August 2023).

Supreme Court in the Rwanda appeals.[11] There have also been a number of changes to the broader rules governing migration to the UK.[12] Given this, these interviews were undertaken against a social and political backdrop where migration has been a matter of considerable political interest and controversy. Some have argued that the focus on migration is a nexus where populist and nativist logics of the radical right have come to be co-opted within mainstream British politics (Worth, 2023). At the least, the centrality which migration has come to adopt within not just UK but broader politics is striking. As just one example, the previous government attempted to run a 'small boats' week as a core focus of government policy and presentation (Townsend, 2023). Given the re-election of Donald Trump in the United States and the ascendency of Giorgia Meloni in Italy, among others, and the concomitant pushing of further political currents that challenge international norms around the rights of migrants, understanding the operations of power and discourse around migration remains one of the most pressing concerns we face.

The timing of this research has meant that the interviews provide insights into the implications of these kinds of highly politicized policy shifts for those engaging with the legal infrastructure on a day-to-day basis. Given this, the interviews offer space to chart the impact of policy change in real time at both a legal and societal level. In part, the engagement with street-level legal practitioners also enables some access to the legal consciousness of those involved with the system allowing us to understand not just the implications of law and policy but also how those working with them engage with the framework. Indeed, some of the most interesting and important insights from these interviews came from matters I had not anticipated, such as the concerns immigration lawyers had around their own safety in light of the tenor and nature of the discourses around migration, especially the statements made by ministers of British government (see, for example, Mason, 2023).

Due to the semi-structured nature of the interviews, they also contain reflections on events as they happened and, as such, this book is able to speak to how highly polarized political narratives impact operational matters and the implications this has for the rights and protections offered by law. In this sense, readers are reminded to be mindful that the situation charted in this book continues to be a live one. If, and when, the political intrigue dies down, regardless of what the system looks like, people will continue to make dangerous journeys seeking protection (Mayblin, 2016). The narratives

[11] See *R (On the Application of AAA and Others) v Secretary of State for the Home Department* [2023] UKSC 42.

[12] The Immigration Rules, available at: https://www.gov.uk/guidance/immigration-rules/immigration-rules- (accessed 9 April 2024).

charted in this book are not static. Nor are they a record of events. Rather, by speaking to those most intimately involved in the day-to-day operation of the narratives, frameworks and rules so often plastered across the front pages of tabloid newspapers or trotted out as Downing Street talking points, this book offers an avenue to access the semiotics of asylum in the UK, to break down the transformation of our legal structures, and to explore the genealogy of a moral panic around asylum. A moral panic that has been, for reasons explored across the chapters of this book, experienced in a particularly salient manner by those asylum seekers whose claims link to their non-normativity.

The desire to explore the semiotics of asylum puts this book into a particular dialogue with the legal consciousness literature (Silbey, 2005). In particular, our exploration of the narratives of legal representatives and staff working within the third sector gives us a means through which to engage with the way that legal representatives understand and make sense of the legal framework within which they are being asked to work.

While the reflections in this book are most directly applicable to those who are claiming asylum due to sexual diversity, they also apply to other groups whose persecution links more to particular non-normative characteristics than any general state within their country of origin. For example, the narratives charted in this book may equally apply to women or religious minorities seeking protection from situations particular to them as women or people of a minority religion within their country of origin. Indeed, it is notable that Braverman's remarks included women alongside sexually diverse people. As such, the focus of this book should not be mistaken for either narrow or niche. Rather, the concerns charted here constitute a threat to all who exist beyond the self-conceptions of normative state and social power, and the arguments deployed here are intended to provide conceptual tools to understand social and discursive dynamics beyond the subject matter directly addressed.

1.1 Migrants (not) welcome here

From Suella Braverman's claim that a hundred million people are seeking to unlawfully enter the UK,[13] to the appearances of the UK prime minister, Rishi Sunak, behind a podium bearing the legend 'stop the boats' (Crace, 2023), the period over which this book was written has been characterized by a singular focus on migration generally, and 'illegal migration' more specifically. Beyond the acts of politicians, the UK has also seen a number of situations which speak to growing hostility within British society. These

[13] HC Deb, 7 March 2023, Vol 729, Cols 151–153.

have included the far-right-inspired attacks on an asylum hotel in Rotherham (Bancroft, 2024), as well as legally produced discrimination and mistreatment, such as the Windrush scandal. A situation where the expansion of the logics of the border into all corners of day-to-day life under what was initially called the 'hostile environment' and later recast as the 'compliant environment' saw huge restrictions enacted with the specific aim of reducing the ability of people entering the UK irregularly to survive (Goodfellow, 2019). These measures, of course, ended up impacting not just those who entered the UK irregularly, but rather, every single person living in the UK. While it is possible for those with documentation to navigate the expansion of the border to regimes of health, employment, education and property, note should be taken that disproportionate affects have been experienced by global ethnic majority UK residents who entered prior to the routine issuing of paperwork to people entering the UK legally. The most obvious of these, being, of course, the Windrush generation (Gentleman, 2020). Here we have seen a group of people, and their children, who entered the UK at the invitation of the government. However, as it was not the practice of the government at the time to provide paper documentation, they were unable to evidence their entitlement to reside in the UK and access services. Many were subject to harms including the denial of medical treatment, threats of deportation to countries they had never visited and the loss of jobs that they had held for decades (Gentleman, 2017). All of these people entered the UK legally and were lawfully resident. However, such was the hunger to be seen to be *'doing something'* to tackle the 'problem' of illegal migration that they were subject to huge penalties which have had devastating and, in some cases, life-threatening implications. Indeed, building on Atkins and Finlayson's insight that, within contemporary populist reason, it is generally thought unwise for a political figure to be going against the stream of 'ordinary' political opinion (Atkins and Finlayson, 2013), the idea of needing to be seen to *do something* about the 'problem' of immigration has often become more central to policy making than the question of whether the policy in question has any realistic chance of securing the goals it seeks to achieve. For example, the government frequently cited deterrence as the motivation for the Nationality and Borders Act 2022 and the Illegal Migration Act 2023 even though Mayblin has demonstrated that reception conditions are rarely a significant factor in the countries where people seek asylum, suggesting that the government's approach was, even on its own terms, founded on false or oversimplified assumptions (Mayblin, 2016).

While the Windrush scandal presents a particularly egregious example, it is only the most clandestine in a number of events which speak to the pervasion of colonial and xenophobic logic throughout British society. The background to Windrush can be found in the 2010 general election where, included within the Manifesto of the Conservative and Unionist Party – who were in government for 14 consecutive years between 2010 and 2024 – was a promise to reduce immigration to the tens of thousands (Scott, 2023). This focus on migration is, of course, not new. Since the 1980s discourses around migration in the UK have pushed conceptualizations of the UK as overwhelmed (Pruitt, 2019). However, the Conservative Party Manifesto from 2010 did provide a government directly returned on a platform which promised significant reductions in migration. As Bonansinga and Forrest have argued, this kind of policy focus speaks to the mainstream co-option of radical right policies around migration within the UK (Bonansinga and Forrest, 2025).

The UK did not have any formal border controls, in the sense which we would now recognize them, until 1905 (see Smith, 2023). And, as the Windrush generation themselves show, the UK during the period after the two world wars actively solicited increased levels of migration in an effort to fill labour shortages. Of course, this is not to suggest that the UK was not deeply embroiled in colonial and xenophobic conceptualizations of both itself as a state, and its population, as well as the many states from which that population was drawn. But rather, it is to point out that the present focus on reducing net migration as an active focus of government – as opposed to a focus of fringe organizations – is reasonably new and worthy of note.

In recent years, many popular commentators have situated migration in general – and the UK government's plan to send those entering the UK without prior permission to Rwanda in particular – as a 'culture war' issue (Cammaerts, 2022). This is to say that the idea of Rwanda, which could be understood as a kind of phantasm, an alternative reality which shifts the way one sees the world (Butler, 2024), has come to be synonymous with a commitment to reducing 'illegal migration'. Cast simply as something that one is for or against, without any particular reference to the effectiveness of the policy in achieving its purported goals. This fits with the pattern of 'complexity reduction', which Mayblin has identified as being central to migration policy making in the UK (Mayblin, 2019).

From political correctness to woke

While the idea of 'culture war' has popularly been framed as something new, many of the contours of the battles waged within this arena closely mirror issues which previously arose around the idea of 'political correctness'.

Hall argued that

> [t]he era of PC [political correctness] is marked by the proliferation of the sites of social conflict to include conflicts around questions of race, gender, sexuality, the family, ethnicity and cultural difference, as well as issues around class and inequality. Issues like life, marriage, and

> sexual relations or food, which used to be considered 'non-political', have become politicized. (Hall, 1995: 166)

Adopting this definition, the links into the contemporary idea of 'culture war' or, as some on right have taken to calling it, 'the war on woke', are clear (see, for example, Dershowitz, 2024). The etymology of the phrase 'woke' is in reference to being awake to racism, which traces back to before the Civil War in the United States as a means for Black Americans to draw attention to their persecution (Davies and MacRae, 2023: 4). The phrase woke – as a sort of folk devil (see Cohen, 2011) – has then been expanded to essentially cover any entrance of politics to areas previously conceived as apolitical, with some theorists identifying the emergence of a whole industry oriented around warning about the dangers of woke (Davies and MacRae, 2023). Given this, it should be apparent that the contemporary 'culture war' maps very closely onto historic controversies over 'political correctness gone mad' (see Tushnet, 1992), forming around the discomfort that arises when cherished norms, often perceived as inherent, are challenged.

Of course, all of the questions marked out as politically correct, woke or an issue of culture war have not actually been politicized in the manner proclaimed. Rather, they have always been political. What registers as politicization is simply the challenging of hegemonic or previously unquestioned power structures (see Bates, 1975). This is why, for example, feminism or queer politics is often seen to be 'politicizing' women or children. Because it is challenging the fundamental assumption that the political norm – the centre our thoughts orient around – fits a certain set of criteria. Namely, they challenge the status of the subject as assumedly white, middle aged, middle class, cisgender, heterosexual and male. In this sense, whatever we call them, the kinds of conflicts we see around issues such as migration are political matters of the first order relating to allocations of power, legal rights and social distribution. Indeed, given that such conflicts relate to struggles over the very concept of the human, they could be referred to as a kind of meta-politics, relating to the structure and nature of political subjectivities themselves (Coleman, 2024: 57–81). That is to say, a kind of politics that functions on the prior question of who the subject of politics is. This topic maps closely on to other debates around who is the human of human rights or who is the human of humanism (Foucault, 2001; Rancière, 2004; Mignolo, 2009).

Such a framing is broadly consistent with conceptualizations of politics after the 'linguistic turn', which has seen a far greater recognition of how discursive productions of subjectivities themselves play a role in how those human beings and institutions are understood and the rights which are allocated to them. In the context of refugees, this framing has long been apparent because, as Hardy has argued, the status of the refugee is fundamentally one of recognition, ultimately dependent on whether a given claimant fits within the discursive and legal frameworks through which the figure of the refugee is understood (2003: 467). Indeed, as El-Enany has argued,

> [t]he framing of those fleeing and seeking protection in the UK as 'illegal Migrants' and further associations with criminality that arises in the language of 'criminal gangs' and 'Foreign National Offenders' could be argued to be a method of foreclosing Empathy: Feelings of empathy are known to encourage cooperation and assistance between human-beings, while an absence of identification with the suffering of others can lead to violence and abuse, both characteristics of Europe's militarised border regime. (El-Enany, 2016: 14)

What El-Enany is describing here, in simple terms, is the character of the other or the subaltern (Spivak, 2004). What Butler would describe as the human who does not register as human (2009: 3). In various frameworks, the character of the other or the subaltern connotes those who are framed as outsiders in a social and political community and who, through this exteriority, are often constructed as a threat. In simple terms, the other is that which is outside the frameworks of recognition operative within a given community or society. The status of other or subaltern are statuses that can be attached and retracted depending on the norms through which recognition as one of the 'the people' is determined. As Judith Butler (2009: 3) has argued: 'To be a body is to be exposed to social crafting and form … in other words, the body is exposed to socially and politically articulated forces as well as to claims of sociality – including, language, work and desire – to make possible the body's persisting and flourishing.'

In this sense, questions over language and the discourses that are employed to characterize groups take on a primary place in the rights and protections afforded to that group with alignment to certain frames of recognition being pivotal to registering as a grievable form of life whose suffering motivates calls for redress (Butler, 2004b: 18–39; 2006). Butler's theorizing of grievable life itself builds on the Foucauldian argument that 'for millennia, man remained what he was for Aristotle: a living animal with the additional capacity for political existence; modern man is an animal whose politics places his existence as a living being in question' (Foucault, 1976: 143). Within the contemporary bio-political state, norms determine whether or not one is regarded as human. Butler encapsulates this situation well in their claim that 'the epistemological capacity to apprehend life is partially dependent on that life being produced according to norms that qualify it as a life' (Butler, 2009: 3).

Tying this together, then, I argue that the issues that are commonly considered to be matters of culture war are fundamentally no different to historic divisions around issues such as 'political correctness'. These issues orient around what might be called a form of meta-politics, that is, politics that relates to concepts and identities and so directly forms a part of the modes in which we become subjects. In this sense, the issues relate to the distinction between the person of 'the people' and the other. In particular, these are issues of epistemology and ontology, begging questions over who is considered to be a legitimate human being, worthy of respect, rights and mourning.

In this register, it may be that contemporary conflations of seeking asylum and illegal migration speak to an attempt to epistemologically construct everyone who is irregularly entering the UK as potentially criminal and, in so doing, as El-Enany suggests, foreclose empathy.

The phantasm of Rwanda

Another salient element of the present political moment lies in the British government's approach to attempting to 'deter' illegal migration. Namely, the agreement with the Republic of Rwanda.[14] At time of writing, this agreement – and attempts to operationalize it as a proposed cornerstone of the UK's approach to 'addressing illegal migration' – has now been the subject of three acts of parliament, a Supreme Court case, numerous government press conferences, and multiple invocations of the 'will of the people' by government ministers (Walker, 2024).

Given that the evidence strongly suggests that the idea of 'pull factors' are not particularly impactful in terms of influencing which countries those seeking asylum travel to (Mayblin, 2016), it is perhaps surprising that a policy which fundamentally centres the idea of deterrence has become such a core centrepiece of the government's focus.

In order to think through how Rwanda has come to adopt such salience, viewed, or at least spoken of, by some figures on the UK political right as a panacea, the only possible solution to the 'millions of people'[15] who allegedly are coming to the UK, we might turn to the conceptual framework of the phantasm as proposed by Butler.

The idea of the phantasm is the conceptual framework that Judith Butler deployed within their 2024 monograph *Who's Afraid of Gender*. Butler deploys the concept to chart how gender has become imbued with manifest forms of conceptual baggage in such a way as to effectively be (mis)attributed

14 UK–Rwanda Migration and Economic Development Partnership (United Kingdom of Great Britain and Northern Ireland and the Republic of Rwanda) (5 December 2023) Rwanda No.1 (2023).

15 HC Deb, 20 March 2023, Vol 730, Col 9.

responsibility for numerous social ills and anxieties, but the general zeitgeist of the concept – the idea that certain modes of thought constitute a sort of alternative reality which comes to colour and condition someone's entire framework for making sense of the world – can also be applied to the proposal of removing people seeking asylum to Rwanda.

The idea of Rwanda is functioning as a phantasm. A dream world where the complex social dynamics which drive people to undertake dangerous journeys in order to seek international protection can simply be 'solved' by deterring people from coming to the UK. This goes beyond the complexity reduction outlined by Mayblin, as the reduction is now even more total, moving from a focus on pull factors to the idea of a single plan as a panacea. The phantasmagorical quality of the Rwanda plan is apparent in the contradictory discourses deployed by its supporters. For example, supporters of the plan simultaneously frame the possibility of being sent to Rwanda as adequately undesirable to dissuade people from coming to the UK, while also arguing that any criticism of the plan is unjust criticism of Rwanda. Such arguments are clearly contradictory in the sense that removal to Rwanda could not work as a deterrent if conditions were not regarded as lesser than those in the UK.

Rwanda and the broader changes brought about within UK asylum law and practice since 2022 operate in an essentially phantasmagorical way. Dualistically, this relies first on the demonstrably false idea that the UK is shouldering some kind of unique burden in terms of the number of people seeking sanctuary in the country. I think here, particularly, of then Home Secretary Suella Braverman's frankly bizarre – and easily disproven – claim that hundreds of millions of people were trying to get to the UK.[16] Here the phantasm is the spectre of a (highly racialized) 'swarm' seeking access to the UK (BBC News, 2015). But, operating alongside this, is a second phantasm. Closely linked to the first, it is a phantasm that ran through the Brexit slogan of 'take back control' (Zotti, 2021). This second phantasm is the idea that we can just 'stop the boats'. That, in a globalized world, any individual state can simply decide that they want to leave a global institution or that they wish now to stop those seeking protection from persecution from coming to this country and do so through a simple innovation such as the idea of sending claimants on to Rwanda.

In this sense, while the research suggests that a policy premised on deterrence is highly unlikely to work (Hassan, 2000), and the policy itself does not for a moment propose to address anything like the volume of claimants who currently present themselves to the Home Office in the UK, there remains, on behalf of the advocates of the plan, an emotional

[16] HC Deb, 7 March 2023, Vol 729, Cols 151–153.

attachment to this policy. This is because, phantasmagorically, the policy is THE answer if only others would get out the way so that they could 'take back control' of 'our' borders.

1.2 Orientalism and (inter)national politics of sexuality

The logics of migration control – often directly organized around stopping 'them' from coming 'here' – are organized around a highly racialized politics that seeks to protect the UK, here conceptualized as highly civilized, from the entry of those who are represented as less civilized (Bowden, 2007). Often, this kind of politics deploys the move that Puar describes as 'homonationalism' (Puar, 2012). In this guise, the homonationalist framing operates by presenting tolerance of LGBTIQA+ rights as a core constituent element of the here (the Occident) and projecting homophobia as something that happens over there (the Orient) (Lalor and Browne, 2018).

A similar operation happens over women's rights. In this guise, refugees, asylum seekers and 'illegal' migrants are often presented as an external threat to the socio-sexual order (De Hart, 2017). This co-production of nationality and sexuality is not new. The conceptualization that sexual pluralism and rights for women are cornerstones of 'civilized' societies which are threatened when the external other is permitted to enter the UK is almost an exact mirror image of the logics of civilization which ran through the UK's history of colonialism (Morgensen, 2012).

During the early colonial period British missionaries were sent to several African communities where evidence is suggestive of highly diverse sexual traditions and cultures (O'Murray and Roscoe, 1998; Amadiume, 2015). These Victorian missionaries saw the sexual cultures among these peoples as a sign of their 'savagery', that they in some sense lacked civilization. This issue around sexual cultures maps more broadly onto the logic of 'development', which long functioned as a justification for states such as Britain maintaining domination over large parts of the world (Salamanca, 2016).

In this sense, the same logics which once operated around the expansion of colonial power now operate around the need for insularity and foreclosure. As such, the modalities of colonialist thought which once fuelled the domination of the British Empire can be argued to remain a core logical foundation of UK migration discourse. These modalities now fuel the construction of the other as a dangerous outsider seeking entry and threatening the progressive liberalism of the UK, which is framed as a unique construction existing only in 'the west' (Latham, 1995). As Bonansinga and Forrest (2025) have argued, this construction is often reified within populist arguments that take a central focus on 'the people' of the UK and which rely on a kind of collective narcissism to frame the UK as uniquely progressive and its people as uniquely tolerant.

This, in turn, plays into the framing of homophobia as something that happens over there, compared to the liberalism found 'here'. In the context of sexuality, Joseph Massad (2002) has outlined how an international framework of activists and organizations have emerged as a *Gay Internationale*. This, he argues, is premised on the assumption that '[h]omosexuals, gays, and lesbians are universal categories that exist everywhere in the world and, based on this prediscursive axiom, the Gay International sets itself the mission of defending them by demanding that their rights as "homosexuals" be granted where they are denied and respected where they are violated' (Massad, 2002: 363).

While it may seem superficially unobjectionable for this kind of international advocacy to take place, it has certain discursive and political effects of which we need to take note. First, the effect of this dynamic, much as Massad identifies, is to posit the idea that categories such as lesbian or gay are pre-discursive. That is, to posit the idea that these are natural categories which exist prior to cultures and societies. However, this universalist framing leaves no conceptual space for autochthonous forms of sexual diversity that do not align with the presentations found in the UK. For example, as I have argued elsewhere, the presentation of sexuality as this kind of flat and simplified form of identity ignores the ruptures and incongruences in sexual behaviour, sexual desire and sexual identity, and how where the priority is placed between these three disparate elements (see Savin-Williams, 2005: 27–48) can have profound implications for which rights are recognized as deserving of protection (Powell, 2021a).

Beyond the crystallization of identities in this way, the other effect that the kind of international pro-LGBTIQA+ rights discourse that Massad is describing produces is the consolidation and (re)production of the kind of here and there dynamics discussed earlier. It is through this idea that there are tolerant 'developed' countries and intolerant 'backwards' countries with regressive social mores that those seeking asylum end up being conceived of as a potential threat to the social and cultural fabric of the UK.

The possibility of unintended consequences is apparent not only within the context of the effects on how sexual and gender diversity, as well as diverse national and cultural traditions, come to be understood in the UK, but also in regard to how sexual and gender diversity come to be understood within refugee countries of origin. For example, when advocating for laws that restrict sexual and gender freedom, it is not uncommon for religious and political leaders to invoke the idea that LGBTIQA+ rights and politics are a form of 'western' imposition and that those advocating for them are being influenced from the outside (Stychin, 2003; Rao, 2015; Mhaoileoin, 2019).

As this suggests, the logics of us and them, the friend and the enemy, the people and the other, are a continuous feature that runs throughout the relationship between nationality and sexual and gender diversity. In this sense, it is important that we remain attuned to the ripples of discourse which can produce unintended consequences far beyond what we may have initially expected.

1.3 From *Shah* and *Islam* to the Illegal Migration Act

As should be becoming increasingly clear, the links between gender, sexuality and nationality run deep. Conceptualizations of nationality have long been gendered within the cultural imaginary (Yuval-Davis, 2000). For example, people from Asia have often been depicted through a feminine lens (Matthews, 2002). Similarly, people of colour, but particularly those from the continent of Africa, have often been depicted in highly masculinized terms (Curry, 2018). As well as being visible in some more extreme examples, such as the construction of Black men as sexually violent (Zounlome et al, 2019). These ideas of sex, gender and sexuality as facets of national character have also played out on a more implicit level, such as through attempts by states to regulate entry into their borders on the basis of sexual identity or behaviour (Luibheid, 2002).

The UK has never directly excluded entry from those who are sexually diverse, unlike the United States, which has directly sought to preserve the heterosexual population from the external 'threat' of sexual diversity (Foss, 1994). However, this should not be taken to mean that the UK has not attempted to conceptualize modalities of proper sexual behaviour as a part of what is expected when entering into the UK population from outside of it. Indeed, as noted earlier, ideas of proper sexuality in its proper place have been central to conceptualizations of 'civilization'.

The regulation of sexuality as a constituent element of border management has operated both as a locus of control and as a limited exception to immigration control. Since 1999, and the case of *Shah* and *Islam*, the UK has generally recognized that forms of sexual diversity – as well as gender – can provide grounds for an asylum claim.[17]

However, the initial protection offered to people of diverse sexualities suffered from an overly conduct driven conception of sexual difference which placed the ability to participate in sexual acts, and not the social and cultural implications of diversity and difference, as the object of protection (Chelvan, 2011: 57). This overly conduct driven approach also contributed to discretion reasoning which, until the 2010 Supreme Court Decision in *HJ (Iran) and HT (Cameroon)*, was one of the central barriers facing sexually diverse people seeking protection in the UK.[18] Resting, in essence, upon a 'reasonable

[17] *Islam (AP) v Secretary of State for the Home Department* and *R v Immigration Appeal Tribunal Ex parte Shah* [1999] UKHL 20; [1999] 2 A C 629 (HL).

[18] *HJ (Iran) and HT (Cameroon) v Secretary of State for the Home Department* [2010] UKSC 31; [2011] 1 AC 596.

expectation that persons should, to the extent that it is possible, co-operate in their own protection'.[19] Indeed, this practice was also common across a number of other jurisdictions, including Australia (Kassisieh, 2008: 64–70).

Rainbow Migration, then known as the UK Lesbian and Gay Immigration Group, estimated that prior to 2010, discretion reasoning resulted in sexually diverse claimants having a rejection rate of 98–99 per cent in initial claims (Rainbow Migration, 2013: 10). In essence, discretion reasoning operated by denying that a claimant had a well-founded fear of persecution on the basis that they could be returned to their country of origin and be discreet in order to avoid the risk of persecution (Millbank, 2010; Wessels, 2013; Powell, 2020). The Australian High Court ruled that this approach was incompatible with the Refugee Convention in 2003.[20] However, it was not until 2010 that the UK Supreme Court followed suit, ruling that the 'Reasonable Tolerability Test', which required decision-makers to consider whether it would be 'reasonably' tolerable for a given claimant to be discrete regarding their sexual diversity, was incompatible with the convention due to its reliance on the suppression of the very characteristic which the Convention sought to protect.[21] Wessels (2012: 815–820) expands on the new test outlined in *HT and HJ*.

Post-2010, issues moved from discretion to disbelief. To unpack this somewhat, the reason for refusal has moved from denying the risk of persecution to instead denying that the claimant is or will be perceived as sexually diverse. In effect, the stance is no longer that the claimant will have no fear of persecution because they can avoid such a fear by concealing their difference from the surrounding society, but rather that they are lying about their difference from the surrounding society. Under these logics, sexual diversity is a fundamental truth which can either be proven or disproven.

1.4 Not gay as in happy

Within queer politics there has been a long tradition of challenging normative structures more broadly than simply those that relate to matters of sexual and gendered diversity. For example, queer figures have long sought coalitions with migrant communities and engaged in struggles to support the rights of migrants, as well as other socially marginalized groups (Cohen, 2020). This has included participation in broader forms of left activism dating

19 RRT Case No V95/03527 [1998] RRTA 246.

20 *Appellant S395/2002 v Minister for Immigration and Multicultural Affairs*; *Appellant S396/2002 v Minister for Immigration and Multicultural Affairs*, [2003] HCA 71, Australia: High Court, 9 December 2003.

21 *HJ (Iran) and HT (Cameroon) v Secretary of State for the Home Department* [2010] UKSC 31; [2011] 1 AC 596.

back to the 1980s. For example, the group Lesbians and Gays Support the Miners – inspiration for the more recent Lesbians and Gays Support the Migrants – sought to build coalitions between queer political activism and the trade union movement. This approach to politics, centring around the formation of coalition, offers a sense of the potential of queer politics in the sense of basing itself not in identities or discreet categories as such, but rather focusing on the building of solidarity and the defence of particular values or philosophical concepts such as autonomy, freedom and workers' rights.

As such, the links between migration and queer politics also runs through the engagement of queer people with pro-migration politics that critically challenges and interjects against some of the narratives perpetuated around asylum seekers. For example, queer activists have frequently opposed attempts to frame migrants as inherently homophobic or misogynistic. Such discursive and rhetorical moves play on the phenomenon Puar has termed 'homonlationalism' (Puar, 2006; 2012; 2013).

The dynamics of homonationalism were outlined earlier. They form part of a broader here and there contrast which is often used as a method of silencing critical perspectives when these are put forward by queer people. Such a move is unsurprising given the relative ubiquity within the social sciences literature of a dichotomy between the idealized European self and the marginalized and demonized other (Buchowski, 2006; Banerjee, 2015). Alongside this silencing function, such narratives also operate to enable the UK to frame itself as more civilized than other cultures or countries. Discursively, this enables the UK to frame itself as both more modern and as an international authority.

As Spijkerboer has argued, such framings are supported via the characterization of European cultures as formed around 'enlightenment, progress, liberty, emancipation and … human rights' (Spijkerboer, 2018: 221). This is contrasted with non-Europeans who are discursively constructed around ideas of 'darkness, stagnation, oppression, subservience' (Spijkerboer, 2018: 222). These framings can be observed in contemporary anti-migrant narratives which frame migrants as a threat to the health of a nation. In its most extreme guises, this may even take the form of white supremacist conspiracy theories such as the Great Replacement Theory (Linders, 2023). Indeed, it is argued that modern right-wing imaginings of a threat to western culture are fundamentally premised on these same constructions, with the idea being that it is through migration and the importation of this constructed 'darkness' that European societies and 'western values' are said to be being undermined. Through these dynamics, Butler argues, the very concept of sexual freedom becomes associated with Europe, contrasted with the conservative politics of non-European nations who, through this, are framed as regressive (Butler, 2008: 3). Further, as Colpani and Habed argue, this establishes Europe as a state of sexual exceptionalism (2014).

This, dualistically, frames Europe as simultaneously under threat and as a space of generally unobtainable freedom. In this sense, the rights afforded to people in Europe – including the UK – are framed less as fundamental rights and more as the fruits of Europe. Not as something those born in other cultures can expect or claim, thus sustaining a hierarchy where only the most extreme forms of harm against sexually diverse people register as worthy of intervention. Otherwise put, as I have argued elsewhere, such harms are characterized as virtually normal (Powell, 2024b). Prior to the UK's outlawing of mandatory discretion in 2010, these dynamics were even more pronounced (Millbank, 2009). But, as Wessels has argued, even since the landmark judgment in *HJ (Iran) and HT (Cameroon)* elements of discretion continue to be an issue, thus showcasing the ways in which the harms to which sexually diverse people are subject are often legitimated within heteronormative legal orders (Wessels, 2023).

While there may be some limited truth to these framings – for example, it is an objective fact that some states impose strict carceral sentences for same-sex sexual activity – it should be noted that it is possible for homophobia to decline without there being a concomitant reduction in heterosexism, heteronormativity and indeed homonormativity (Duggan, 2002: 175–194). As I expand on in Chapter 2, the fact that the UK has far fewer incidents of overt homophobic violence does not mean that sexually diverse people do not face difficulties due to the rigidity of social norms. Indeed, it can be argued that the here and there narrative prevents attention being drawn to the ways in which the UK remains structured by fundamentally heterosexual norms. Thus, even though the research is clear that homophobia has fallen significantly since the 1980s and 1990s (Clements and Field, 2014), the continuing and pervasive reach of heteronormativity cannot be ignored as a salient social factor which structures lived experiences.

Through the ideas of civilization and the contemporary here and there logic, sexuality has been continuously suffused by nationalism. Whether this lies in the rejection of sexual diversity conceptualized as civilization or their embrace as a part of the broader discourse of human rights, the dynamic remains the same. This dynamic involves states such as the UK setting which forms of human conduct are viewed as modern, permissible and worthy of protection. Indeed, as Spijkerboer notes, those seeking asylum on the basis of their sexual diversity often need to engage in the practice of disclaiming their countries of origin as places of violence and regressive structures (2018: 223).

This, of course, does not just serve the UK in terms of providing discursive and rhetorical weight in issues directly related to gender and sexuality. Rather, this provides a way of framing arguments and approaches across a broad swathe of areas. For example, when arguments were raised against British forces being engaged in the bombing of Islamic State in Syria, a part of the response hinged on the idea that Islamic State enact violent death upon LGBTIQA+ people (Schotten, 2016). This is, of course, true (Tschantret, 2018). However, the deployment of this fact in this context is, in effect, an attempt to render illegitimate entirely appropriate questions relating to both the moral and practical value of UK intervention on another continent, in a context where the chances of harms to civilian populations are extremely high.

Indeed, it could be argued that the changing dynamics reflect a continued coloniality within the context of what Attwood has identified as a more overtly sexualized culture. Such a sexualized culture leads to, for example:

> A contemporary preoccupation with sexual values, practices and identity; the public shift to more permissive sexual attitudes, the proliferation of sexual texts; the emergence of new forms of sexual experience; the apparent breakdown of rules, categories and regulations designed to keep the obscene at bay; our fondness for scandals controversies and panics around sex. (Attwood, 2006: 78–79)

The one area where Attwood is, I would argue, mistaken is in characterizing the preoccupation with 'sexual values, practices and identity' as new. Far from being new, such institutions were a fundamental driver in the self-conception of Europeans across history, as I will further explore in the next chapter.

In this sense, a queer theoretical approach to questions of refugee protection for sexually diverse people faces a number of issues and challenges. In the next chapter, I expand on some of these issues, considering how the adoption of a queer theoretical perspective – and specifically the practice of queering – maps onto questions oriented around progressive law reform and analysis.

1.5 Chapter roadmap

The remainder of the book develops across six substantive chapters which, together, offer a comprehensive and multi-perspectival overview of the state of play for asylum claims by LGBTIQA+ people in the UK. Chapter 2 offers a deeper exploration of queer theory, outlining the counter-normative theoretical framework which informs the analysis undertaken in the subsequent chapters and which, I argue, is essential to enabling queer theory to be used in order to generate policy-oriented proposals. This then leads into Chapter 3 which looks at the experiences of sexually diverse people with lived experience of navigating the UK asylum system. Specifically, the chapter draws on eight semi-structured interviews with people who have secured asylum in the UK on the basis of being LGBTIQA+, arguing that there are a number of mismatches between the lived experiences of sexually diverse people and the expectations operating within the UK asylum system.

Chapter 4 looks at the perspectives of legal representatives, arguing that the discourses deployed by government have actively contributed to producing dangers for legal practitioners which has, in turn, undermined the ability of those practitioners to support refugees and asylum seekers in navigating the mismatches identified within Chapter 3. Chapter 5 then brings in the experiences of people working within third sector organizations. Through seeking to outline the role that third sector organizations are playing, the chapter explores some of the particular vulnerabilities that sexually diverse people seeking asylum face and considers how some of these difficulties intersect with the theoretical issues discussed within Chapter 2.

Finally, Chapter 6 offers an overview of the state of play for asylum claims on the basis of sexual diversity in the UK, bringing the theory of Chapter 2 into closer conversation with the narratives explored across Chapters 3, 4 and 5 in order to critically consider the future of LGBTIQA+ asylum and chart the likely implications of the changes we are seeing across the UK asylum and migration landscape.

2

Queering Refugee Law

As identified in the title, this book is a work of queer theory. This is in the sense that it seeks to render obscure the assumptions on which both the law and 'common sense' are based and to draw attention to the lived diversity of human experience and identity in regard to sexual and gender diversity and the asylum system. As Zanghellini has suggested, there is an extent to which

> [w]e would not be queer theorists if we were not narcissistically invested in a version of ourselves as romantic antiheroes. This is one of the reasons that accounts for some of the deliberate silences and ambiguities in our work: we try to avoid spelling out some assumptions or judgements that align with normative exercises of practical reason, lest we should come across as a little pedestrian, a little too uncool relative to our impossibly queer academic colleague[s]. (Zanghellini, 2020: 540)

Perhaps this could be summed up, in potentially kinder terms, by saying that as theorists engaged in drawing attention to the forms of violence and occlusion that both underpin and are produced by norms regarding sex, gender and sexuality, those of us who identify as queer theorists are often opposed to setting out norms through which membership of the group calling themselves queer theorists could be determined. If your theoretical position is directed towards challenging existing norms, then it can appear threatening to come out in favour of any norms at all.

Despite this, given that this book seeks to reconcile queer theory with empirical socio-legal work, I wish to expand on what it means to queer law and more specifically what it means to queer refugee law. My use of the term queering is synonymous with the phrase to queer. Drawing on Halberstam, I consider the purpose of queering as fundamentally about disrupting underlying assumptions, most often with regard to gender, sex or sexuality (1998: 13).

This definition is also consistent with that adopted by other scholars. For example, Abes and Kasch, writing in the context of education, argue that 'queer theory critically analyses the meaning of identity, focusing on the intersections of identities and resisting oppressive social constructions of sexual orientation and gender' (2007: 620). At the very core of this definition is the idea of resisting oppressive social constructions. These constructions are the frameworks on which people and institutions base their conceptualization of the world. This form of resistance is important because 'gay identity itself can serve the forces of normalisation … sexual orientation is itself a normalising force' (Dean, 2018: xix). Given this, I argue that queer theory is a framework that seeks to subtend, disrupt and dismantle underlying assumptions and create greater conceptual space for different ways of being.

Put simply, to apply queer theory to refugee law is to seek to disrupt the underlying assumptions that are deployed and created within this area of law, to subject them to empirical scrutiny, and to draw attention to the issues that arise when such underlying assumptions do not correspond to the lived realities of those the legal system is tasked with recognizing. As it was put by one refugee at a symposium at Oxford Brookes University in 2023, '[t]he Home Office [and society more broadly] has little tick boxes they want you to fit into'. My interest here is in what happens to those who do not fit neatly into such boxes.

2.1 LGBTIQA+ rights in theory and practice

In undertaking to disrupt the underlying assumptions of refugee law, it is first necessary to detect both what these assumptions are and where they come from. In my previous work, I have argued that refugee status determination has increasingly come to be based on a conception of sexuality as, first and foremost, an identity (Powell, 2021a). This is expanded on in section 2.4 of this chapter. However, at this stage it is helpful to draw out my argument that the development of LGBTIQA+ rights in the UK has created a context within which the rights, realities and experiences of sexually diverse people have come to be understood as a matter of protecting identities that exist independent of social and historical context. That is to say, the underlying assumption of LGBTIQA+ rights in the UK is fundamentally that, for example, gay men and lesbians were 'born this way' and that, as such, they should be protected by law and safe from social exclusion or ill treatment (Johnston, 2015). This has been referred to as the 'immutability defence' by Yoshino (2000).

The deployment of the Born This Way narrative carries other implications for the way in which sexual diversity is understood. For example, the idea of being gay as a form of identity in and of itself suggests that this is a category with a level of stability, something that someone either is or isn't

(Stychin, 2005). The purpose of deploying an argument such as Born This Way is to stress the immutable and prior status of LGBTIQA+ identities (Draz, 2017: 372–373). This is a form of strategic essentialism that involves a decision to present a given category in a simplified manner which ignores differences within the category to achieve a given political goal (Spivak, 1985: 175–187). Because, once you configure a range of characteristics into a stable identity, that identity group can 'speak on its own behalf, to demand that its legitimacy of "naturality" be acknowledged, often in the same vocabulary, using the same categories by which it was ... disqualified' (Foucault, 1976: 101). Foucault argued that, in the case of homosexuality, the main formulation came within the discipline of medicine with an attempt to convert behaviours such as sodomy into taxonomizable ways of being. As he put it:

> [T]he machinery of power that focused on this whole alien strain did not aim to suppress it, but rather to give it an analytical, visible and permanent reality: it was implanted in bodies, slipped in beneath modes of conduct, made into a principle of classification and intelligibility, established as a raison d'être and a natural order of disorder. (Foucault, 1976: 44)

Some, such as Gleeson, have argued that Foucault's model for understanding the development of sexuality is overly medicalized, instead she posits that the law was the main vessel through which the concepts of sexuality that we now commonly deploy to place ourselves within the world were developed (Gleeson, 2007). Regardless, the exact genus of sexuality is not important here, all that matters at this stage is some level of acceptance that our present concepts and categories for the organization of sex(uality) emerge from specific histories and geographies (Weeks, 2015), and the fact that these have been taken up by activists and those seeking law reform does nothing to undermine this. Subjectivities are not just a reality on which politics is enacted, but themselves the product of forms of meta-politics arising from various disciplines ranging from medicine to education to social etiquette.

Born This Way and strategic essentialism

Born This Way itself is an example of strategic essentialism that arises from the US context, where it was deployed as a response to the religious right who presented an argument premised on gay men making a sinful choice, being morally culpable, and the legitimate recipients of critique and forms of punishment (Fetner, 2001). As such, the purpose of Born This Way was to present a counter-argument that minimized the role of choice and instead presented gay people as 'virtually normal', different only by accident of birth

(Sullivan, 1996). This fits more generally with what might be termed an assimilationist approach, focused on gaining legal rights within the existing model of society rather than trying to challenge that model. Assimilationist strategies might create space for homosexualities, but they do so in a way that is fundamentally homonormative, a concept which Duggan introduces to connote the depoliticized quality of contemporary gay and lesbian identities that do not challenge the fundamental institutions of patriarchy or heterosexuality such as marriage or the market (Duggan, 2002). Puar further explains how later instantiations of homonormativity have even built towards what she terms homonationalism, whereby 'arrangements of … sexual exceptionalism – homonormativity … complicates the dichotomous casting away of the nation as only supportive and productive of heteronormativity and disallowing of homosexuality' (Puar, 2006: 68). Thus, under the assimilationist model, the focus becomes disclaiming differences and stressing how normal the group in question is really.

As Johnston has argued, the Born This Way myth, like all other myths of origin, has a tendency to provide a totalizing view of the world (2015: 141). An example of this can be seen in recent articulations made around the rights and status of transgender people. For example, the claim by the LGB Alliance that gender affirming care for young people is a form of 'transing the gay away'[1] is partly contingent on an idea of sexuality as a 'natural status' in comparison to the presumed artificiality of gender identity. Only by adopting such a view, of sexuality as a natural status that is innate, in comparison to gender identity as some kind of external imposition – a social construction – does the idea that one could 'trans the gay away' make sense. Such a perspective is, of course, based on a fundamental misunderstanding of social constructivism. Specifically, such arguments mistake the argument that something is a social construct for the argument that it is not real. This is either bad faith, or a misunderstanding of social constructivism and queer theory. No queer theorist contends that sex, gender or sexuality are not real. Indeed, the entire framework focuses on deconstructing these entities because they are such a monolithic and hegemonic reality that to challenge them on an analytical or moral level becomes almost inconceivable. It is because of the very reality, and violent enforcement, of these institutions that they are such a target within queer theory. Thus, as Rubin and Butler argue, the scripts that govern gender and sexuality have been crafted over a long time and often shape the very frameworks through which people make sense of the world, they literally shape and contour our realities, and so moving out of them is a long and fraught process (Rubin and Butler, 2012). This example

[1] See written evidence submitted by LGB Alliance [GRA1647], available at: https://committees.parliament.uk/writtenevidence/17828/pdf/ (accessed 30 April 2025).

is salient because the idea of sexuality as innate speaks to how successful the strategic essentialism of Born This Way has been in the context of rights for those who are sexually diverse. However, it also speaks to the problems with such an approach, insofar as identities that are less easily tethered to biological essentialism quickly become targets to be distinguished from the biologically validated and acceptable forms of sexual difference.

It is, of course, normatively desirable that diverse sexual subjectivities are protected from harm and mistreatment. However, the underlying assumption that such identities are, in effect, innate, as if they exist independently of social context, is potentially harmful to those whose forms of diversity link to more culturally specific articulations. Indeed, such a view, in situating sexually diverse people as virtually normal, leaves a problem well-articulated by Tim Dean, specifically that '[w]hen assimilationist gays pass as normal, presenting themselves as "just like everyone else", the social pressure to comply with normative models intensifies against anyone who still counts as queer or somehow beyond the pale' (Dean, 2018: xl). This is an issue that I expand on further in Chapter 3, identifying areas of 'mismatch' where the assumptions underlying what it means to be sexually diverse within the refugee status determination framework do not align with the lived realities of those seeking asylum. For now, it is sufficient to say that the focus of Born This Way, the idea that there is no, or at least a limited role for, choice or socialization within the development of sexual diversities, ties the rights of sexually diverse people to forms of biological essentialism and assimilationism that are, I argue, beyond their strategic utility.

This idea is reflected by some within wider discussion of the protection of sexually diverse people under the asylum system. For example, Spijkerboer has argued that asylum policy adopts a limited conception of sexual diversity that is only able to account for performances of diversity that are consistent with a limited range of fixed categories of sexual identity (2013). The result of this is that, as he puts it, 'LGBT people are assigned to specific and quite narrow space where we can be LGBT – but only one category at a time, preferably for life, and only to the extent that they identify with one of those exact categories' (Spijkerboer, 2013: 224–225). As I develop over the next three chapters, the implications for anyone not meeting with this assignation are serious and can be highly detrimental to the chances of success in any given asylum claim.

Evidence of the issues sexually diverse claimants face in regard to proving their identities has long been apparent. For example, Rainbow Migration identified that between 2011 and 2013, 86 per cent of rejected claims were denied on the basis of a lack of credibility (Rainbow Migration, 2013). Put another way, 86 per cent of claims were denied on the basis that their narrative was not regarded as being adequately plausible and consistent. As the literature makes clear, one of the most difficult elements of asylum claims founded on sexual diversity is proving that the claimant is or would be perceived as a sexually diverse person (Lewis, 2014; Powell, 2021a). This difficulty is particularly acute when the widespread absence of 'objective evidence' is considered. Given this, the extent to which a claimant's narrative is viewed as credible can often be central to establishing their need for protection (Murray, 2016).

Weeks has argued that 'the sexual categories and languages we deploy to place people, and place ourselves, in a complex and diverse world, have become critical factors in shaping contemporary structures of sexuality and gender' (Weeks, 2015: 1092). This shaping has, in turn, contributed to a pattern that Stychin has recognized as the 'universalizing of same-sex sexualities as identities' (2005: 954). To see this universalization, consider for a second those who would prefer not to attach an identity-based category to their gender or sexuality. For example, look at the experiences of non-binary people, those who do not identify with either the masculine or feminine gender role, or who otherwise operate between them in one or another formulation. Despite their lack of positive identification with any gender, non-binary people will find themselves gendered by others. An example of this could be as simple as a cashier in a shop referring to them as sir or madam. In that moment, their non-identification is cast aside as they are assigned a category by another. The same also applies to sexuality. Think, for example, of highly stereotypical games such as gay or European. Such games again use a basis of presumed traits to assign a category to a person. Indeed, the ascription of taxonomies and categories is a core feature of language. For example, Sedgwick deploys the methods of Foucault to demonstrate the constitutive role that binaries, such as that between hetero- and homosexuality, often play within our systems of logic (Sedgwick, 2008). The result of the wide deployment of social categories is, of course, that these categories are often mistaken for being natural or innate, with their performative nature being erased (Butler, 1999: 31–39, 175–190). Put another way, because we structure our communications through these categories, we mistake them for being innate or ontologically prior and struggle to recognize their socially constructed nature (White, 1999: 158). This goes back to the idea of meta-politics discussed in Chapter 1. It is not that politicizing these categories is new, it is rather that the categories through which we understand them are so ubiquitous that they give the impression of something given or prior.

As should be apparent, this process of ascription is social. It links back to the very underlying assumptions that queer theory seeks to challenge. For example, in the case of our non-binary scenario, the shopkeeper makes a series of assumptions to arrive at the conclusion that the person in front of them is a man. First, they assume that there is a gender binary, or at least that there are different genders between which distinctions can and should be drawn. Second, they assume that there are particular traits or characteristics which mark someone as being of a particular gender. Third, they assume the person before them displays the traits consistent with a particular gender. This is all generally unconscious. Given the pervasiveness of the gender binary the assumptions are automatic. Because gender has itself become part of the framework through which we make sense of the world. We assume the subjectivities of man and woman are given and that anyone we might meet will fit with one or the other of them.

While social ascription can be deeply problematic and harmful, additional issues arise because the social assumptions which I have just outlined are also pervasive within legal frameworks. Staying with the example of sex and gender, we register children with a legal sex at birth.[2] This legal designation is contingent on their body conforming to certain sexed expectations of what is a male or female body. In this sense, from the moment of our birth, we are subjected to others' underlying assumptions. To the point that it has almost been forgotten that these assumptions are themselves the product of a scientific and social taxonomy that has not been the same across all communities and is not essential or innate (Fausto-Sterling, 2000). Rather, these categories are themselves a product of the particular history and culture of the UK. Indeed, adopting a Gramscian view, it's the very pervasiveness of these ideas that renders them invisible (Bates, 1975; Gramsci, 1998). The adoption of these ascriptions within legal frameworks is a part of the process by which they form hegemonic institutions. Thus, law is often invested with, and based on, forms of knowledge that – despite their widespread and pervasive nature – remain social constructs. To be clear here, I am not claiming that the phenomena which science analyses do not exist independently of science. Such a claim would be unsustainable. Rather, my argument is that science is itself a discipline which humans have constructed, a filter through which information is passed to generate knowledge (Foucault, 1971; 2001). Put another way, my claim is simply that given the pervasive, performative and hegemonic nature of categories such as sex or sexuality, it is difficult to understand their referents in a way not ideologically inflected by existing structures.

Legal categories

As Grabham has noted, within the law, there is a 'propensity to categorise' (Grabham, 2008: 186). This is because law effectively constitutes a deployment of certain discursive categories in order to make sense of

[2] Births and Deaths Registration Act 1953, s1.

social phenomena. That is, law can be conceptualized as a discipline or set of discourses within which social battles are waged. As Butler has argued, the binding nature of law and legal judgments itself operates to cement particular arrangements and systems of power/knowledge (Butler, 2020: 132). Indeed, Loizidou argues that a Foucauldian conception of law essentially sees the legal system as performative in nature (Loizidou, 2007). In this sense, just as with the example of gendering by a shopkeeper earlier, legal systems effectively function by installing themselves into discourse as necessary grounds (Butler, 1999: 16). When discussing legal disciplines such as asylum law, this can be viewed as a pre-eminent example of bio-politics, because law here is functioning to determine which lives are fostered and which are disavowed (Foucault, 1976: 136–138). In this context, note should be taken of the set of policies originally labelled as the Hostile Environment, and then renamed the Compliant Environment (Wemyss, 2018). These policies are designed to disavow certain categories of people by blocking access to various forms of state provision (Agamben, 1998).

Law becomes framed as if it were neutral or pre-determined. It acts as a foundation of our subjectivities. The role of humans in authoring the law, and its interaction with disparate forms of knowledge, are occluded by the very act of legal judgment which proclaims itself as unearthing a form of truth (Foucault, 2000). Thus, legal and social frameworks interlink to produce the concepts through which people make sense of the world. In this sense, the role of sex, sexuality and gender as underlying institutions which themselves play into the underlying assumptions on which legal judgments are based is occluded. Instead, the categories of law and society are seen as natural or freestanding, mere tests which one either does or does not meet, rather than the deeply contingent frameworks they actually are.

This is not the same as asking whether or not law takes account of moral perspectives. Even the most ardent legal positivist would have to recognize that law is, ultimately, founded in language. Indeed, an appreciation of language and arguments founded on the meaning of words was central to Bentham's efforts to sketch out the positivist legal framework (Bentham, 1970). As such, one can hold that the law is a simple question of recognizing those rules which pass a secondary rule as law, in the Hartian sense, without needing to argue that laws do not have reference to linguistic or social issues (Hart, 1961). The point here is to establish that whether you conceptualize law as a science determined without reference to morals, or a manifestation of God's rule on earth, law remains just one social institution among many that operates through instilling itself as a fundamental basis of our society and, therefore, hides its own status as contingent and produced. Thus, the categories through which it operates are always at risk of being engaged by other disciplines.

In the context of asylum, the framework of the Refugee Convention[3] and its 1967 Protocol[4] provide numerous categories through which one must pass to be recognized as a refugee and thus entitled to all of the rights detailed under the Convention. As addressed in Chapter 1, the Refugee Convention definition of a refugee, according to Article 1A(2), outlines that a refugee is a person who is fleeing a well-founded fear of persecution based on one of the five grounds: race; religion; nationality; membership of a particular social group; and political opinion. As this shows, categories are fundamental to law not just in regard to sexual diversity, but also the Convention framework. For example, the harms experienced by a refugee must be categorized as persecution, this means that they must be presented in a recognizable form, which both individual decision-makers, and the established legal framework, recognize as a form of persecution. Similarly, the claimant must be able to show that their fear of persecution is based on the reasons provided under the Convention. For example, if they are claiming that they fear persecution on the basis of religion, then they need to show that their beliefs are or are perceived as a religion. Given the need to fit within the categories provided by the Convention, many people with whom we might commonly associate the term refugee, such as those who are fleeing war or climate change, will often not meet the Convention definition.

As Baars has noted, when the law offers categories of being – such as the gender categories male and female – violence is often enacted against those who do not fit into those categories (Baars, 2019). In the refugee example, this can mean that those whose claims do not fall within one of the recognized categories provided by the Convention are subjected to the violence of being denied status and potentially returned to the threat of serious mistreatment. In regard to those whose status hinges on their sexual diversity, the issues are greater still, with a need to align their enactment of diversity with the available categories of sexual diversity. As such, questions of refugee status are intrinsically tied up with categories. In this sense, as Crawley has argued, the question of whether or not one is a refugee can often be a matter of how one's experiences are analytically characterized (Crawley, 2000). The fundamental issue is whether one's experiences are capable of being read as legible by the established processes and knowledge frameworks in a country.

In drawing this out, I do not seek to argue that categorization is prima facie bad. Indeed, it is recognized that the forms of complexity reduction

3 Convention Relating to the Status of Refugees, 28 July 1951, 189 UNTS 137.

4 Protocol Relating to the Status of Refugees (adopted 31 January 1967, entered into force 4 October 1967), 606 UNTS 267 (Protocol).

that categorization permits are a virtual necessity for law, which is called on to mediate the full spectrum of social complexities into a format where decisive outcomes can be reached. However, I argue that the improper deployment of categories, such as when they are falsely universalized or adopted in too rigid a manner can result in various forms of what I have characterized as 'administrative violence' (Powell, 2023a; 2023b). In particular, this form of violence often figures as symbolic violence arising from the issue of misrecognition, such as the Home Office categorizing a lesbian as heterosexual because her performance of sexual diversity does not correspond to their expectations (Bourdieu, 1992: 127).

Thus, the problem with categorical and identitarian conceptualizations as a means for protecting the rights of sexually diverse people is not an outright objection to their deployment, but rather an argument that violence can occur when there are mismatches between the categories provided by legal and social systems and the lived realities of people who are forced to engage with those categories. In particular, these problems might relate to the various models that claim to offer decision-makers a means to ascertain whether a given claimant falls within a particular category (Dawson and Gerber, 2017). But, more generally, issues arise from the very structure of the particular social group ground, particularly through the test provided under the Nationality and Borders Act 2022. These are matters I return to in Chapters 4 and 5.

2.2 Queer theory and the practice of queering

Queer theory is frequently accused of lacking conceptual clarity and of being overly drawn to linguistic discussions that lack concrete purchase on the world. Indeed, as Martha Nussbaum once said of Butler – who is widely regarded as one of the intellectual cornerstones of queer theory – when characterizing the new form of feminism they represented: 'It is the virtually complete turning from the material side of life, toward a type of verbal and symbolic politics that makes only the flimsiest of connections with the real situation of real women' (Nussbaum, 1999). However, as I have outlined earlier, when one considers that the legal system is itself contingent on the way in which experiences are analytically characterized and categorized, it becomes clear that the contestation of language, identity and concepts is where fundamental contestations over what is an acceptable form of life are undertaken. The point here is that what Nussbaum understood as 'verbal and symbolic' politics is actually the space within which disputes over what kind of lives are liveable and grievable are waged (Butler, 2009). It is within this verbal and symbolic realm that the day-to-day subjectivities around which what Nussbaum and other liberals would see real politics as orienting are contested and formed.

In this register, queer theory offers an analytic tool that provides critical purchase to challenge the assumptions on which current UK asylum practice is built. This kind of critique is vital precisely because the critical questions queer theory enables us to raise constitute questions that go to the very core of our societies. As such, queer theory is never about symbols or linguistic games, but rather is an interjection into the very concepts that make up the day-to-day of our politics. A meta-politics that gets to the core building blocks on which concrete law and policy is conducted. Taken in this sense, far from being symbolic or verbal, queer theory gives us access to the ways in which political subjectivities are formed.

Counter-normativity

However, in order to use queer theory in this way, one further issue must be clarified. Namely, it is important to chart the relationship between queer theory and normativity. Some adherents of queer theory have aligned themselves with a position that Zanghellini (2009) identifies as 'anti-normative'. They have deployed queer theory as a form of pure critique, identifying problems with existing normativities, but not offering solutions or ways to resolve those issues. Indeed, such approaches are often dedicated to challenging all normative systems. And, to be clear, this approach is consistent with the fundamental idea of queer theory I have sketched earlier, that which focuses on the disruption of underlying assumptions regarding the nature of sexual and gender categories.

However, it is argued that, in aligning with the anti-normative position, one loses the ability to defend certain fundamental positions, concerns or ideas. To be truly anti-normative, one must effectively accept a position of nihilism. This is because, to the truly anti-normative theorists, any norm, up to and including the prohibition of murder, cannot be given intellectual justification. Rather, such a norm must be critiqued for the violences and incongruences that it produces. Given this, the anti-normative theorist is also unable to justify why, for example, the ill-treatment of sexual and gender diverse people is wrong. When faced with a situation such as someone facing torture for their non-conformity with gender norms, one can say that the norms themselves are wrong and violent, but they cannot say that the torture is wrong. To do so would be contingent on an a-priori moral norm against torture. However, an anti-normative theorist is forced to reject such a norm as arbitrary or itself a source of violence. So, in this sense, an anti-normative approach to queer theory entirely blunts its usefulness as a tool to advocate for rights and protections.

Given this, it is argued that the nihilism of the anti-normative position leaves it unable to do what queer theory initially set out to do, that is, to create more conceptual space for different subjectivities. In this work, the aim is to assess, through the various narratives I will explore in Chapters 3, 4 and 5, the extent to which the categories provided by legal and administrative processes correspond to the lived realities of claimants and the extent to which the system is able to effectively and fairly process claims for protection by sexually diverse people. If I were to adopt an anti-normative stance, then this question would, as Nussbaum suggests, effectively not have a purchase on reality. This is because, having ascertained, for example, that the categories do not map well onto lived realities, I would be unable to raise any suggestions for what may fit better. If I were to suggest improvements, then what I would be engaging in is a form of normative reasoning.

For this reason, I reject the idea of anti-normativity. Indeed, while I would not endorse the words of Nussbaum, it is difficult to avoid the conclusion that an entirely anti-normative position does constitute a refusal to engage with material reality insofar as it places theoretical purity above the concrete change of material conditions for those suffering harm on the basis of their sexual or gender diversity. Instead, I adopt what Zanghellini (2009: 1–4) has termed counter-normativity. Counter-normativity still involves the challenge and repudiation of dominant norms. However, it does not do this from a standpoint that all norms are inherently wrong or unjustified. Rather, a counter-normative stance is one which deploys the critical tools of queer theory to make concrete proposals for alternative norms. Thus, for example, in my previous work I have proposed a conceptual shift from LGBTIQA+to sexually diverse in regard to how sexual difference is understood within the context of asylum claims (Powell, 2021a). Put another way, I have proposed an alternative norm, which, I argue, addresses many of the harms caused by the current conceptual framework. In this sense, adopting a counter-normative position involves considering how less violent norms could be constructed.

Such an approach not only allows for the making of sustained normative claims but also, I argue, makes for a more comfortable fit between legal scholarship and queer theory. In particular, it creates space for the embrace of certain rights within a queer theoretical frame. This is significant because some have argued that queer theory – and its intellectual forerunners such as Foucault – are not compatible with human rights (Pickett, 2000). However, as Hooke has argued, 'it is fair to say that Foucault supports a vague sense of the right to be different' (1987: 47). Further, as Gordon argues, towards the end of his life, Foucault endorsed a suite of wide-ranging relational rights and recognized the utility of law for resisting certain forms of governmental power (2020: xxix–xi). Like the work of Foucault, queer theory is generally focused on resisting forms of governmental and disciplinary power. As such, much as Zanghellini proposes, I utilize the counter-normative framework of queer theory to enact the 'repudiation of dominant norms' (2009: 1) without falling into an anti-normative 'renunciation of prescriptive projects'

(2009: 4). In this regard, I endorse Zanghellini's (2020) approach in turning to queer theory in pursuit of what are fundamentally humanistic aims

Across the subsequent chapters, I will seek to challenge underlying assumptions regarding the nature of sexual diversity. However, in doing so, I will adopt a position of counter-normativity. Enabling me to propose alternative norms that will contribute to the construction of a legal framework which is more compatible with the lived realities of asylum claimants. Within this, I include reflections on practical elements of the asylum process. As such, while this might be considered a work of what I termed meta-politics – that which deals with concepts, identities and ideas – it is also very much addressed towards the concrete, day-to-day, operation of law and administration.

2.3 Homonormativity to homonationalism: conceptualizing sexuality, nation and the politics of normativity

As a work of queer theory, focused on matters of meta-politics, I have identified this book as fundamentally engaged in a critical process of counter-normative work. That is, as challenging existing norms around sexual diversity and the way in which these norms form a part of the refugee status determination framework. Before norms can be challenged, they must be identified and outlined. As such, this section looks at the way in which sexuality, nation and the wider normativities within which they are deployed have developed.

LGBTIQA+ rights in the UK

The development of LGBT rights in the UK is relatively well-trodden ground. Detailed legal histories can be found, such as in the work of Jeffrey Weeks (2016). However, as a brief summary, buggery was criminalized in England and Wales from 1533 onwards, initially on penalty of death.[5] In 1885, Henry Laboucher, a Liberal MP, introduced an amendment to the Criminal Law Amendment Act. The amendment resulted in Section 11, which created the offence of 'Gross Indecency'. This offence effectively meant that from 1885, until the introduction of a partial defence in 1967, all male same-sex sexual activity was unlawful. Only male same-sex activity was directly criminalized. However, Derry (2020) has usefully charted the relationship between women who have sex with women and the criminal law.

[5] See Buggery Act 1533.

While the law may have been intended to banish same-sex sexual activities from the public sphere, the prosecution of a number of high-profile people across the late 1800s and the early 1900s meant that it actually contributed substantially to greater public awareness of same-sex sexual activities. For example, it was for the offence of Gross Indecency that Oscar Wilde and Lord Montague of Beaulieu, a member of the House of Lords, were imprisoned. Both cases, the trial of Oscar Wilde and that of Lord Montague and his co-defendants gained substantial media attention. Indeed, reports detailed that sympathetic crowds gathered outside the court when Montague and his co-defendants were sentenced (Mars-Jones, 2017).

In light of the substantial media attention that prosecutions for Gross Indecency were receiving, Lord Wolfenden, then chancellor of the University of Reading, was instructed to undertake a report into how the 'homosexual problem' could be dealt with, recommending partial decriminalization. The Wolfenden Report was not a liberatory moment, but rather an attempt to banish homosexuality to the domain of the private. Indeed, following the Sexual Offences Act 1967, which introduced a partial defence to Gross Indecency, and thus offered the first step towards decriminalization, Lord Arran, who had introduced the Bill to the House of Lords, said 'I ask those [homosexuals] to show their thanks by comporting themselves quietly and with dignity … ostentatious behaviour now or in the future or any form of public flaunting would be utterly distasteful'.[6] As this shows, far from a moment of liberation, the move was more focused on rendering diverse sexual behaviours and identities 'quiet' and within the realm of the private. Indeed, it is notable that the number of prosecutions for gross indecency actually went up in the aftermath of the partial decriminalization (Tatchell, 2017). This speaks to how the license provided to those engaging in the behaviours in private also strengthened the interdiction against more public displays.

Writing in the US context, Adler (2020) has charted how many of the landmark developments in regard to LGBT people were contingent on rights to privacy. Similarly, in a UK and European context, the decision in *Dudgeon v UK*, which saw the European Court of Human Rights rule that the continued criminalization of homosexuality – under the framework of Gross Indecency – constituted a violation of the Article 8 rights to private and family life, again rested, in essence, on the idea that sexuality was something that belonged to the private sphere and, thus, was not a matter of legitimate legal regulation for the state.[7] As this suggests, a large part of the early logics behind the protection of sexual diversity lay in the location of sexual and

6 HL Deb, 21 July 1967, Vol 285, CC-522–524.

7 *Dudgeon v UK* (App no 7525/76), ECHR, 22 October 1981.

gender diversity within the home and thus outside of the legitimate purview of the liberal state. This, in turn, has contributed to the view that sexuality is not legitimately a characteristic that requires social change, but rather a facet of private life which should not be interfered with.

Echoes of this same logic can be seen in both the discretion reasoning that governed in sexual diversity claims until 2010 and in the more contemporary instances of disbelief. In the case of discretion, what the state is saying is that the claimant will not be persecuted because they will be able to engage in their sexual diversity without interference provided they do so exclusively within private spaces. As should be clear this, in effect, situates sexual diversity as a private matter within the home rather than as something which has implications for public behaviour and identity. In a similar register, contemporary literature has traced the success of claims as being deeply linked to open performances of identity such as engagement in pride parades and attendance at particular kinds of space (Dhoest, 2019; Luibhéid, 2023). In this sense, ideas of the public/private divide continue to be of profound relevance to our understanding of sexual diversity, mirroring the demand for privacy with a requirement for public displays.

Over time, activists sought to move from legal toleration contingent on privacy to public acceptance. This led to shifts towards a more unified 'gay rights' movement which focused on presenting a strategically essentialized (Spivak, 1985: 175–187) formulation of gay men and lesbians as a group who were born gay and deserved respect for 'who they are'. As proposed, this essentialism served a significant social utility, enabling gay people to present themselves as 'virtually normal' (Sullivan, 1996). This is not to say that certain differences were not pivotal to the construction of a certain core or essentialized constituency of gay men and lesbians. Far from it. Rather, it is to say that while sexual difference was pinpointed as a point of organization, what Foucault termed a 'raison d'être' (1976: 44), this difference was framed as an accident of birth. A morally arbitrary fact about people which, while confining them to a certain classification of people, nonetheless was not something that rendered them as incapable of forming useful and productive parts of a tolerant and liberal society (Brickell, 2001). In this sense, it was possible for the 'gay rights movement' to campaign for specific rights, deploying a virtual normality, which presented sexuality as a situation which anyone could find themselves in and something which should not be a ground for someone to be treated differently from surrounding society. Simply put, the logic was of the person who should have access to exactly the same rights as everyone else.

As Clements and Field have presciently drawn out, any notion of a linear progress narrative around LGBTIQA+ rights must be abandoned (Clements and Field, 2014). Indeed, social attitudes surveys demonstrate that 1987 was the most homophobic year on record in the UK. This, 20 years after the UK's partial decriminalization, demonstrates the often-incongruent relationship between law and social attitudes. Of course, one of the central drivers of the increase in negative attitudes towards gay men was the HIV pandemic, which was at its peak in the mid-1980s with very large numbers of – shockingly young – gay men falling ill and dying (Cook, 2016). In this context, Susan Sontag spoke of a social death that precedes the physical, with gay men becoming marked as potentially contagious and seen as a threat to the broader population (Sontag, 1989). In this sense, the 1980s can be viewed as a historical inversion, cutting across the narrative of 'virtual normality' and the dictum of privacy to draw visual and spectacular attention to the marked differences of men who have sex with men. This spectacular difference arises both from the numbers who lost their lives, but also from the physical manifestations of late-stage HIV and Aids, manifesting in forms of body horror that physically marked those who had the virus out from the surrounding society (Engelmann, 2016). In this sense, the peak in fear, anxiety and disgust towards LGBTIQA+ people coincides with events that challenged the narrative of virtual normality and drew attention to the diverse sexual practices of such communities. Indeed, this shift also allowed space for the religious right and other figures of what Ronald Reagan called the 'moral majority' to intervene with narratives of personal responsibility (Sparke, 2016) and seek to blame gay men themselves for the harms experienced during the period (Morris, 2021).

In response to these challenges, one can detect a doubling down on the ideas of homonormativity. That is, an active attempt by organizations, particularly in the context of highly effective treatments which have effectively brought an end to the HIV pandemic in countries such as the UK, to present LGBTIQA+ people as 'virtually normal' (Ashford et al, 2020). This can be seen both in the forms of activism adopted and the targets on which that activism focused. For example, the UK's largest LGBTIQA+ organization, Stonewall's slogan 'some people are gay, get over it' operates by pushing two countervailing discourses that correlate to the patterns of essentialism and normativity outlined earlier. First, the claim that 'some people are gay' seeks to validate the sexual identity of being gay as a way of being, as a fact about who someone is. This can be viewed as a form of strategic essentialism, operating to give permanent and stable content to the category of 'gay' and hinting – though subtly – that this is a form of biological existence and thus naturalizing that category. In essence, the purpose here is to gesture once more to the morally arbitrary nature of being gay. While, at the same time, through the statement 'get over it', hinting that this is something inconsequential, like the idea that a person has green eyes or brown hair. Through these two countervailing discourses, it is argued, sexuality is presented in a homonormative framework that sets it out as both fundamental to who someone is, while presenting the acceptance of it as fundamentally compatible with existing social orders (Powell, 2021a). In simple terms, someone being gay does not change the fact that they are just like you.

Thus, the primary thrust of discourses around sexuality has been to attempt to shroud sexuality in a politics of the normative. This is to say, that the focus has been on casting sexual diversities as essentially compatible with existing normative orders and therefore capable of being inculcated and properly fostered within the nation. In this register, while the UK has undoubtedly been in a position to include a number of sexual diversities within the range of acceptable identities, it has done so in a highly normativizing manner. As such, there remains a real problem with embracing those whose sexual diversities do not fit within frameworks familiar to the UK. The result of this, in the context of the asylum system, as I develop in the next section, is that the UK is only able to recognize the identity performances and persecution faced by those who perform their identities in highly normativized and specific ways.

2.4 Gay enough for the government? Queer theory and the identity-based refugee

Recalling that, as addressed at the outset of this chapter, queer theory is concerned with disrupting underlying assumptions, it is argued that it provides vital critical purchase for challenging the limited and highly identitarian conceptions of sexual diversity currently deployed within the UK. The asylum system is a place in which these conceptions are particularly harmful because it is one of the few contexts within which the state seeks to make authoritative decisions as to whether or not a given person is, or would be perceived as, a given form of sexual diversity.

As argued earlier, when considering the topic of what constitutes a sexual identity the law has few answers. Instead, there is a need to look outside of law to inform decision-makers on what sexual identities are. In this sense, the law adopts the underlying assumptions of the surrounding society regarding what sexual identities exist and what they mean. The operation of evidence and credibility within refugee status determination, based almost exclusively in narrative, very directly draws on how society has conceptualized sexual diversity in order to tether ideas of plausibility when approaching credibility considerations.

Given this, queer theory under a counter-normative approach provides this text with the critical purchase to challenge the way in which refugee status determination in regard to sexually diverse refugees is conducted. In particular, it allows the space to critically consider whether the normativities through which sexual diversity is understood are able to adequately translate to other social, historical, geographical and political contexts.

In the UK, we have now reached a point where there is a widely held social perception that identities such as gay and lesbian are effectively ontologically prior, that they exist irrespective of the particular social and historical contexts within which they have emerged and, as a corollary, that such identities are effectively the same in every context. As a result of this, the question of refugee status as it relates to sexually diverse people often comes to be based on what is effectively an assessment of the extent to which the narrative of the particular claimant is sufficiently close to a gay or lesbian identity in the UK to read as credible.

As I have argued elsewhere, this may correlate to wider facets of sexual identity such as the social engagements a person has or the types of space they inhabit (Powell, 2024a). Regardless, the salient issue here is that the ability of claimants to gain refugee status is often tied to their correspondence with a narrow and identity-focused conception of sexual diversity. Often, conceptions of sexual identity will be informed by the wider day-to-day manifestations of sexual diversity that both decision-makers and policy makers observe in their own lives. Indeed, it can be argued that some of the models proposed to assist decision-makers to determine whether or not a given person is in fact gay have themselves contributed to the narrowness of the frames of reference through which claimants are required to pass.

The Difference, Stigma, Shame, Harm model

One example of this is the Difference, Stigma, Shame, Harm model (Chelvan, 2011; 2018). This model, often abbreviated to DSSH, claims to provide a helpful tool that enables decision-makers to more easily identify those claimants who are or would be perceived as sexually diverse. The first stage of the model calls on decision-makers to consider whether the claimant has a narrative of difference. Though this is claimed to be focused generally on feelings of difference from the surrounding society, claimants in systems such as the UK's – noting that materials such as the Home Office's 2016 Asylum Policy Instruction: Sexual Orientation in Asylum Claims are clearly influenced by the DSSH model – have reported being expected to offer highly developed emotional narratives of realizing their identity (Rainbow Migration, 2018). Further, the third part of the model, which calls for a focus on the claimant's experiences of shame resulting from the stigma they have experienced due to their difference from the surrounding society, can also be seen as having circumscribed the emotional responses of claimants (Åberg, 2023). While it is accurate that many will respond to experiences of stigma and social hostility by experiencing shame, this is not an inherent reaction and there are other emotional responses a person may experience. For example, some people may instead respond to stigma with a sense of outrage. Otherwise put, the idea of shame effectively relies on the person responding to their experiences of stigma by viewing themselves as the problem and thus feeling shame for who they are. However, some people, particularly in the context of a more globalized world where examples of open sexual diversity can often be freely seen online, may instead view those who are stigmatizing them as the ones who are in the wrong. As such, rather than feeling shame, they may be motivated to make change or may feel a sense of outrage.

Dawson and Gerber (2017) have drawn attention to the shortcomings of the model in regard to its inability to accurately represent the experiences of sexually diverse women. They also go on to identify that when the model is applied it often quickly comes to be applied as a form of calcified check boxes, rather than the set of helpful prompts it was originally framed as. This corresponds to my own findings and speaks to how the deployment of certain models can themselves contribute to a more fixed conception of sexual diversity being relied on within the context of the asylum system.

Fundamentally, the issue with these models is that they perpetuate largely fixed ways of conceptualizing sexual diversity. This, combined with the forms of biological essentialism that have been deployed by both opponents to and supporters of the rights of sexually diverse people, has resulted in the relatively fixed conceptions of sexual diversity which I have outlined here. In turn, it is argued, these fixed conceptions come to be represented within legal systems that end up being called on to determine whether or not someone is within a given category, such as gay men. This is particularly the case in a system that is heavily based on narrative and credibility, in the way the refugee status determination system is.

Given this context around how sexually diverse people have been constructed in the UK, it is argued that queer theory serves as a useful corrective that enables a critical examination of the ways in which sexual diversity is conceptualized. When undertaken from the counter-normative orientation adopted within this book, it provides a critical purchase that enables consideration of where there are mismatches between the frames of recognition deployed by the asylum system and the lived realities of claimants. In the next chapter, these mismatches are drawn out via a dialogue with the lived realities of refugees.

3

The Narratives of Refugees

Often legal research, written from a formalist or doctrinal perspective, can be said to be overly concerned with rules and policies and, in so doing, can ignore the lived experiences of those engaging with legal institutions as both a relevant feature to understanding the operations of legal apparatus and as holders of knowledge regarding the nature of those apparatus. In the case of asylum claims by people who are sexually diverse, lived experience of the asylum system carries a particular and important form of knowledge. Specifically, such claimants are able to show, through their experiences, how specific forms of knowledge – framed by decision-makers as given and objective – are implicated within decision-making processes. For example, those who have claimed asylum in the UK are able to speak to how gender and sexual diversity were conceptualized by decision-makers, and how these conceptualizations interacted with the legal framework as well as the Home Office's Asylum Policy Instructions (APIs), and can therefore offer critical insights into how forms of social/scientific knowledge and reasoning operate within what are often presented as objective – quasi-scientific – legal and administrative decision-making processes.

This chapter draws on eight semi-structured interviews with people who have lived experience of navigating the UK asylum system with a claim based on their sexual diversity. These interviews were undertaken between 2018 and March 2020, and focus on the self-conceptions of the claimants and how these self-conceptions were understood by those considering whether they were entitled to international protection. Semi-structured interviews were used because, as Elam and Fenton have argued, semi-structured interviews are often the best approach to undertaking research on sensitive topics given that they are a form of research where the researcher is directly on hand to intervene and ensure appropriate action is taken if the participant becomes uncomfortable, and because the open nature of such interviews enables any the participant to have space to explore their own narrative and experiences with the impact of any prior assumptions on the part of the researcher being minimized (Elam and Fenton, 2003: 19–20). The interviews were undertaken in semi-private locations such as cafes. Participants were invited to choose the locations, enabling them to select places where they felt they would be comfortable. The creation of an environment where participants felt calm and safe was of paramount concern due to the risk of potentially retraumatizing participants. The interviews were approximately two hours in duration and adopted an open-ended approach. While there was a set list of questions all participants were asked, space was given to the natural development of the conversation, with the responses of participants leading the direction of conversation.

While this part of the study drew on a small sample, the adequacy of the sample was assessed with reference to the concept of 'information power' (Malterud et al, 2016). Information power focuses, in particular, on criteria such as the specificity of the sample and the methods of analysis which will be utilized in exploring the findings. Given that the aims of these interviews were on assessing whether the UK asylum apparatus could comprehend the heterogeneous nature of the ways in which people seeking asylum experience sexual diversity, a deep analysis of the data was required, this therefore tended towards the engagement of a smaller sample.

The analysis of the interviews deployed an ethnographically informed phenomenological narrative analysis approach. The focus of phenomenological narrative enquiry is on understanding the meanings which participants attach to their own experiences (Koven, 2014: 500). This approach also favours smaller samples as 'the aim is to reveal something of the experience of each of a set of individuals based on very careful examination of each individual' (Black et al, 2011: 52). Ethnographic approaches focus on situating the experiences within participants' own cultural worlds and ensuring that such experiences are articulated on participants' own terms (Roulston and Choi, 2018: 235). In short, combining the two approaches sought to understand the experiences of participants in their own terms to facilitate determinations as to the extent to which the participants' own experiences were consistent with how the Home Office understands those same experiences.

While the interviews were undertaken prior to the profound changes made to the UK's system for refugee status determination between 2022 and 2024, their experiences of sexual diversity offer a useful benchmark against which the shifting processes can be evaluated (Powell, 2024b), particularly when taken alongside the third sector and legal practitioner narratives analysed in Chapters 4, 5 and 6. These subsequent chapters are based on eighteen further interviews with legal practitioners and volunteers and staff working in third sector organizations which support asylum seekers and were undertaken in 2023. Those interviews were again undertaken in semi-private settings on a semi-structured basis with the focus being on exploring the experiences of actors within the UK asylum system as a means to access the operation of everyday legal consciousness within the UK asylum system (Sarat, 1990). In order to access this a phenomenological narrative analysis approach was again applied to these interviews. As such, the three different participant groups offer a significant body of experienced expertise regarding the functioning of the UK asylum system.

Rather surprisingly, given the volume of change across the rest of the UK asylum system, the API on Sexual Orientation in Asylum Claims has not been updated since 2016.[1] This means that, while the broader legal framework has shifted significantly, the policies and guidance to be applied when seeking to determine whether a given asylum claimant is or would be perceived as sexually diverse remain unchanged from its position at the time when the interviews were undertaken. However, some of the changes – such as those made to the standard of proof by Section 32 of the Nationality and Borders Act 2022 – will have implications in regard to how the APIs are applied in practice. To reflect this, I have in places sought to address how the shifts made to the asylum system since 2022 would likely impact the asylum claimants who I spoke to were they to make their claim under the new framework. In most cases, the higher standard of proof would simply exacerbate the issues participants identified during the interviews by making matters of credibility and proof even more onerous.

3.1 Sexuality as identity: exploring sexual diversity

One of the first issues arising when trying to discuss LGBTIQA+rights – particularly within the context of the international or global plain – arises from issues around languages and concepts. In the UK, as in other states forming a part of the presumed unity known as 'the west', we have a conception of sexual diversity or difference as constituting a series of discrete identities – such as gay or lesbian – which offer a stable way of understanding and socially situating particular groups of people based on an idea of sexual object/subject choice. Indeed, the question of whether one accepts these discrete identities as a fundamental truth or sees them simply as strategically useful within a given context could be argued to be the predominant lines of separation between queer theorists and advocates of LGBTIQA+ equal rights. However, to see that this framing is a product of a particular set of discourses, you need only look at the history of the UK. As Foucault has argued, it was during the Victorian period where the social category of the homosexual came to be constructed as the primary way of making sense

[1] UK Visas and Immigration, 'Asylum Policy Instruction: Sexual Orientation in Asylum Claims' (Home Office, 2016), available at: https://assets.publishing.service.gov.uk/government/uploads/system/uploads/attachment_data/file/543882/Sexual-orientation-in-asylum-claims-v6.pdf (accessed 20 September 2024).

of sexual diversity (Foucault, 1976). Specifically, during this period, non-normative sexual desires were transformed through a series of logics and narratives which re-configured an aberrant behaviour (the act of sodomy) to a fundamental status that one holds, marking them out as a particular kind of person, that is, the homosexual person. I have charted the history in the UK context in the previous chapter.

However, what we need to take forward here is simply an idea that the way in which we understand sexual diversity is not inherent or natural. Rather, it is a product of particular historic discourses and institutions and that, despite this, it functions as a benchmark of intelligibility through which access to rights and institutional fostering is regulated. Otherwise put, knowledge, including our knowledge regarding subjectivities, is always historically and socially constituted and yet that knowledge forms the epistemological grid through which we come to understand who the human of human rights is. To put this more simply, how we understand categories such as gay and lesbian is the result of the history and culture of the UK and we should not expect these categories to look the same in places with different histories and cultures.

Proving sexuality: sexual diversity in the asylum system

The refugee status determination system offers one of the key locations within which conceptions of sexual diversity take on concrete legal effects. This is because, in order to succeed in an asylum claim on the basis of sexual diversity, a claimant needs to show not only that they fear persecution, but that their fear of persecution is a result of their sexual diversity. Within the broader literature, this is referred to as the nexus criterion (Nilsson, 2014). For example, a claimant who was fleeing persecution as a gay man would, as a part of their claim, and to the appropriate standard of proof, need to show that they were a gay man or would be perceived as one. Note should be taken here that International Refugee Law, and the guidance given by the United Nations High Commissioner for Refugees, anticipated a low standard of proof being applied,[2] with claimants given the benefit of the doubt where their narrative appears to generally display the hallmarks of credibility. However, some organizations have argued that, in practice, a higher standard of proof is being applied within the current practices of the

[2] United Nations High Commissioner for Refugees (UNHCR), Note on Burden and Standard of Proof in Refugee Claims, 16 December 1998; United Nations High Commissioner for Refugees (UNHCR), Handbook on Procedures and Criteria for Determining Refugee Status and Guidelines on International Protection Under the 1951 Convention and the 1967 Protocol Relating to the Status of Refugees, Reissued February 2019, UNDOC HCR/1P/4/ENG/REV.4 43–47.

UK (Freedom From Torture, 2019). Indeed, there is extensive evidence of a pervasive 'culture of disbelief' operating within the Home Office and functioning in a way that has significant implications for how claimants experience the asylum system (Jubany, 2011; Gibson, 2013; Schuster, 2020; Ferreira, 2022). Obviously, this raises immediate issues insofar as the forms of evidence required to demonstrate or 'prove' a characteristic such as sexual diversity cannot be easily identified and require a number of extrinsic forms of knowledge to be engaged within the production of legal truth. It is these forms of knowledge, and the extent to which they correspond to the lived realities of asylum claimants, that we turn in this chapter.

In this sense, the refugee status determination process offers an interesting site within which questions of epistemology are contested and re-formulated. As Bruce-Jones has argued, the way in which sexual diversity is presented within one case may have implications for how it is understood in future (Bruce-Jones, 2015). While the Home Office offers guidance to decision-makers regarding how cases founded on sexual diversity should be approached,[3] it remains the case that, with regard to defining sexual diversity, law has few answers. As such, decision-makers often look to broader disciplines of knowledge when attempting to discern whether there is adequate evidence, and indeed whether the evidence which has been offered is credible. Indeed, as I have argued elsewhere, many of the frameworks through which sexual diversities are understood arise from media depictions of sexual diversity which help to cement, in the minds of decision-makers, particular envisionings of what it means to be of a diverse gender or/and sexual identity, orientation or behaviour (Powell, 2021b: 276–287). These media representations, of course, draw on the historical and social facets we have discussed previously.

While some immigration judges have claimed that sexual diversity asylum claims are 'easy to make and impossible to disprove',[4] academic commentators have pointed out that 'decision-makers still have no idea what claimants need to do to prove their sexual orientation' (Lewis, 2014: 963). Of course, the reality underlying both of these positions is that there is no way to provide an objective answer regarding how they could be proved, because the answer is, ultimately, indeterminate. Given this, as I will argue in what follows, it is advisable for administrative frameworks seeking to discern matters in relation

---

[3] UK Visas and Immigration, 'Asylum Policy Instruction: Sexual Orientation in Asylum Claims' (Home Office, 2016), available at: https://assets.publishing.service.gov.uk/government/uploads/system/uploads/attachment_data/file/543882/Sexual-orientation-in-asylum-claims-v6.pdf (accessed 20 September 2024).

[4] *Krasniqi v Secretary of State for the Home Department* [2001] UKIAT 01TH02140 [2].

to sexual diversity to adopt an open-textured and flexible approach to issues around showing group membership.

This could encompass using self-identification, as Jansen has proposed in the Dutch context (Jansen, 2019). However, such an approach still risks marginalizing those who do not understand their sexual diversity through the framework of identity. As such, there is also a need to be open-textured and thoughtful in regard to the forms of evidence which will be considered, while remaining mindful of the need to ensure that claimants are properly extended the benefit of the doubt. In this regard, there is a real risk that those asylum seekers seeking to avoid removal from the UK under the new processes established by the Illegal Migration Act 2023 – should this be brought into effect – would be at a real risk of removal from the UK notwithstanding the substantial vulnerabilities they may have due to the compression of timeframes that this legal framework brings about. Further reflections on the issues posed by the changes brought to the UK asylum system between 2022 and 2024 are included in Chapter 6 of this volume.

Given this, reflections around the inter-relations of law and knowledge of sexual and gender diversity addressed in this chapter are pertinent not just to the claim of refugee status, but also to issues such as the operation of the suspensive claims process envisaged by the Illegal Migration Act 2023. Within both processes, the essential issue is that, as Nelken has claimed, '[w]hat counts as legal knowledge, or knowledge for law, is something that changes over time. And this mainly happens outside the courtroom' (2006: 602). In this sense, the conceptualizations of sexual diversity deployed within the administrative process often speak to broader socio-cultural frameworks that cannot be captured within administrative guidance or legal frameworks. Put simply, decision-makers will look at claims around sexual diversity through lenses which are conditioned by the representations of sexual diversity which they see every day within their own lives and the historical and social narratives which they have been taught.

In this register, the purpose of using a queer counter-normative framework is to attempt to cast sunlight on to these representations in order to demonstrate their incongruences with the lived realities of people and therefore to provide critical impetus for less harmful representations and conceptualizations to emerge.

Discordant sexuality: sexual identity, sexual orientation and sexual behaviour

The change in how sexual diversity has been conceptualized within the UK since the Victorian period is well-articulated within Foucault's work on the *History of Sexuality* (Foucault, 1976; 1986; 1990; 2021). In this work, Foucault is effectively seeking to document how during the Victorian era the discipline of medicine, through the deployment of the scientific method, worked to generate new subjectivities, that is, sexualities which subjects came to claim (Foucault, 1976). As explored earlier, these identities were generally viewed as stable, fixed, and for life. However, this framing perhaps fails to fully engage with the internal complexities and contradictions of sexual diversity. Savin-Williams argues that sexuality carries within itself three constituent parts which can be, and often are, discordant with one another. Specifically, he argues that sexuality contains the three distinctive elements of sexual identity, sexual orientation and sexual behaviour (Savin-Williams, 2005: 27–48). There is, Savin-Williams argues, no inherent reason for these different characteristics to cohere. For example, someone could identify as a straight man while having sexual desires for, that is, be oriented towards, exclusively other men and engaging in sexual activities with both men and women.

In this sense, the first issue which we need to address is the presumed coherence and simplicity of 'sexuality'. As the narratives of the refugees I spoke to attested, sexuality is rarely a clear or coherent concept. Rather, the frameworks through which we understand sexual diversity speak to the particular histories and cultures from which it has emerged and, in the UK context, this has led to the focus on a particular range of (neo-)liberal cosmopolitan identities. However, this is neither inherent nor necessary and decision-makers should not assume that people from different social and political contexts will understand themselves in a manner that corresponds either to this identity driven logic, or to the forms of sexual diversity, which they encounter within their own day-to-day experiences.

The 2016 Asylum Policy Instruction

Unfortunately, such perspectives are, as we explore in this chapter, reinforced by the API on sexual diversity which – with its focus on the presentation of 'narrative of difference'[5] – presents sexual diversity as if it were a form of identity or fundamental status which conditions all elements of claimant's social life.

Sweeney identifies that 'the APIs … are influential but not-legislative documents designed to help decision-makers by drawing together law and good practice' (Sweeney, 2009: 704). As such, the APIs are often the first port of call for decision-makers, offering them guidance on both the law and

[5] UK Visas and Immigration, 'Asylum Policy Instruction: Sexual Orientation in Asylum Claims' (Home Office, 2016), available at: https://assets.publishing.service.gov.uk/government/uploads/system/uploads/attachment_data/file/543882/Sexual-orientation-in-asylum-claims-v6.pdf (accessed 20 September 2024).

how it should be applied in practice. This means that their content can be crucial to the functioning of the asylum system. The 2016 sexual diversity API provides little guidance on what questions and forms of evidence decision-makers should use when trying to determine whether or not a given claimant is or would be perceived of as sexually diverse, instead focusing on the idea of a narrative of difference as outlined earlier.

Turning to the API itself, the policy begins by looking to issues of language and terminology.[6] In doing so, it also immediately touches on some of the conceptual issues which I have already addressed. The premise of the policy in stating that 'LGB is an acronym used in many Western Cultures for lesbian, gay or bisexual'[7] is that there is a stable referent to which these terms can be applied. This is helpful insofar as it seeks to make decision-makers aware that language around LGB is a product of specific history and may not be utilized by those who have been socialized within different contexts (Massad, 2002; Nasser-Eddin et al, 2018). However, it is also flawed as it functions to universalize the referent – that is, sexuality as identity – and particularize the terminology. Of course, as addressed in Chapter 2, the reality is that the referent, like the language through which it is expressed, is not stable but rather is itself a product brought about through the interaction of a range of different countervailing discourses and forms of power across particular histories and cultures. As such, this section can be seen as contributing to a sense that the referent is universal and that differences are likely to be only linguistic in nature.

Moving on from this, the API identifies that LGB will often be used in order to 'encompass a person's social identity and community'.[8] While the policy is clear in stating that the terminology of LGB 'does not suggest that LGB people are a homogenous group with a shared or collective identity, representation or experience of linked issues',[9] I would argue that

---

6 UK Visas and Immigration, 'Asylum Policy Instruction: Sexual Orientation in Asylum Claims' (Home Office, 2016), available at: https://assets.publishing.service.gov.uk/government/uploads/system/uploads/attachment_data/file/543882/Sexual-orientation-in-asylum-claims-v6.pdf (accessed 20 September 2024), p 6.

7 UK Visas and Immigration, 'Asylum Policy Instruction: Sexual Orientation in Asylum Claims' (Home Office, 2016), available at: https://assets.publishing.service.gov.uk/government/uploads/system/uploads/attachment_data/file/543882/Sexual-orientation-in-asylum-claims-v6.pdf (accessed 20 September 2024), p 6.

8 UK Visas and Immigration, 'Asylum Policy Instruction: Sexual Orientation in Asylum Claims' (Home Office, 2016), available at: https://assets.publishing.service.gov.uk/government/uploads/system/uploads/attachment_data/file/543882/Sexual-orientation-in-asylum-claims-v6.pdf (accessed 17 June 2024), p 6.

9 UK Visas and Immigration, 'Asylum Policy Instruction: Sexual Orientation in Asylum Claims' (Home Office, 2016), available at: https://assets.publishing.service.gov.uk/government/uploads/system/uploads/attachment_data/file/543882/Sexual-orientation-in-asylum-claims-v6.pdf (accessed 17 June 2024), p 6.

the close alignment which it makes between sexual diversity and forms of social identity and community is problematic in presuming that sexuality presents in a unified manner that effectively presupposes identification as a core component of sexual diversity. This is because such a conceptualization presumes that sexual diversity will correlate to a form of group identity or a way of being, even if the exact terminology and formulation of the group identity is not the same as those we might commonly see in the UK.

This ignores the fact that, for some, sexual diversity is not viewed as a form of identity at all, but in fact as a form of behaviour or a type of attraction (orientation). Where this is the case, the framing of the policy is immediately setting decision-makers towards a set of expectations with which claimants may struggle to correspond, creating a mismatch that harms the ability of sexually diverse people who experience their sexual diversity in a manner that does not mirror those seen in the UK to navigate the process. For example, Abdullah told me:

> I never really identified with my sexuality. I recognized my sexuality, I accepted it, I was okay with it. I even lived with it. But the thing is, here is where it gets more complicated, identity is a very difficult word to identify. In every culture there is a certain set of values associated with identity. (Abdullah, Omani refugee)[10]

As this narrative shows, sexual orientation, desire and identity is a multivalent phenomenon. It cannot be assumed that it will present in the same way within different contexts. For Abdullah, the idea of his sexual diversity constituting a form of identity did not correspond to his lived experience. Indeed, he then explained that identity can often be viewed as highly culturally specific with different values and norms attaching to different ways of being within different contexts.

Abdullah went on to tell me about how, within the culture of his country of origin, Oman, identity was more likely to be linked to characteristics such as one's faith group, tribe or nationality. However, with regard to sexual behaviour or orientation, these were not generally viewed as fundamental or as framing who someone is. Rather, such characteristics were associated with behaviour. Specifically he told me:

> In the Gulf Region, or lets say in the wider region, so let's say in the Middle East, in a sense, identity is not who you associate with or what you feel. Identity is your faith group, your tribe, your nationality. …

10 Please note that pseudonyms are used throughout this book in order to protect the identity of all Participants

> So, when you say what do you identify as … if you ask any Omani to identify themselves, even if they were the proudest and outest gay man or woman, they wouldn't even end up saying that they are gay. … Sexual identity is viewed as something you do. (Abdullah, Omani refugee)

For Abdullah, the idea of sexuality as a form of identity was a Christian or European notion. This framing did not correspond to his lived realities. While it is important not to generalize from a single experience, Abdullah's words here correspond to literature around how sexuality is understood in certain Middle Eastern contexts (Nasser-Eddin et al, 2018; Allouche, 2020). Given that the section we are presently discussing is intended to make decision-makers aware of the potential factors which may limit the ability of claimants to advance a coherent narrative within the context of a substantive asylum interview, it is concerning that such a universalizing worldview – which may function as a source of cognitive dissonance for or imposition upon claimants – is asserted and encouraged as the approach which decision-makers should take to conducting interviews with asylum claimants.

Indeed, Abdullah went on to directly address the disjunction between his own conceptualization of his sexual diversity and that of the Home Office. Specifically, he said:

> [The Home Office's] understanding of homosexuality was that of a gay person. To me gay is so different than homosexual. I mean homosexual is just your sexual attraction, full stop. But when you are gay it is not just your attraction; it is also how you express your attraction, and the slogans which you use to express that attraction, and the way you conduct yourself in relation to that attraction. So, basically, you have to re-culture yourself in relation to that attraction and if you have not re-cultured yourself yet, then you are not gay yet. You are just homosexual. (Abdullah, Omani refugee)

The drawing of this distinction between gay and homosexual is an interesting one. It reflects the development of gay identities in the period after criminalization across the UK,[11] US[12] and much of Europe (Westrate and McLean, 2010), and contrasts it with the highly conduct-driven conceptualization of the homosexual which existed prior to this and has

[11] The Sexual Offences Act 1967.

[12] In *Lawrence v Texas* the US Supreme Court held that all laws criminalizing sodomy between consenting adults were unconstitutional. See *Lawrence v Texas* 539 U.S. 558 (US Supreme Court).

been recorded by scholars as continuing to predominate within particular cultural and social contexts (Caplan, 1989). In this sense, his narrative draws direct attention to the disjuncture between the sexuality/sexual orientation as identity conceptualization of sexual diversities that we have developed in the UK and contrasts these to a conceptualization of sexual diversity far more rooted within sexual behaviour which more readily corresponds to his own self-understanding.

As this suggests, my argument is that in the UK context, as Abdullah identifies, sexuality is generally viewed as a form of identity. It is understood as something that conditions how you express yourself and as a fundamental element of 'who you are'. It is only within this logic that the narrative of 'coming out' makes sense, an announcement to the world of who you are. However, for him, sexuality was more about attraction, desire and behaviour. In this sense, Abdullah called himself a homosexual to connote that he was attracted physically and emotionally to men. To draw on Sara Ahmed, his orientation (desire) called him towards other men as objects of desire (Ahmed, 2006: 16–21). However, he stopped short of adopting a view that his attractions made him a particular type of person.

In this sense, Abdullah's narrative reflected a mismatch with the expectations of the Home Office. The Home Office expected a narrative of identity, that Abdullah would chart how his experiences of desire had made him realize that he was a particular kind of person. Indeed, as the literature outlines, they will also have expected a highly developed outline of his emotional responses to becoming aware of this identity, and a rationalization of how it has affected other areas of his life and relationships (Rainbow Migration, 2018). As such, the forms of evidence expected under the API, which broadly focus on eliciting a narrative of how someone is different from surrounding society, did not -fit with Abdullah's self-conceptualization, which focused instead on his being someone who engages in particular forms of behaviour. For Abdullah, who conceptualized himself as fundamentally the same as others from his country of origin, but merely attracted to people of the same sex, the API undermined, rather than supported, his ability to frame his claim. Note should be taken here that, clearly drawing on the Difference, Stigma, Shame, Harm (DSSH) model, the primary focus underlying the API is on locating a 'narrative of difference' within the lived experience of the asylum claimant (Dawson and Gerber, 2017). However, for someone who, like Abdullah, understands their sexual diversity more as a form of physical and romantic attraction than as an identity, such a narrative would be difficult to provide. In this sense, the way that sexual diversity is conceptualized within the UK asylum system actively harms the chances of claimants like Abdullah being able to navigate that system.

Other participants noted similar concerns around the assumption of a universal sexuality on the part of the Home Office. For example, Babu stated:

> One of the most interesting things is like how gender identity and sexuality, all these things, like you know homosexuality and on the broader scale in these countries such as Egypt were influenced by colonialism. Because, prior to colonialism sexuality was not an issue. Like, a lot of Arabic literature actually talks about men falling in love with other men and how absolutely fine it was hundreds of years before colonialism. And then once the colonial powers overtook those countries, they change the laws and regulations that they put in place to make them perceive the things that Europe was perceiving at the time and among them was the idea of sexuality; that homosexuality was wrong. (Babu, Egyptian refugee)

As this suggests, a further issue that arises within the context of the API's focus on a narrative of difference is that for some claimants it carries resonances of colonialism, imposing the idea that sexual diversity is a significant and defining characteristic which forms a core part of who 'someone is'. Such a feeling of imposition within the asylum system is problematic because the system is intended to embed a shared responsibility in regard to the burden of proof, expecting that decision-makers will work with claimants and support them. This includes by means of creating a comfortable and supportive interview environment. However, the imposition of culturally unfamiliar or uncomfortable frameworks can encumber the ability of people to feel comfortable (Birks et al, 2007; Koven, 2014). The idea that conceptualizing sexual diversity as an identity is a form of 'western imposition' or is not common outside of a European context was not one which was shared by all participants. For example, Abeo said:

> I think there is a universality of identity, that gay men are always in love with other man and gay women are always in love with other women. So that is a universality of identity. Now, how we then socially express it, depends on the environments where we find ourselves. (Abeo, Nigerian refugee)

As this suggests, even though Abeo viewed sexuality as being an essentially universal identity, he still saw space for social and cultural variation in how this might be expressed. In this sense, while some claimants were able to, in effect, articulate a narrative of difference in the manner anticipated by the policy, there remain issues insofar as the framing of the policy seems to presuppose that the existence of such identities will function as a basis for community formation. Indeed, looking to the text of the API itself, the underlying assumption seems to be that the main differences in regard to how sexual diversity will be understood within different cultures are linguistic. In this regard, Abeo expressed frustration with the process, telling me:

> If you ask me do I go to gay parties, and I say yes there are gay parties, and you say do I go, and I say no I don't go to gay parties and you say oh so you are not gay, that is a disservice. Because you can say oh people here go to gay clubs, but people here go to gay clubs because there is freedom to do so, and even if you don't want to go there is freedom. (Abeo, Nigerian refugee)

As such, despite the fact that Abeo understood his own sexual diversity as being a form of universal 'gay' identity, which he shared with others from around the world, without depending on time, location or specific socio-cultural context, he still felt frustrated that decision-makers had not seemed able to understand the impact that culture and other social factors might have on how sexual diversity manifests itself and on the type of experiences and evidence offered during the substantive interview process. Indeed, he told me that his experiences of the asylum process had left him feeling both frustrated and disrespected, particularly due to the disbelief displayed towards his experiences.

Similar mismatches between the way decision-makers anticipated and understood sexual diversity were present for other refugees who I spoke to. Indeed, one of the biggest problems which faced Masani, a Ugandan lesbian refugee, was the expectation that sexuality was a fixed and stable phenomenon. This expectation is implicit in the links between sexuality and truth. As explored by Foucault, the act of 'coming out' could be linked back to ideas of the Catholic confession, confessing your identity to the streets in the sense that people who are sexually diverse are seen to be revealing something fundamental about themselves (Foucault, 1976: 53–76). This is then viewed as a declaration of a fixed, stable and permanent identity. For Masani, this proved to be problematic as her previous marriage to a man was interpreted by the Home Office as evidence to support the contention that her claim to be a lesbian was not credible. As she said:

> I was forced to marry. I had no choice. Because if I had refused, then my sexuality would have been suspected. But, when I came here, they said I was not a lesbian because I had been married. The letter made it sound so simple, you had a husband … therefore, it is not credible that you are a lesbian. (Masani, Ugandan refugee)

Masani struggled in the UK asylum system, having her initial claim denied and facing a long period of uncertainty before being granted refugee status. In her case, the lack of a clear narrative of fixed sexual diversity proved to be extremely problematic. Her previous partner of the opposite sex was viewed as incompatible with the fixed terms in which sexual diversity was expected to manifest. This issue around expectations of fixed, permanent, monosexual identities has been noted by other scholars such as Rehaag, whose work on the problems which face bisexual asylum claims has similarly documented the additional disbelief related hurdles faced by claimants whose identities and orientations or behaviours encompass desire for or engagement with a wider range of sexual partners (Rehaag, 2008; Lopes Heimer, 2020).

Indeed, this was an issue some participants noted that their legal representatives had warned them about. For example, Abasi told me that, 'One of the things my solicitor mentioned was that if I confuse them with any of the questions I answered during the interview and my statement says something else … that would make a problem' (Abasi, Egyptian refugee). In this sense, changes in how a claimant identifies, or more complex narratives, seem to be something which the Home Office struggles to comprehend. This applies not just to marriage, but also to matters like learning or identifying with new terminology during the claim process. For example, the concerns that Abasi's lawyer noted could also apply to someone who initially said that they were gay but who, upon gaining greater familiarity with the frameworks utilized in the UK, later identified that they are bisexual.

The disbelief which Masani encountered also ignores the extent to which heterosexual marriage is often one of the main strategies which those seeking to keep their sexual diversity secret from the surrounding society adopt (Giametta, 2017: 45). Indeed, here it is worth reflecting that sexually diverse people within contexts where there is a fear of persecution cannot simply avoid that persecution by passively not engaging in particular forms of behaviour, but instead must often consciously undertake positive actions in order to avoid persecution (Wessels, 2023). For example, in order to avoid persecution, it may be necessary to engage with institutions such as marriage or expectations around having children. Not engaging with such institutions may, in and of itself, produce the risk of the person being viewed as undermining an established social order and may therefore put them at risk of persecution. As such, it creates a double bind for such behaviours to then potentially be read as evidence of a lack of credibility in regard to the asylum claim which has been made. Indeed, this more complex interaction in regard to the actions people must undertake in order to avoid attention within their country of origin is a part of why the practice of discretion reasoning has been so problematic.

The literature around sexual diversity has long established the idea that human sexual behaviours and desires are generally fluid in nature (Diamond, 2000; 2005; 2008; Savin-Williams, 2017). In a seven-year study, Savin-Williams found that 'nearly two thirds of women changed their sexual identity at least once because the label did not adequately capture the diversity of their sexual and romantic feelings' (Savin-Williams, 2006: 42). Indeed, Dustin and Held argue that the inability to engage with the fluidity of human sexuality is one of the biggest weaknesses of the DSSH model on which the API is based (2021). In this sense, expectations around a fixed status are not in accordance with the broader literature regarding the nature of sexual diversity and should be avoided if the asylum process is to offer a fair and evidence-based exploration of asylum claims.

Other participants, such as Abasi, told me about how he felt that his queer identity 'is more than just being gay or lesbian … it's a spectrum', but he also noted that due to his own perceptions of how the processes operates he had 'just kept things standard' for the Home Office and, following the advice of his lawyer, pretended to be 'straightforwardly' gay (Abasi, Egyptian refugee). In this sense, the idea of fixed and simple identities creates what are effectively unwritten social rules and expectations that asylum claimants have to navigate when framing their claim.

In regard to Masani's personal experience, note should also be taken that the intersections of the different social identities which she occupies may also have impacted how her claim was understood. For example, as a woman, she is likely to have faced additional pressures to marry and reduced agency to avoid heterosexual relationships than a man in a similar situation may have done. This, while an important consideration, does not pull us away from the broader point that the API appears to be advancing a particularistic conceptualization of sexual diversity as being an identity which carries connotations and implications for every element of a person's life. Rather, it points out how these oversimplified expectations become even more dangerous when intersectional dimensions are considered.

3.2 Proving an identity: social role and official expectations

Beyond the idea of a fixed status that is core to who someone is and is seen as having implications for both where they go and who they spend time with, the conceptualization of sexual diversity adopted within the asylum system also appears to put significant weight on people framing their social engagements around their sexual diversity. This is clear on the face of the API, which advises decision-makers that

> [t]o enable claimants to present their case, it may be necessary to ask questions about where claimants have socialized or whether, for example, they have been members of clubs, groups or organizations. … Where a claimant has indicated that they have interacted with the LGB community, questions enabling the claimant to detail their

> knowledge and/or interactions with LGB contacts, groups and activities ... may be useful.[13]

As such, decision-makers within the UK process are guided towards an expectation that sexual diversity will manifest in social identities and communities that govern who people associate with and the spaces and places which they occupy. As such, we now turn to consider the wider expectations of officials around how sexual diversities will be presented and how this, again, corresponds to the lived realities of sexually diverse refugees and asylum seekers.

In the US context, McGuirk has offered an analysis which explores how forms of conspicuous consumption have come to structure LGBTIQA+ subjectivities (McGuirk, 2018). Similarly, within the narratives of the refugees I interviewed there was a clear focus on engagement with spaces and places that link a claimant with particular forms of capital. Indeed, drawing back to Chapter 2, which – among other things – set out the role of hetero- and homonormativity as structuring forces in our conceptualizations of sexual diversity, one can argue that the clearest encapsulation of the kind of de-politicized, nationalist, pro-market figure that can be accepted and embraced within the normative order is the middle-class white gay man motivated by consumption and engaging in fixed relationships and social situations which do not challenge the privileged status of heterosexuality (Juss, 2015). Indeed, writing in the French context, Bouchet-Mayer and Ferez (2024) have deployed Morris' concept of Gay Capital as a way of understanding the operative assumptions of French refugee status determination processes. This concept frames certain forms of knowledge about gay subjectivities as a form of Bourdieusian capital that can, within certain contexts, confer forms of advantage (Morris, 2018). In this sense, the social scripts which structure official expectations closely link to particular ideas about the spaces, relationships and forms of knowledge which are seen as part and parcel of contemporary LGBTIQA+ subjectivities.

Engagement in LGBTIQA+ communities

One clear expectation throughout my interviews with refugees was the expectation of engagement with and active participation in a broader LGBTIQA+ community. This fits with the idea of conspicuous consumption

[13] UK Visas and Immigration, 'Asylum Policy Instruction: Sexual Orientation in Asylum Claims' (Home Office, 2016), available at: https://assets.publishing.service.gov.uk/government/uploads/system/uploads/attachment_data/file/543882/Sexual-orientation-in-asylum-claims-v6.pdf (accessed 17 June 2024), p 23.

explored earlier and speaks to the particular modalities of sexual difference which are intelligible within normative logics of identity designation along the lines it is understood in the UK. For example, Masani told me:

> My lawyer had told me to do things like go to a lesbian bar and take photos and go to pride and take photos, but I was just doing that to try and satisfy them that I was a lesbian. In the end, this was what made me not successful in my first application. (Masani, Ugandan refugee)

As this shows, there is a clear expectation around social participation in LGBTIQA+ spaces regardless of the extent to which this reflects the actual, self-directed, desires of those attempting to navigate the asylum system. In Masani's narrative, this seemed to function not only as an opportunity for the presentation of positive evidence, but also as a source of incredulity. Indeed, note here should also be taken of the broader literature which has outlined how such decision-maker expectations can lead to double-binds where a lack of evidence is viewed as indicative of the lack of support for the claim but the presence of the evidence is viewed as self-serving or non-probative (Shaw and Verghese, 2022). Indeed, the issue of double-binds was raised by Damian, one of the legal representatives, who told me that '[I]f we didn't have it, the Home Office query it, if we do have it, they say well that doesn't prove anything' (Damian, legal practitioner). Masani went on to tell me:

> When I met with the Home Office for my interview, they asked me a lot of questions like, are there any lesbian spaces in Uganda and then what about Nigeria? They asked me about the LGBT community and then all these questions about what bars I go to in London and Manchester and where do I meet other lesbian people. (Masani, Ugandan refugee)

This expectation was repeated by multiple participants. For example, as we have already heard from Abeo, he faced incredulity and disbelief from those who felt that his claim was not believable due to the fact that he had not engaged with gay clubs or other LGBTIQA+ venues. Indeed, writing in the Belgian context, Dhoest argued that '[i]f you don't engage in associations, if you don't build up LGBT networks that strongly affects your credibility. So, those people are, so to speak, forced to march in the pride parade … purely for this file' (Dhoest, 20197: 1085). This was clear across all participants with engagement with a broader LGBTIQA+ community forming a key focal point in terms of the kinds of evidence which decision-makers anticipated and expected claimants to be able to show. Indeed, all of the refugees who I spoke to had been asked to provide evidence of attendance at pride events, venues regarded as being for the LGBTIQA+ community, and groups designed to provide support for LGBTIQA+ refugees and asylum seekers. In this sense, much as Held (2023: 1899) has argued, there seems clear evidence that '[w]hen LGBTQ+ refugees arrive in Europe and claim asylum, decision-makers and others often assume – in a homonationalist vein – that they find safety liberation and freedom and are happy and keen to go to gay prides and queer spaces'.

This expectation is particularly problematic given that, as Held has also argued, such spaces are often deeply racialized (Held, 2017). Indeed, as they have further argued, such spaces could be seen as ambivalent in the sense that they are both important potential sources of support while also being shaped by deeply unequal power relations (Held, 2023: 1900). For example, Adroa told me about his experiences of racism in LGBTIQA+ venues, explaining that 'you go to a club for gay people and they look at you differently … they say what's up Black man, what's up Black boy'. In this regard one of the forms of ambivalence at play in these scenarios is the role of racism. As Hunter (2010) has argued, queer spaces are often coded, implicitly or otherwise, as white. This can mean that, for ethnic minorities, such spaces may actually be experienced as hostile (Ruez, 2017). For example, Babu noted that he was made to feel uncomfortable specifically on the basis of his status as a refugee, stating:

> I used to be open about myself being a refugee, in the beginning. Then I stopped, because of the way people look at you. It's different and they think, 'Oh you're a refugee so most probably you are claiming benefits, you're taking advantage of our resources' and doing this and that. (Babu, Egyptian refugee)

Further, as discussed in Chapter 5, note should be taken that a range of issues around where refugees are located and the forms of support which are provided to them significantly impact their ability to engage with spaces generally identified as being for the LGBTIQA+ community. For example, if a refugee is dispersed into a very rural area, then simple proximity may mean that it is not possible to engage with LGBTIQA+ spaces even if they wanted to (see Danisi et al, 2021). As Griffiths and Yeo have argued, policies such as dispersal can also contribute to divisions and tensions between refugees and the host societies, which, in turn, construct refugees as potentially suspicious and difficult to integrate (Griffiths and Yeo, 2021). Queer spaces, like the broader community, are not immune to these dynamics.

Of course, for some, LGBTIQA+ spaces are anything but ambivalent. For example, Eko, a refugee from Indonesia, said that he had enjoyed joining Pride and other LGBTIQA+ spaces, telling me that 'I always joined Pride London from 2013, so my lawyer provided pictures of the Pride I was joining'. While Chataluka said:

> Going out to gay clubs, I enjoyed that. When I come to London also, I have been to gay clubs for the first time as, like, being curious. I took some pictures there and I have them since I moved here. So, that was also good that I have documented it with dates. (Chataluka, Egyptian refugee)

As this suggests, for some claimants the experience of attending Pride and other LGBTIQA+ spaces was broadly a positive one. However, even for these claimants, the need to take repeated photos and in essence 'prove' that they were there can still be seen to create a kind of structured artificiality to the experience and it is notable that those refugees who reported having found the process less problematic also identified themselves as people who liked to keep a lot of records and take a lot of photos, this not being a trait that all people share, particularly if they have previously been in a context where the keeping of such photos and records could place them at risk of persecution.

Indeed, as I have argued elsewhere, the focus on attendance in particular kinds of space hints at the central role which liberalism plays in shaping how sexual diversities are conceptualized (Powell, 2024a: 175). Principally, the expectation reflects a sense that there is a clear, coherent and stable way to be LGBTIQA+ and that a claimant either does or docs not align with this framing. In principle, this expectation reflects the view that there is a particular 'way of life' which can be tested for (Weeks, 2012: 53). The link to liberalism here arises from the decontextualized nature of these ideas, viewing humans as free individuals able to form an identity and occupy spaces without considering the role of culture, history and society more broadly in how we are constituted as subjects. In essence, then, the issue is a lack of attention to the meta-politics we have already outlined and how these meta-politics shape the subjectivities through which we make sense of one another and the world around us.

Relationships and romantic attachments

These same expectations can be seen as being at play in the story of Yew Fook Sam. Sam's story made national headlines in the UK after the Home Office argued at tribunal that he could not be gay as he had never had a 'same' sex relationship (Pidd, 2019). As this suggests, official expectations govern not only engagement with institutions and social activities, but also mediate visibility in regard to the need to be able to demonstrate active engagement in romantic relationships. However, as addressed in the next section, this form of relationship building cannot be primarily behavioural in nature,[14] but rather is presumed to be along the same lines as a heterosexual

[14] This is, in effect, the implication of the A, B and C decision. See Cases C-148 to C-150, *ABC v Staatssecretaris van Veiligheid en Justitie* [2014] ECRI- 2406.

relationship, revolving around a deep attachment and prolonged engagement with a given individual. Similar expectations were clear in Eko's narrative where he identified that the central evidence in his claim was a 'statement from my partner … about I am gay' (Eko, Indonesian refugee). Similarly, Chataluka told me that '[p]robably the second half of the interview … was more about my boyfriend. … Also, what the passion will be when you talk about your boyfriend' (Chataluka, Egyptian refugee). Similarly, questions around relationships were also reported by Abasi and Babu. In this way, the official expectations at play within the refugee status determination framework could rightly be said to be both heteronormative, in the sense that queer relationships are expected to be romance-centred, like heterosexual kinship, and homonormative in the expectation that queer romantic relationships are expected to be lasting and singular, again mirroring an essentially heterosexual model.

The focus on stable identities and stable relationships could be said to reflect the inherent homonormativity of the UK asylum system, capable of engaging with and comprehending only those identities which correspond to normative liberal logics of romance, and which are, therefore, stripped of political potentiality and instead form depoliticized constituencies that can be taken up by the normative order (Duggan, 2002). Of particular note here is the risk that, within the strictures of these normative official expectations, culturally specific articulations of sexual diversity will be disavowed, with only those who are able to articulate highly particularistic accounts of sexual diversity, which map closely on to those we might commonly see in the UK, able to genuinely rely on protection. This is consistent with broader critiques of human rights. For example, Brown (2004) has argued that human rights embody a false promise as they conceal the conceptual baggage associated with particular choices and, as such, risk displacing emancipatory political projects in a manner that fundamentally props up an unequal status quo. In this case, the false promise is of freedom, with asylum systems instead providing only a surrogate accessible to those whose sexual diversities bear a familial resemblance to those commonly seen in the UK. Hopgood has similarly argued that human rights apparatus fundamentally seeks to embody and support those identities which are compatible with a neoliberal world order (Hopgood, 2000). In this sense, again, the forms of identity fostered within the asylum process could be said to be those which map most closely onto the highly liberal consumerist framing of LGBTIQA+ identities we have come to expect in the UK.

A further concern regarding these expectations is that, much as Dawson and Gerber (2017) suggested in their analysis of the DSSH model, it seems that decision-makers' expectations have become fixed and calcified into a particular model for determining whether or not a given claimant is LGBTIQA+. Indeed, much as Rainbow Migration found in their 2018

Still Falling Short report, officials seem to expect claimants to have clearly thought out narratives of self-realization which clearly and specifically articulate how their sexual diversity is a core component of their lives, and which links to their broader social and romantic engagements (Rainbow Migration, 2018).

In this register, the engagement with spaces and romantic relationships both map on to a broader set of conceptualizations of the meanings of sexual diversity in the terms addressed within Chapters 1 and 2 of this volume and are the kinds of knowledge formations, calcified as components within legal apparatus, that a counter-normative queer framework enables us to begin to unwind.

Legal representatives' role in promoting attendance and community engagement

As well as coming from the decision-makers, participants' narratives also made clear that their own legal representatives would often have a role in promoting the centrality of engagement with the broader community as a central element to a successful claim. For example, Chataluka told me that '[w]hat my solicitor helped me with was that she asked about certain things should be in my, err, my evidence. For example, I would have to attend Pride and take pictures there. Which was the first time ever I went to Pride'. Obviously, it is logical that legal representatives want to do all that they can to ensure that their own client's cases are as strong as possible. However, this perhaps speaks to a further ambivalence insofar as the provision of this kind of evidence cements it as an expectation for decision-makers when they come to look at subsequent 'similar' cases. The same dynamic can be seen in Masani's story around attending bars, as explored earlier, with her lawyer advising her that she needed to attend lesbian bars even though this was not something she would have done of her own volition.

As I have argued elsewhere, 'there is a need for practitioners to be wary that the way in which they support their own clients has the potential to contribute to the fixing of decision-maker expectations' (Powell, 2024a: 178). This expectation goes back to the issue we were exploring in the first section of this chapter, the reduction of complex phenomena such as sexual diversity to a simplified formulation of identity. As Adroa told me:

> They [Home Office decision-makers] don't understand that maybe Black people can be gay. And even if they think you can be gay, they want you to behave like a white man … they expect you to go to gay clubs … they expect you to behave in a basically European way. (Adroa, Nigerian refugee)

At the root of these expectations lies the same problem Juss raised in 2015, that refugee rights are formulated around ideas of consumption, hyper-visibility and public proclamations of identity (Juss, 2015: 134). These expectations are promoted both by decision-makers in terms of how they think through matters such as credibility and the burden of proof, as well as by the API, and by legal practitioners seeking to support their clients to navigate through the process.

3.3 Repressing desire: law's occlusions

Much of this chapter has focused on the role of speech and actions in articulating particular formulations of sexual diversity and how these formulations were subsequently interpreted by decision-makers. However, as well as speech, we should consider the way in which silences structure and support formulations of identity. Understanding the role of silence, the repression of desire and how asylum law privileges certain forms of knowledge while occluding others is, I argue, key to understanding the experiences of sexually diverse refugees and, therefore, key to promoting counter-normative solutions.

Silence holds a dualistic role marking both the occlusions within the decision-making process and the conditions which many claimants strive to escape. For example, in describing her own experiences of interviewing refugees, Fobear has argued that '[f]or many who have lived in silence for most of their lives because of homophobia and transphobia, being able to share their story with outsides can induce a sense of pride and accomplishment' (2015: 103). However, others, such as Abdullah who we discussed earlier in this chapter, may find themselves silenced, forced to take another path, by the weight of official expectations within the asylum encounter.

Often, within the discourses of liberal democracy, silence is framed as an absence or a lack. However, as Tamale has argued:

> [There are] different meanings attached to the concept of silence. Though in the dominant Western tradition voice is valorised and silence constructed as a total blank, in many African cultures silence can be as powerful and empowering as speech. For instance, studies have shown that there is a legitimate silence surrounding the sexualities of some African women, one that is ambiguous and not able to be engaged. (Tamale, 2011: 13)

In this sense, silence may not merely be the blank which we often presume it to be but rather an act of communication or a discursive framework which carries its own meanings. Indeed, one could connect this framing of silence to the work Sedgwick has undertaken around the structural role of ignorance in regard to queer modes of being. Specifically, Sedgwick argues that

> [i]f ignorance is not – as it evidently is not – a single Manichean aboriginal maw of darkness from which the heroics of human cognition can occasionally wrestle facts, insights, freedoms, progress, perhaps there exists instead a plethora of ignorances, and we may begin to ask questions about the labor, erotics and economics of their human production and distribution. Insofar as ignorance is ignorance of a knowledge – a knowledge which may itself, it goes without saying, be seen as either true or false under some other regime of truth – these ignorances, far from being pieces of the originary dark, are produced to correspond to particular knowledges and circulate as particular regimes of truth. (Sedgwick, 2008: 8)

Given this, we perhaps need to re-think the forms of evidence which are not accepted as evidence of a sexual diversity as forming a constituent part of a broader regime of truth promoted within the asylum system.

As addressed previously, sexual diversity is commonly framed as being a matter of identity, with issues relating to both desire (orientation) and behaviour being largely ignored or framed as not relevant to being sexually diverse. This framing is partially embedded by a structuring silence in regard to sexual activity. Specifically, following the decision of the European Court of Justice in *ABC*,[15] direct questions on sexual activity are not permitted within the refugee status determination system. There are obvious reasons relating to maintaining dignity which support strict limits being applied to the asking of questions regarding sexual activity. However, this does not suspend a need for critical examination regarding how the prohibition of discussions around sexual behaviour establishes a form of ignorance or silence as being at the very centre of the process. Specifically, the prohibition of discussion on or around issues of sexual behaviour re-diverts the regime of truth around sexual diversity to its focus on sexual identity.

Because behaviours and desires are disallowed as legitimate forms of evidence for sexual diversity, the conceptualization of sexual diversity on which the asylum system operates is pushed to prioritize narratives of self-realization and social participation. This focus, of course, poses problems for those who do in fact understand their sexual diversity primarily in terms of either behaviour or attraction. However, it also generates issues for those who are not out, or who are, as of yet, unable to advance a complex narrative of self-realization.

As Eko's example shows, the API on its current terms gives those who have particular social ties and associations a clear way to bring forward evidence

[15] Cases C-148 to C-150, *ABC v Staatssecretaris van Veiligheid en Justitie* [2014] ECRI- 2406.

of their identity. But, in so doing, it also exacerbates the difficulty those unable to showcase such ties face.

Practical issues with community engagement

In regard to social activities within one's country of origin, it is reasonably obvious why people who fear persecution for an activity would not want to keep significant volumes of evidence regarding their engagement in that activity. Indeed, a further issue may arise insofar as many social activities within refugee countries of origin may be focused on sexual activity and thus fall foul of the discussion topics permitted within the refugee status determination process. While, in the UK context, the expanded use of large accommodation facilities, taken alongside the dispersal policy which allocates accommodation on a 'no-choice' basis, is likely to significantly limit opportunities for social participation (Fletcher, 2024). As Fletcher documents, many people detained in large-scale asylum accommodation seek to avoid disclosing or discussing their identities due to fears concerning the possible views of those who they are accommodated alongside.

Attendance at LGBTIQA+ spaces can also be prohibitively expensive for refugee populations. The current rate of support for those determined to be destitute is barely more than £50 per week. The terms of support set out under Sections 95, 98 and of the Immigration and Asylum Act 1999 mean that engagement with many spaces coded as LGBTIQA+ is inaccessible for those claimants who do not have independent means. This means that for many of the most vulnerable asylum claimants there are a range of structural defects within the asylum system itself which deprive them of the opportunity to provide evidence to support their claims. However, the kind of decontextualized expectations around evidence, as themselves a form of structuring ignorance or silence, mean that this is something which is rarely taken account of by decision-makers.

Consideration should also be taken of the increasing digitalization of LGBTIQA+ spaces. Specifically, while there has been a general reduction in the range of available LGBTIQA+ social venues existing in-person, academic literature has drawn attention to the role that applications and other social media networks play in providing spaces for sexually diverse people to gather (Mowlabocus, 2010). However, these spaces are also noted for often being highly sexualized (Albury and Byron, 2014). Given the current policy in regard to sexually explicit materials, this can cause problems in terms of claimants wanting to deploy the use of applications and websites as a form of evidence to support their asylum claim. Indeed, Babu reflected the difficulty of meeting people, telling me that: 'One of the things I wanted to mention is that there is very limited resource for actually meeting people who are gay, or who have been through the same thing from a similar background.' Linked to this, other participants raised concerns about the cultural unfamiliarity of LGBTIQA+ spaces. For example, Chataluka noted that such spaces were deeply fuelled by alcohol and, given that he didn't drink much, identified that this sometimes caused issues for him in terms of navigating these spaces and engaging with his friends. In this sense, there are a number of complexities around the idea of engaging in social spaces which complicate evidential expectations.

The focus on the evidence in relation to developed narratives of identity and community engagement occupies the conceptual space around sexual diversity in a way which itself produces the forms of silence and structural ignorance outlined in this chapter. This is to say that the conceptualizations of sexual diversity deployed by decision-makers, in policy documents and in society more broadly, are, in a sense, so hegemonic that they leave little conceptual space for the lived realities of people as they are actually experienced. So, in this sense, the elements of LGBTIQA+ subjectivities that we do not discuss also structure interactions within the refugee status determination system. They limit the forms of question which are asked and provide support for the idea that the identity and emotion based models are the only way to determine whether or not the person before the decision-maker 'is' a sexually diverse person.

3.4 Some routes: refugee proposals for improving the refugee status determination framework

Across the interviews with refugees, many also offered suggestions towards how to address the issues within the refugee status determination framework. Given the importance of lived experiences to understanding what traversing the UK asylum system is like for someone whose claim arises on the basis of their sexual diversity, I include these suggestions as accounts of what the people I spoke to thought would create a more effective system. These suggestions are not policy proposals, but they offer insights into the kinds of concerns that people navigating the refugee status determination had about the process and the way in which it operates.

The most recurrent suggestion presented to me was the need to include greater attention to the mental health of people seeking asylum. All of the participants noted the serious implications that their experiences had had for their mental health. They also raised how difficult it was for them to be expected to recount these experiences to decision-makers without first having received proper care to address the harm caused to their mental health.

The point here is reasonably clear. For those fleeing fear of persecution, many of whom may have previous experiences of persecution, experiences of distress are common. Yet, despite the well documented impact of trauma on memory (Herlihy et al, 2002), and the significant body of research outlining the risks of retraumatization (see Shidlo and Ahola, 2013), institutional efforts from the Home Office to address the trauma of people seeking asylum remain limited. As participants made clear, the lack of attention to this can be seen to exacerbate the other issues we have discussed in this chapter. In this sense, the provision of properly funded mental health interventions for people seeking asylum could be a way of improving the refugee status determination system in a manner that benefits both the wellbeing of asylum claimants and the reliability of the decision-making process.

As well as the possible inculcation of greater mental health support and treatment, other refugees I spoke to recommended that greater reliance be placed on self-identification. This is also a frequent proposal by others working on how to improve refugee status determination processes within the context of claims by sexually diverse people (see, for example, Jansen, 2019). It is true that placing greater weight on self-identification would help to address some of the instances of administrative violence – such as where an asylum claimant is told that, notwithstanding their own lived experiences, they are in fact not gay or lesbian – that currently occur within the refugee status determination system.

However, given what we have already explored around how the forms of evidence and types of expectation which are deployed within one asylum claim can then impact how decision-makers approach subsequent asylum claims, there is also a need to be cautious here as while greater reliance on self-identification may indeed improve the system for those claimants who already understand their own sexual diversities as a form of identity, this could also make the asylum process more difficult for people who do not currently deploy an identity framework as a way of conceptualizing their own sexual diversity.

Another solution proposed by the refugees who I spoke to revolved around improved training for asylum decision-makers. The suggestion of improved training and the problematization of poor knowledge and understanding on the part of decision-makers arises frequently with the asylum literature across a range of jurisdictions (Affolter, 2022). Indeed, while there is significant disagreement about how the quality of decision-making in this area might be improved, there is general agreement that it is likely to include improved provision of training. This could also be extended to having higher requirements in place for who is able to sign up to work as a decision-maker.

While the call for further training is well made, it does need to be borne in mind that there is limited agreement regarding the content of the training which could be deployed and that, therefore, it is difficult to make any substantial assessment of how viable this would be as a solution to the problems identified in this chapter. Indeed, note should be taken that some forms of training could exacerbate issues. For example, some current suggestions for training might focus on models such as the DSSH model.

However, given the issues we have noted regarding the expectation for claimants to be able to advance deeply developed and highly emotionally considered and driven narratives regarding their realization of a narrative of difference from the surrounding society, it is arguable that further training based on a framework such as this may actually exacerbate the issues outlined. In this sense, while there is doubtless merit to the deployment of further training, it is important that critical attention is paid to the nature of that training to ensure that some of the current problems within refugee status determination processes do not end up becoming reified.

None of these suggestions featured as a sought out recommendation. So, as noted, it is not possible to consider them as detailed solutions. However, given that they came from participants who themselves have experienced the UK asylum system, it is important to include these proposals so that readers are aware of the kinds of suggestions that participants raised and the things which they would like to see to ensure that the process works better for those who will go through it after them.

4

Narratives from Practice

4.1 What we are going to need: expectations and evidence

As explored in the previous chapter, one of the central issues which faces people claiming asylum on the basis of their sexual diversity is the need to prove that they are, or will be perceived as, sexually diverse. The problems this poses for claimants were clearly and consistently recounted by all participants from practitioner and third sector backgrounds. Further, the coincidence between these narratives and the matters which we explored in the previous chapter speaks to the widespread nature of the issues which people seeking asylum continue to face in evidencing sexual diversity.

Whether speaking to claimants themselves, legal practitioners or the extensive range of third sector volunteers and workers who try to support people seeking asylum, the most frequently addressed issues related to credibility and evidence. For a legal practitioner, supporting a sexually diverse person through the refugee status determination process, a central part of their role is to assist the person seeking asylum with how they can provide the Home Office with adequate evidence that they are, for example, a lesbian. Put another way, they need to advise the people they are supporting on how to satisfy decision-makers that they are or will be perceived as LGBTIQA+.

The general consensus among those working to support asylum seekers, whether from the third sector or legal practice, was that the current framework utilized to determine whether or not someone is sexually diverse is deeply flawed and creates difficulties for claimants. For example, some participants reported continuing examples of simplistic stereotyping relating to appearance. In this regard, Mia told me that '[t]here are things that are going to make your life easier. If you can articulate ... why you need protection and if you visually look like the Home Office expects gay people and lesbians and bisexual and trans people to look, you are going to have an easier ride' (Mia, third sector worker). Although they are not permitted under the Asylum Policy Instruction (API), the literature documents recurring instances of stereotypes being relied on across different jurisdictions (Topel, 2016; Vogler, 2016; Powell, 2020). As such, even though, explicit examples around appearance were not commonly raised by participants, the evidence seems to support the continuing role of stereotypes in shaping experiences of navigating the asylum system for LGBTIQA+ people.

While other participants did not directly mention appearance in the way Mia did, there was a broader sense that the system had some very specific expectations around the kind of narrative sexually diverse asylum seekers would present. For example, in agreement with the refugee narratives explored during the previous chapter, Amelia said:

> The whole framework for assessing sexual identity in asylum claims is problematic, because how does one assess sexual identity? And the Home Office have to make a decision about whether they believe your sexual identity or not. So then you are left with how do I prove that to you … they are looking for evidence that that person felt different, evidence that that person feels stigmatized and they feel shameful. (Amelia, legal practitioner)

For Amelia, who also had experience of working in the third sector, the approach adopted by the Home Office presented significant issues in that it rested on expecting a highly particularistic narrative of sexual identity development. As they outlined, this conception was deeply dependent on an articulation of feelings and emotions linked to a recognition of one's difference from the surrounding society. This links with some of the experiences of seeking asylum that we explored in the previous chapter and also shows how the conceptualizations of sexual diversity that we outlined in Chapter 2 often become universalized as the framework through which sexual diversity is understood within refugee status determination.

Simplification and the Difference, Stigma, Shame and Harm model

In this regard, one cause that practitioners frequently cited as being core to this is the Difference, Stigma, Shame, Harm (DSSH) model, which significantly informed the 2016 API on sexual diversity asylum claims.

As Sophia reflected, far from being a nuanced model, this approach seems to fail to comprehend both the complexity of sexual diversity, and the diversity of the experiences which people seeking asylum have had in their lives prior to arriving in the UK. Specifically, they told me:

> There isn't any sort of real understanding I think in terms of the nuances as to how identity might work and how different types of identity might function. I don't think that's something that really has

> sort of got any real understanding in terms of the subtleties, there's still very much, the idea of working to a particular narrative. (Sophia, legal practitioner)

As this suggests, although the questions the Home Office ask may not relate to matters such as appearances or sexual behaviour, they still reflect a lack of nuance and some highly oversimplified expectations around how people might behave or feel. Returning to the themes discussed in Chapter 2, this highlights the meta-politics which have formed the subjectivities through which everyone, including those who work at the Home Office, make sense of sexual diversities.

For Amelia, as well as several other participants, the blame for this lay with the deployment of models such as DSSH. The DSSH model is intended to be a helpful tool to assist with understanding refugees' experiences (Chelvan, 2011: 60–62). It focuses the compilation of evidence around four key themes: the recognition of oneself as different from the surrounding society; experiences of stigma from the surrounding society for that difference; feelings of shame associated with that stigma; and experiences of harm as a result of the shame and stigma. However, as Amelia told me:

> That framework [the DSSH model] I really struggle with, because I've had clients who don't necessarily feel different, so no I don't feel different, that's just how I always felt. ... So that doesn't fit with the category and they also want to see you kind of tell the story and this kind of like journey and people don't have one clear, they always say when did you realize you were gay, and that's a really problematic, heteronormative question and it's impossible to articulate for some people. I've seen it used in refusals. (Amelia, legal practitioner)

Of particular note here is Amelia's recognition that the DSSH model is being used in refusals, even though its original framing was as a helpful tool which may support some claimants to demonstrate that they are, for example, gay. As I have argued elsewhere, this is problematic as the model does not necessarily fit with the way in which refugees understand their own sexual diversities (Powell, 2021a). Further, as Dawson and Gerber have argued, there was always a risk with a model such as this that it would become calcified as an expectation and that, therefore, rather than being a helpful tool, it would instead become the justification for refusing claims (Dawson and Gerber, 2017). Amelia was not alone in expressing this point of view. Lucas also noted their concern, stating:

> I really hate um ideas of models ... obviously there is a danger that people go well this is how a claim is. Now the truth is and I don't really

> like it, is that a lot of people though, the Home Office look for that kind of thing. … [I have an outlier client] He really is very unusual in that he had a boyfriend in Pakistan, they were both Pakistani. The man married a British woman, they … continued a kind of very clandestine relationship here in Britain for a number of years, they've never broken up. Our gay man doesn't really seem to have any interest in meeting anybody else. He doesn't really go to anything … it's really quite hard … that will make the Home Office go, you're not gay. (Lucas, legal practitioner)

As this suggests, it may well be the case that, for many claimants, approaches such as the DSSH provide a framework that is applicable and helpful to frame their claim. However, for those who do not live a particular kind of cosmopolitan gay life, as explored in the previous chapter, it can also provide reasons for rejection. In this sense, a counter-normative conceptualization of queer theory offers the tools to challenge the restrictive modes through which models such as DSSH conceptualize sexual and gender diversity.

Similarly, Zadia raised concerns over the requirement for an emotional journey, saying that 'it's really frustrating … I think for them [the Home Office] the alternative that they don't want to do is believe people, that's too radical' (Zadia, legal practitioner). This point was further drawn out by Ava, who said:

> The vast majority of refusals I see on the basis of refusing sexuality is, you didn't express emotional journey, you didn't explain why you're different, you didn't explain how that felt, you didn't explain the emotion of it and that all does come from DSSH, there's no question about it. (Ava, legal practitioner)

As all three of these participants make clear, the DSSH framework was repeatedly deployed by decision-makers across the cases which they were engaged in. However, far from being a positive tool for helping claimants to prove their status, these narratives suggest that it had formed a defined set of expectations which could provide the basis for the refusal. For example, in explaining why one of their clients had been refused in their initial asylum claim, Sophia reflected on how the fact that '[h]e supported Chelsea Football Club and wanted be a plumber' had been 'like the worst case scenario for the Home Office' (Sophia, legal practitioner). In particular, issues had arisen because the person she was supporting did not see himself as different from other men within his country of origin and, as a very quiet person, did not speak effusively about his feelings regarding his being gay. The result of this was that his initial asylum claim ended in refusal. In this sense, models such as DSSH were seen by practitioners as having contributed to highly restrictive conceptualizations of sexual diversity which often operated as reasons for doubt or disbelief that people seeking asylum were sexually diverse people.

Given this, while Chelvan (2020) has argued that the DSSH model is a way to move beyond stereotypes and assumptions, there is a need to consider the assumptions which the model has itself embedded within the decision-making framework. In particular, as Dustin and Ferreira (2021) have argued, these participant narratives can be seen to suggest a need to return to a focus on the fundamentals of refugee law, including persecution over and above identity. As such, much as has been argued in other national contexts, these narratives could be seen to suggest a need to depart from the use of the DSSH model (Zisakou, 2024).

Similar issues were identified by Elijah, who told me about one particular case:

> [There was a] woman from Uganda years ago and they didn't accept that she was a lesbian. The reason was because she was so marginalized … in every aspect of her life and she lived amongst the Ugandan community. So she didn't tell them that she was a lesbian, because she knew she would literally lose her home. … So I mean the Home Office were saying why aren't you running down Old Compton Street with a rainbow flag on your head and it's like a) I can't afford to go to Old Compton Street, b) I don't want anyone in here to know I'm a lesbian, c) there is actually a lot of racism in the LGBT community, like there is everywhere, and d) I don't drink. (Elijah, legal practitioner)

In effect, there was a shared conception from across the participants that it was those who were, for whatever reason, not openly expressing identity as a sexually diverse person who were the most likely to have difficulty in framing their claims in a manner which decision-makers could make sense of. As explored earlier, this may relate to the way in which sexual diversities within the UK have been defined around their relationship to forms of conspicuous consumption, as well as the forms of evidence which have been encouraged by the reliance on models such as the DSSH model in response to the fact that there is, in effect, no objective way to determine sexual diversity.

Legal representatives, ambivalence and reification

Some participants also expressed a concern about the role they may be playing in terms of guiding their own clients and how this may itself reinforce the expectations of decision-makers. For example, Lucas told me:

> I don't really like models and I don't like stereotyping and yet, god, in my work, I play the game and what I'm doing is, I'm acting in the best interest of my clients, that's what I'm doing. So, my narrative looks very good for the Home Office and my evidence looks very good for the Home Office, but there is a danger that I'm reinforcing these ideas and that the person who doesn't fit into the pattern actually is even more harmed. (Lucas, legal practitioner)

This corresponds to the arguments made by Bruce-Jones (2015) regarding the need to be aware of how the way in which concepts and identities are framed in one claim shifts the expectations and understandings of decision-makers when it comes to adjudicating on subsequent claims. In effect, the point here is that all of the work that goes into supporting a client does not just have implications for that client. Rather, advocacy has implications for everyone else engaging with the refugee status determination system. This is because utilizing methods such as models has the effect of naturalizing those models as 'the' way that category should be understood.

Indeed, this issue links into the problem of models more broadly in that the use of models has implications for the way in which decision-makers conceptualize sexual diversity. In this sense, the use of a model in one case could be understood as a broader meta-political act which also functions to shift the way that decision-makers in subsequent cases understand sexual diversity. In this way, the engagement of models, whether within Home Office guidance or through their deployment by legal practitioners, can be understood to shift the ways in which sexual diversity is conceptualized, often contributing to the more restrictive identity driven conceptualizations that we highlighted across the previous three chapters.

Accommodation, dispersal and practical issues

As well as the concerns around consolidating the expectations of decision-makers, participants also sought to draw out how the expectations of openness and engagement with a broader LGBTIQA+ community do not take account of the structural conditions people seeking asylum live in. Specifically, openness is only possible when someone is within conditions which facilitate that openness. For example, Elijah's client had been unable to be open about her being a lesbian as she lived among the Ugandan community. Similarly, Isabella recounted how the claimants who they supported had struggled to provide evidence due to the fact that they were sharing Home Office accommodation with people from a diverse range of backgrounds, whose politics they did not know. Specifically, they said:

> They were in a shared accommodation with other young people from other parts of the world and fully aware that they could put themselves at risk, so had intentionally been very discreet, you know having to hide themselves in that part of their sexuality. So they couldn't provide anything like, oh yeah I go to this place, or I associate with, you know. (Isabella, legal practitioner)

In this sense, there is also a need to be attentive to how practices undertaken by the Home Office may undermine the ability of claimants to dispense with evidential expectations. For example, in this case, the fact that accommodation is allocated on a no-choice basis with asylum claimants often required to share rooms or at least premises can create conditions within which asylum claimants do not feel comfortable in being open about their sexual diversity (Fletcher, 2024). Therefore, issues arise not just from the models which are deployed in order to facilitate decision-makers in determining whether the person in question is or would be perceived as a sexually diverse person, but also from the material conditions within which people seeking asylum are placed.

Amelia further raised concerns around the policy of dispersal, which may also have implications for showing expected engagement with LGBTIQA+ coded spaces and organizations. Indeed, the limited range of LGBTIQA+ services and greater social difficulties can be seen in the urban flight phenomenon widely catalogued among British, European and American LGBTIQA+ people (Hubbard et al, 2015; McGlynn, 2018). In this regard, Amelia told me:

> Regarding to dispersal [to areas outside of cities] … I am thinking of one lesbian woman, a young woman never really had left her village in Nigeria before having to flee, very vulnerable and just kind of looking for any sort of support with her own sexuality, looking for LGBT+ groups and we just couldn't find anything for her … you know it's just really, really tricky. There aren't those places you can go to and then the Home Office kind of goes there's an absence here of any evidence of you participating in this community. (Amelia, legal practitioner)

As this makes clear, there are issues not only over who someone is accommodated with, but also where that accommodation is located. It is extremely difficult for people dispersed into rural areas far away from LGBTIQA+ focused spaces to demonstrate the expected engagement with organizations even if they wanted to do so. Indeed, Ethan set out how some of the people they worked with did not feel safe outside of the city, telling me that:

> I think there is definitely a desire to be in a city. They feel safer in a city. And I think explaining that to the Home Office, I don't think they take that seriously. It's almost like they think it's some kind of ridiculous request that you're just using the LGBT aspect of things to try and get something. (Ethan, third sector worker)

It is notable here both that Ethan's perception was that people seeking asylum might not feel safe outside of the city and also that this was not something that the Home Office would seriously engage with. As this suggests, the dispersal policy creates some particular vulnerabilities not only around access to support and spaces, but also in terms of whether people can be themselves within the areas where they are being accommodated. Issues such as these have previously been identified within the Swedish context (Wimark, 2021). The prevalence of such issues points to a need for greater consideration to be made as to how policies around accommodation and similar areas disproportionately impact sexual and gender diverse people within the asylum system.

Indeed, given what has previously been noted around the role of conspicuous consumption in framing the conceptual frameworks through which we make sense of sexual diversity, it could be argued that LGBTIQA+ identities are implicitly conceptualized within an urban context (D'Emilio, 2012). This, of course, has a particularly pernicious interaction with the Home Office's broader dispersal policy.

Ezra further drew out how it was not just the Home Office, but also other support organizations, which might problematically engage with the ability of asylum claimants to be open in their day-to-day lives. Specifically, they told me:

> For a lot of refugees and asylum seekers the local Islamic organizations, or mosques would be again one of the places where they would find support in community, which is not a safe place for a lot of LGBT people that are fleeing that, whether it's a church in their home country, or things to do with religion and sexuality of course. (Ezra, third sector worker)

Here the issue is that many of the support services provided to refugees and asylum seekers are – in the absence of proper state support – instead provided by charitable and religious organizations (Williams et al, 2012; Coyle, 2021). This can result in a double-bind between the need to avoid openly and clearly displaying sexual diversity in order to be safe and the need to openly evidence engagement within particular kinds of spaces in order to provide evidence in support of their sexual diversity within the asylum system.

This point was also well made by Mia, who told me that, when they had worked in a refugee-focused organization with no specialist background supporting sexually diverse people, '[i]f someone had no recourse to public funds, it would be a religious organization or religiously inspired group that we would be able to refer to, because they didn't have the beureaucracy of like the box ticking exercises, as a lot of them do' (Mia, third sector worker). This may mean that – regardless of the actual views of any individual religious organizations – people may not feel comfortable being open about their sexual diversity. Where religious organizations are key sources of support, this can cause serious issues insofar as the continued reliance on the social and support networks provided by these organizations may mean that they do not feel comfortable being open. This can, in turn, compromise their ability to provide evidence and a narrative of a form that corresponds to the expectations of decision-makers. Such issues can also arise where a person seeking asylum is living in a diaspora community, or maintains contact with family members.

Indeed, this kind of double-bind can place claimants in potentially dangerous situations where they have to choose between lacking adequate evidence to present to the Home Office, or risk compromising the support structures which they rely on for accommodation and other forms of day-to-day support. Part of the reason that this can be so problematic is that, as we have learned from the lived experiences of claimants we explored in the preceding chapter, decision-makers often have strong expectations that claimants will be able to evidence significant engagement with spaces and people who are clearly associated to and a part of the LGBTIQA+ community. For example, Ezra went on to tell me that the kinds of evidence they would commonly see clients deploying included 'attendance at Pride … LGBT venues, where there is like very visible Rainbow flags, etc, attendance of LGBT circles, or organizations. So again we continuously get requests from the refugees to get like a photo at the end of the meet up and like in front of a Rainbow flag' (Ezra, third sector worker).

These expectations of both extensively and highly evidenced engagement with LGBTIQA+ communities was also outlined by Aisha, who worked with a third sector organization which was particularly focused on support for lesbian refugees and asylum seekers. They particularly stressed how the expectations about visibility and participation in community spaces placed particular burdens on women. Specifically they identified that

> [the] Home Office's expectations seems to me to involve things like being on the gay scene and you can't do that on 40 quid a week, being in a relationship – well a lot of the women I've worked with don't feel while they are so insecure that they can offer anything to a permanent relationship. If they do get into another relationship it's very often with

> another person seeking asylum, who is then much too frightened to write a letter of support. (Aisha, third sector worker)

Aisha went on to tell me that the expectations around presence in particular spaces was particularly problematic for women due to the lack of women's focused queer spaces and due to the fact that women's experiences of sexuality are often experienced more within the private realm, particularly due to the socialization which women will have experienced (Valentine, 1997). These findings around the asylum system are broadly consistent with Dawson and Gerber's concerns around the DSSH model (Dawson and Gerber, 2017). Aisha further pointed out:

> Throughout history men have lived in the public sphere and women in the private sphere, so it was with the gay community. Certainly in my young days, and back in the day, most lesbian social life took place in other people's houses. Yes there was a gay street in London, yes there were various clubs and later on there were club nights, but no, lesbian space has always been very restricted. (Aisha, third sector worker)

This raises a further interesting point around how the evidential expectations embedded within Home Office decision-making processes may mean that certain claimants are disadvantaged in terms of framing a claim on the basis of sexual diversity. This would impact not only women, but also those whose identities are more complex or culturally specific, such as those who do not align their self-conceptions with the forms of sexual diversity commonly seen in the UK. The expectations for claimants to be able to show significant engagement with groups and spaces was also repeated by Amelia, who said:

> There's a real assumption that if you are part of an LGBTQ advocacy group, or something like that, then that is real good evidence that you are gay and I see that regularly. So the Home Office, we might have given all of the evidence in a lengthy statement about someone's sexual identity and the Home Office one year later are like, hi thanks for that, can we have evidence of any LGBTQ+ groups you are part of. (Amelia, legal practitioner)

As addressed in the previous chapter, the expectation to engage with a particular kind of space and for claimants to be part of support groups reflects an expectation on the part of decision-makers for claimants to present with a form of identity that is a fundamental part of who they are, something that has implications both for where they go and who they spend time with.

It is also important to have regard to the fact that claimants who have just come to the UK from a place where they may have been attempting to conceal their sexual diversity are suddenly expected to articulate complex narratives regarding how they feel about their sexual diversity and how this is a key factor in where they go and who they spend time with. For example, Amelia explained:

> [If] your experience is that you are not allowed to talk, you don't see any gay people in your place that you've grown up with, there's no language for it, your first time being able to be in anyway open is when you are in the UK, it's really, really difficult for people to articulate. And I've seen people who, one of the questions the Home Office ask, is how do you identify yourself, how do I refer to you, your sexuality and people don't know what to say. (Amelia, legal practitioner)

The expectations of decision-makers, and indeed of the API itself, often ignores the fact that people have not had a language through which to conceptualize their experiences and may have only recently come from a space where they are unable to speak openly regarding those experiences. As such, expectations around developed narratives of emotional self-reflection and engagement with organizations centred on that specific identity ignore the context that claimants are, generally speaking, fleeing persecution and may not be ready to engage in gatherings which centre on being LGBTIQA+.

Similar expectations around attendance at particular venues and spaces were also expressed by Lucas, who told me that '[t]hey do expect you to go to some kind of LGBT venue or clubs as they call them, you know are you a member of any clubs and I never quite know what they mean by that, or organizations' (Lucas, legal practitioner). This point was repeated again and again by participants, strongly suggesting that attendance in spaces coded as LGBTIQA+ has become one of the central determinants in the success or failure of an asylum claim (see, further, Powell, 2024a).

Media representation and decision-maker socialization

An interesting point raised by Avery in terms of these expectations on the part of decision-makers relates to the socialization of decision-makers and the fact that they are living in a society where they are routinely seeing examples of sexual diversity. Of course, as they are used to seeing these kinds of identities, this will cement an idea that these are inherent and fixed ways of being – adopting here a Butlerian idea that the everyday repetitive nature of these performances both naturalizes them and obscures their performative dimensions (Butler, 1999; White, 1999) – and may further inform the expectations which decision-makers then go on to apply when asked to determine whether a given claimant is a person who is sexually diverse. Specifically, Avery said:

> Once you start with LGBT, I don't think they know what it means. It's really interesting and … because the Home Office caseworkers are human and they've grown up in the UK and they understand what LGBT means, they assume that other people do and they don't all necessarily understand. It's a very western concept. (Avery, third sector worker)

The point Avery raises here is interesting in the sense that it speaks to the fact that the ideas around socializing in venues arise not just from the API, but also from the broader representations of LGBTIQA+ identities that decision-makers socialized in the UK will be familiar with. Indeed, as Berlant has argued, these ordinary representations, due to their 'ordinariness', express a kind of emblematic knowledge (Berlant, 1998: 109). In this way, it is to be expected that the conceptual baggage within which decision-makers have been socialized would impact on their approach to decision-making. Indeed, as Hilton-Morrow and Battles have argued, for anyone born after the late 1980s, representations of LGBTIQA+ people in media are ubiquitous (Hilton-Morrow and Battles, 2015: 70). The result of this is that decision-makers will have strongly contoured preconceptions of what a 'gay' or 'lesbian' narrative looks and sounds like.

As explored through the narratives of claimants themselves in the previous chapter, there also seem to be expectations of a fixed identity. For example, Elijah told me:

> My client had been married and that just, the decision-maker couldn't get over the fact that he had been married and he was very clear he had to marry, there was pressure from his family. He lived in a country where it's, homosexuality is illegal. … But the decision-maker absolutely could not get over it. (Elijiah, legal practitioner)

As this narrative, like Masani's before, suggests, the idea that sexuality is fixed over a lifetime seemed to be a strongly held misconception for many decision-makers (see Diamond, 2000; 2005; 2008; Savin-Williams, 2017). Further, as Elijah's narrative notes, such expectations not only fail to account for the reality of human sexuality, but also to take account of the active steps people may need to take in order to comply with social norms within their country of origin. This is to say that avoiding being perceived as sexually diverse is not just about 'discretion' but requires active engagement with institutions such as marriage and childrearing (Giametta, 2017: 45).

Translation and language

Another problem participants raised was how translation can, in some cases, intersect with the expectations around evidence. For example, the complex interaction of gender and sexuality can become confused due to the inherent overlaps between these concepts and how the language within which they are expressed differs between societies. Sophia said:

> Translation can make a huge mess of this, particularly where you get cases where gender identity is linked to sexuality. … The use of language can be just a bit of a mess. I've certainly had to unpick interview records where it's not been clear what the question was about at any time, because the way terms have been used … it's just assumed the interpreter and that there are words for various things. (Sophia, legal practitioner)

Issues around interpretation and translation were also something which Babu, and other refugee participants, raised. Specifically, there are concerns regarding both the quality and nature of the translation work and how this will impact the narrative to be analysed by the decision-maker, as well as how this will impact on the comfort of people seeking asylum, who may find that concerns regarding the quality of the translation, and the views of the translator, impacts their ability to speak openly during the interview encounter. This can, of course, have significant implications for the ability of claimants to present a narrative which accords with the expectations of decision-makers. Such issues have also been noted in the Canadian context (LaViolette, 2013). Mia also related that they had 'heard things in terms of … people won't want to say what our service users are saying, because it goes against their belief systems' (Mia, third Sector worker). This is concerning in the sense that it also raises questions around whether interpreters may alter the narratives given by asylum claimants due to their own comfort around certain topics.

Though it is to be explored more fully in Chapter 6, as we explore the new and emerging legal and political framework within which asylum claims are being adjudicated, it is also pertinent to note that the rise in the standard of proof from the reasonable degree of likelihood standard to the balance of probabilities standard was raised by some participants as an area of concern in relation to the issues posed earlier. For example, Riley identified that

> [t]he person also has to prove that they have a characteristic that would cause them to fear persecution on the basis of one of the refugee convention reasons and so that means proof that they come within a particular social group, to that higher standard of proof. LGBTQI+

> people who are applying on that basis must meet that higher standard of proof at the first test. (Riley, legal practitioner)

Notable here is the fact that there is already a highly documented culture of disbelief in the Home Office (Jubany, 2011; Schuster, 2020). This culture of disbelief is particularly problematic for claims which are being made on the basis of sexual and gender diversity (Lewis, 2014; Ferreira, 2022). In this sense, there are reasons to be particularly concerned that the change, introduced under Section 32 of the Nationality and Borders Act, might lead to particular difficulties for this already vulnerablized group of claimants (Powell and Rifath, 2023).

The essential point here is that by raising the standard of proof to the balance of probabilities for key elements of the claim, the amount which is required for a claimant to prove in order to secure refugee status has been increased. This, in turn, exacerbates many of the expectations and issues which we have explored across this chapter and the preceding one. The net result of this is that the already extensive range of, often conceptual, difficulties claimants face in proving that they are sexually diverse people are likely to get worse as the impacts of the legislative changes introduced across the period 2022–2024 become clearer through their applicability to a wider range of claims.

4.2 Legal aid

The issues posed by the cuts to legal aid introduced as a part of the broader programme of government austerity between 2010 and the current moment are well established within the literature (Newman and Robins, 2021; Mant et al, 2024). To recount this in short, legal aid fees were extensively cut in the early 2000s, with restrictions to the provision of legal aid immigration and asylum support then being introduced as part of the Legal Aid Sentencing and Punishment of Offenders Act 2012. This has caused particular difficulties in relation to legal aid asylum and immigration, as has been documented by Jo Wilding (2021). Recently, the specific issues that such cuts and limitations pose for sexually diverse claimants has also been explored by a research team led by Edward J. Alessi, who outlined how the situation around legal aid immigration and asylum support posed particular difficulties for sexually diverse people in terms of finding appropriate legal support and advice (Alessi et al, 2024).

Those seeking asylum are able to put forward a claim for exceptional case funding from the Legal Aid Agency in order to support them in claiming asylum in the UK. However, as Wilding has documented, the UK not only has issues with the overall availability of legal aid but also faces significant problems with the existence of legal aid deserts (Wilding, 2021: 121–149).

This, again, has problematic interactions with the UK government's dispersal policy because people are often accommodated in areas where there are very serious issues with accessing in-person legal advice. Further, as I go on to show, this also creates specific difficulties for sexually diverse claimants who may be accommodated in a location which does not allow them access to legal representatives with expertise in sexual diversity claims.

Legal representative capacity and trust building

On one level, this creates risks for claimants in the sense that it leads to significant difficulties accessing legal advice, particularly within the timelines set by the Home Office. But it also creates difficulties for practitioners. For example, an issue which a number of participants recounted was how the huge volume of cases individual legal practitioners were carrying at any given time – sometimes several hundred (for example, Sophia recounted how most people in their team had 150 to 200 cases each at any given time) – limited the ability of legal practitioners to build relationships with claimants. Specifically, they identified that

> [p]retty much every type of asylum claim that you could imagine comes to us. I mean we've got hundreds of clients actually, so I've got a caseload of about 150 cases, which isn't ideal and I supervise two people with 100 cases each and we've got about 100 people on the waiting list, because … detention centre closed down and then people were relocated to hotels … and we are the only legal aid firm and they're all asylum seekers, but there's just no capacity. (Sophia, legal practitioner)

This presents a significant issue in regard to sexual diversity claims because building the trust and relationship with a claimant that is needed to properly support them to discuss experiences which are likely traumatic takes time and engagement (see Alessi et al, 2024). As Riley noted, it is those claimants who are rendered vulnerable due to the social status and categories which they inhabit and the area they are placed into who are the most likely to face the negative effects that the lack of time representatives are able to devote to each individual generates within the asylum system. Specifically, they stated:

> Now I'm not saying that someone needs to have a great deal of legal expertise to do an LGBTQI+ claim … but it might be the case that people assess in really complex cases, whether they do, or whether the person would best be represented by someone else who has better knowledge. I do think that the people who are most adversely affected by the lack of capacity and the restraints on legal aid are those who

> are the most vulnerable. … From these areas we know that people often disclose their reasons for their persecution relatively late in the stage of the claim so would also likely to be impacted if they don't have a representative who they feel that they can trust. (Riley, legal practitioner)

The point here is that claimants who inhabit particular social categories are more likely to need additional support in navigating the asylum process. For example, for claimants who are sexually diverse this might be additional support in understanding the categories and forms of evidence decision-maker will expect to see, but with which they are not currently familiar. This may not even be strictly legal, instead it may relate to helping the claimant to understand the conceptual frameworks through which sexual diversity is made sense of in the UK.

However, this kind of support – or indeed the necessary work of building a relationship so that someone feels comfortable opening up to the legal representative about elements of their life which they may consider to be deeply intimate and personal – is often not possible within the current financial and time constraints that the system creates. It can therefore be said that the negative implications which the changes to the legal aid framework have had for all people seeking asylum are particularly pronounced for sexually diverse people. This point was articulately drawn out by Muhammad:

> The essence of … any successful asylum claim is credibility. To me the essence of a credible asylum claim is a coherent and detailed narrative and how do you get a detailed coherent narrative from a vulnerable applicant … it's true probably to say that most LGBT+ refugees are more vulnerable, have a vulnerability there, or vulnerabilities, getting that narrative from people and presenting it in a way that's coherent and is credible and can withstand Home Office kind of disbelief is not something that you can get done in an hour or two. (Muhammad, legal practitioner)

Indeed, Isabella outlined how most of their job is experienced as a form of firefighting, dealing with immediate disasters and fielding enquiries, quite often from very distressed asylum claimants, to the point where even working on the longer-term elements of the job could be difficult. Specifically, they outlined that,

> [t]here's such poor funding from the Legal Aid Agency for adult claims that it's not financially viable to have that many workers. So we all have large caseloads, yeah incredibly large caseloads and it's often, most days it's firefighting, it's what is happening today and tomorrow that I need

> to action and that, you often know that you've got those bigger projects like preparing a fresh claim, or writing a brief to a council, which you kind of need to sit, it's like a kind of more academic process. But you think when can I do that, because currently my phone is ringing and my emails are coming in and out and I'm meeting people. (Isabella, legal practitioner)

The issues with practitioners having such large caseloads are not just in regard to matters such as the ability to form a relationship with claimants, but also the problems this can pose for claimants who may need to urgently contact their legal representatives. For example, as explored further in Chapter 6, many asylum claimants experienced significant anxiety and fear in regard to the UK government's announcements around the plan to send asylum claimants to Rwanda (see Sen et al, 2022). For those claimants already in the system, this anxiety could have quickly been addressed by their legal representative confirming that the changes to the law would not have an impact on them. However, the excessive caseloads that representatives carry means that providing such reassurance will often have been beyond their capacity, or at least that they will not have been in a position to immediately communicate with their (often well over 100) clients regarding the implications of the change, which the government was promoting as one of its central policy achievements, for them and their claim for protection in the UK.

Concerns about capacity were ubiquitous across participants, with some impressing the severity of the situation. For example, Amelia told me:

> South Wales I think we are at a point where, I had a think about it the other day, because a friend of mine left legal aid and I think we're at a point where one person leaving is 7 to 10 per cent of the Legal Aid capacity for Wales. Every one of us leaves a hole. (Amelia, legal practitioner)

They went on to identify that, 'if the person in Plymouth quits, we're stuffed, because there is one person in Plymouth. So if they quit the whole region goes down'. As this shows, as well as the overall issue with access to legal aid, there are particular issues presenting in particular areas, with large geographic areas being covered by exceptionally small numbers of lawyers. Indeed, Jessie outlined a sense that the lack of available legal support specialized in the field of asylum and immigration had opened up some claimants to a risk of engaging predatory lawyers who were charging them significant amounts, but who were then not offering proper legal support.

Of concern here is the possibility that legal representatives who are not experienced in sexual diversity asylum claims may not be aware of the range of decision-maker and conceptual expectations which we have already outlined in this book. This may, in turn, mean that they are not well placed to provide a person seeking asylum with the legal advice they need in terms of how to frame their claim and the kinds of evidence which the Home Office will be looking for.

Government policy and legal aid capacity

Some participants identified that these issues had been exacerbated by recent policy directives. For example, the movement towards housing asylum seekers in hotels, and other mass accommodation centres such as the Bibi Stockholm had, Riley suggested, created new issues for legal aid practitioners such as the fact that the Legal Aid Agency would not cover the time and opportunity costs associated with travelling to take instructions from those you are to be representing. Specifically they outlined that

> hotels pop up across England and Wales… and there may or may not be the legal representatives in that area to provide in-person advice and this is where the legal aid deserts become relevant … what's the likelihood that your client will be able to travel to you? … Whilst the Legal Aid Agency covers some costs like a person travelling to see their legal representative, it doesn't cover other loss, for example people aren't going to be remunerated for their time. So a fee earner, who is losing money because they are spending five hours on the train to get to Napier Barracks isn't going to be remunerated for that … for example with the barges that we're talking about, as the south west only has four legal aid representatives, so for this barge in Portland, if we are talking about in-person advice on the barge, how many people are going to have access to it, likely not many. (Riley, legal practitioner)

Having already noted that those working as legal aid lawyers often have caseloads of more than 100 clients, there is a real need here to consider accommodation policies can impact the ability of legal representatives to properly support their clients. Indeed, Wilding has argued that the lack of attention to legal aid deserts can be seen as a kind of strategic ignorance, which she argues may be incompatible with the statutory duties incumbent on the Lord Chancellor (Wilding, 2021). While Burridge and Gill have argued that the combination of dispersal and legal aid deserts results in luck and uncertainty coming to play a key role in the success or failure of asylum claims (Burridge and Gill, 2017).

Given this, legal representatives face a difficult double-bind where they either do not meet clients in person and instead speaks with them remotely, which poses a range of issues explored in what follows. Or, in travelling to meet one client in order to give them support, the legal representative incurs extensive opportunity costs in the sense that the unremunerated time they spend travelling is time during which they are not able to engage with the huge range of other clients and tasks they need to be working on. This affects not just them in the sense that it has huge implications for the ability of them personally and their firm to bring in fees, but also their clients as the time they are spending further inhibits their ability to support other clients who they may be working with at that time.

When considering issues around digital or remote meetings, aside from exacerbating the issues with building trust and rapport that we have already addressed, an increased use in remote legal advice poses a further concern. Specifically, it is often difficult for those housed in large-scale accommodation to access private space. However, if a claimant is needing to keep their sexual diversity secret from those with whom they are accommodated (Fletcher, 2024), how are they to take proper legal advice if they are required to do so remotely within their accommodation? In this sense, as with the other issues we have addressed earlier, it is not that the issues with legal aid and access to justice are specific to sexually diverse people, they present a profound issue for everyone seeking sanctuary in the UK. However, due to a complex interplay of social factors those who are sexually diverse may experience greater difficulties as a result of these general problems.

In relation to claimants in large-scale accommodation centres, the issues facing sexually diverse people relate not only to their ability to take advice, but also to their ability to fully advise their legal representative of their situation. In short, any legal representative seeking to give advice is going to need the client to share details of their basis of claim, this will include extensive details of the experiences which have led them to claim asylum. Without this, it will not be possible for the legal representative to advise them on how their claim should be framed. However, many asylum claimants in large-scale accommodation may not be able to speak openly, as they may not feel safe to be open about their sexual diversity. As such, the interaction of the policy on legal aid and the move towards larger-scale accommodation centres, taken together, pose particular issues for sexually diverse people seeking asylum.

Some participants went further still, for example, Jessie identified a distinct fear that the system as a whole had effectively collapsed. Specifically, they stated:

> There's a real risk, I feel from my perception of sitting here in my city office, that there's a real risk that the whole thing is just at kind of collapse point and you know that all has to then be weighed up against what the government are planning on doing, to try and speed up asylum cases and so on. (Jessie, legal practitioner)

In this regard, it should be noted that in many ways government policies across the period 2022–2024 contained the potential of significantly exacerbating existing issues. For example, the initial focus of the Nationality and Borders Act 2022 was on creating a form of differential treatment in regard to refugee status between those who had entered the UK with prior permission, such as a visa, and those who had arrived irregularly. One of the core differences envisaged between what were termed group 1 and group 2 refugees was that those in group 2 would only receive their grant of status for a period of 30 months, as opposed to the five years granted to those in group 1. The net effect of this would have been to effectively halve the period in which someone could remain in the UK without having to re-engage with the asylum system. In short, this change would not only have been harmful to people seeking asylum in terms of exacerbating levels of uncertainty and restricting their ability to build a life in the UK, but would also have significant capacity implications both for immigration practitioners and the Home Office, exacerbating existing issues around legal aid support as well as potentially exacerbating delays in regard to decision-making, by dramatically increasing the volume of cases which the Home Office had to reconsider.

While this group distinction was ultimately scrapped (Right to Remain, 2023), even the proposal and short-term enactment of it consumed large amounts of practitioner time in regard to thinking through the effects of the change and preparing to support clients in regard to it. In this sense, consideration should be taken of how these kinds of 'tough' policies may actually compromise the ability of both legal practitioners and the Home Office to create a workable system which is able to give the kind of prompt decisions which are needed.

As I will explore later in this book, the changes proposed by government – seemingly more focused on appearing tough than creating a legally workable system – could easily be argued to have significantly contributed to the capacity issues which have faced the UK asylum system, creating delays, associated significant costs, and undermining the ability of the UK to comply with its international obligations. I further explore these issues in Chapter 6, but at this stage, the main issue to bear in mind is the fact that these changes have been made within a wider context of legal aid cuts which have hugely reduced the capacity of legal representatives to support their clients and generated particularly difficult situations for those who are already vulnerabilized.

The issues in regard to legal aid were not perceived as being ubiquitous across the UK. For example, Brogan, who worked for a non-governmental organization in Northern Ireland, said, '[y]ep, because the thing is … one of the biggest differences in Northern Ireland, compared to the rest of England, Scotland and Wales is there's free legal support and it's very available. It's like there's no asylum seeker that goes without any legal support and advice' (Brogan, third sector worker). During the course of the research, three of the participants were based in Northern Ireland and all three shared a perception that there was greater availability of legal support within Northern Ireland than other parts of the UK.

This presents an interesting issue and raises a broader question regarding how the different nations which make up the UK each play their own part in creating the conditions which are experienced by people seeking asylum as well as those granted refugee status. This is beyond the scope of this book, but it is nonetheless interesting to note that within the legal aid regime of Northern Ireland the clear sense was that the issues often experienced in England, Wales and Scotland were not present.

4.3 Concerns regarding practitioner safety and the role of lawyers

One major part of the contemporary asylum landscape is the embrace of narratives that are hostile to lawyers by a range of leading political and media actors, including those within the UK government. This sits as part of a broader hostility directed towards people seeking asylum and what has (incorrectly) been branded as 'illegal migration'. This has included the government deploying language such as 'lefty lawyers' (Mason, 2023) and 'activist lawyers'[1] to imply that legal representatives are acting in a politicized or improper manner. Indeed, this idea fits into a broader zeitgeist. For example, following the decision of the High Court in the first *Miller* case,[2] the *Daily Mail* ran with a now infamous headline declaring that the judges were 'Enemies of the people' for their, entirely orthodox, holding that a Royal Prerogative power could not be used to trigger the UK's exit from the European Union when doing so would directly contradict the European Communities Act 1972 (Slack, 2016). Both the Law Society and the Bar Council have been active in pointing out the dangerous nature of these narratives and the threats they may pose to both practitioners as people and, more broadly, to the rule of law in the UK.

Example of the hostile narratives directed towards lawyers working in this area can be seen in the then Home Secretary Suella Braverman's briefing that migration lawyers were supporters of people-trafficking (BBC News,

1 See International Bar Association, 'UK government's "activist lawyers" and "playing politics" rhetoric undermines the rule of law say IBA and IBAHRI' (23 November 2020), available at: https://www.ibanet.org/article/bb258df4-b878-41b1-b255-0f9690fbfefa (accessed 17 October 2024).

2 *R (On the Application of Miller and Another) v Secretary of State for Exiting the European Union* [201] UKSC 5.

2023). This is, of course, a dangerous misrepresentation which could potentially endanger lives if people were to take it at face value and associate legal practitioners with the kinds of harm arising from human trafficking. While others have identified human rights lawyers as blocking the removal of dangerous criminals from the UK (Barrett and Bartlett, 2020). This again situates the act of practising law, which is central in regard to ensuring that the actions of government are undertaken in a manner that is in accordance with the legal framework set down by parliament, as adjacent to engagement in criminal activity.

While the politicization of lawyers is, in and of itself, nothing new, the embrace of these narratives by a government is clearly incompatible with the United Nations Basic Principles on the Role of Lawyers.[3] Specifically, principle 16, which states that:

> Governments shall ensure that lawyers (a) are able to perform all of their professional functions without intimidation, hindrance, harassment or improper interference … (c) shall not suffer, or be threatened with, prosecution or administrative, economic or other sanctions for any action taken in accordance with recognized professional duties, standards and ethics.[4]

Unfortunately, in the routine statements of government ministers which criticize lawyers for simply applying the legal framework as set out either directly by parliament, or by another body in accordance with powers given by parliament, the government itself has not only failed to ensure, but directly contributed to, intimidation and hindrance of lawyers discharging their functions. Indeed, in some cases – such as that of Jacqueline Mackenzie – this has even extended to the level of identifying individual lawyers within government dossiers (Syal, 2023). Many of the participants in this study felt that the government had directly contributed to the creation of a narrative and a context which directly threatened their safety. In stating this, it is important to remember that, ultimately, it is not just the safety of individual lawyers which is compromised when practitioners feels unsafe, but also the ability of people to ensure that their legal rights are not violated and that public bodies, such as the Home Office, are acting according to law. As such, the narratives repeated by participants have implications for legal

3 United Nations Office of the High Commissioner for Human Rights, Basic Principles of the Role of Lawyers Adopted by the Eighth United Nations Congress on the Prevention and Treatment of Offenders, Havana, Cuba, Adopted 7 September 1990.

4 United Nations Office of the High Commissioner for Human Rights, Basic Principles of the Role of Lawyers Adopted by the Eighth United Nations Congress on the Prevention and Treatment of Offenders, Havana, Cuba, Adopted 7 September 1990, principle 16.

practitioners themselves but also for constitutional fundamentals such as the rule of law and the supremacy of parliament.

Indeed, other actions of government here should also be noted. Paragraph 18 of the same set of principles identifies that '[l]awyers shall not be identified with their clients or their clients causes as a result of discharging their functions'.[5] Despite this, on multiple occasions, government statements have implied that lawyers bear responsibility for who they represent. Of course, at least in terms of barristers, practitioners are expected to follow the cab rank rule and take any client who requests support.[6] Despite this, the current or former clients of legal representatives have frequently been deployed as a political tool to question their legitimacy.

Turning to the participants themselves, some argued that the narratives deployed by government representatives had actively placed them in danger. For example, Elijah said:

> I remember Priti Patel saying something inflammatory and I know then there was a knife attack in Duncan Lewis … and then again Suella Braverman said something which I thought that is actually a personal attack on the work I'm doing and my colleagues and it's incredibly dangerous for our safety. (Elijah, legal practitioner)

Considering the sections of the Basic Principles on the Role of Lawyers discussed earlier, it is striking that participants felt that there was a direct correlation between the statements made by government ministers and incidents of actual violence aimed at lawyers. Indeed, following the August 2024 riots, the president of the Law Society of England and Wales stated that 'we have serious concerns about the safety and wellbeing of our members following names and addresses of a number of solicitors firms and advice agencies being shared on a list of targets' (Law Society, 2024). As this suggests, the equation of lawyers with clients can lead to very serious and very real dangers.

Damian also reflected on the levels of hostility faced and the implications that this has for them and their colleagues in terms of speaking openly about their jobs. Specifically, they told me that '[c]learly there is hostility … you might have to think about saying what you do in particular contexts … you can't just be open and say yeah I'm a lawyer I deal with

5 United Nations Office of the High Commissioner for Human Rights, Basic Principles of the Role of Lawyers Adopted by the Eighth United Nations Congress on the Prevention and Treatment of Offenders, Havana, Cuba, Adopted 7 September 1990, 18.

6 The Bar Council, 'Cab rank rule: Statement of the Four Bars' (26 May 2023), available at: https://www.barcouncil.org.uk/resource/cab-rank-rule-statement-of-the-four-bars.html (accessed 17 October 2024).

asylum seekers … because is it safe for me to say this in this context' (Damian, legal practitioner). Other participants also felt that government narratives about both migration and lawyers had contributed to creating a situation within which legal practitioners felt unsafe. For example, Riley said:

> I think there is an increasing concern that the media and the government are aligned in their misrepresentation of lawyers and practitioners who are working in this field and that that might be a threat to their safety and also their ability to best represent their clients. If they no longer feel that they can do so safely without jeopardizing their own safety, or their family's safety, then for example the Bar Counsel's position in that case was that they could withdraw from the case. (Riley, legal practitioner)

The fact that Riley refers to practitioners responding to the narratives with concerns about their own safety and this possibly leading to them withdrawing from cases is striking and speaks to how the implications of these concerns go beyond the impact on individual lawyers and instead threaten the entire edifice of the rule of law. Put simply, legal rights and rules do not mean a great deal if they cannot be enforced by a court. The enforcement of rights is, therefore, dependent on people being able to access the legal representation needed to ensure their rights are respected. This, in turn, is dependent on lawyers feeling they can represent their clients without their safety or welfare being undermined.

Even beyond the rhetorical invocations of government ministers and the media, other participants reflected a sense of anxiety around sharing what they did at work. For example, Amelia stated:

> Whenever I've spoken to anyone actually about the day to day, what I do, people are always shocked and they can't believe these things are happening and are far more empathetic than I might imagine otherwise people to be. But yeah I think there is this kind of increasingly hostile approach to legal aid lawyers and especially with the idea of this invasion of people on dinghies literally landing on the shores and if you say yeah I represent some of those, I mean I can imagine if I'm, not amongst my friends, or friends of friends, probably that would be a much more hostile thing. (Amelia, legal practitioner)

Given that during the period where these interviews were being undertaken, we were working in a political epoch where politicians frequently attempted to present practitioners as synonymous with their clients, it is perhaps unsurprising to hear such anxiety regarding revealing the nature of their job roles to people who they did not know. It is also interesting to note here how Amelia's narrative reflected a sense of the 'small boats' narrative having conditioned public understanding of the issue, possibly contributing to greater hostility towards asylum seekers, refugees and those working to support them.

Indeed, it is worth noting that, as some participants reflected, the interviews were undertaken during the course of a period in which two Members of Parliament were murdered (Cobain and Taylor, 2016; BBC News, 2022). With one of the killings being directly linked to far-right anti-migrant sentiments of the kind the government could be argued to have stoked up. This came alongside a number of other very public far-right or conspiracy theory linked actions, ranging from protest to actual violence (Ekman, 2022). As such, it is perhaps unsurprising that some participants reflected particular anxiety regarding the possibility of lawyers being targets. For example, Muhammad said:

> If I was working still at [name of organization] I think I might feel a little bit edgy to be honest. I think that we know that the far right have become more violent, we know that they've killed an MP, that they've got it, they've attacked other people, they attacked an asylum office, of an asylum lawyer. You know fascists have always been violent and so that's a worry to be honest and I think what's also a worry for me politically is that it's going, it's tipping over into something different now, which is that the far right are fusing with you know, and this is the Trump thing, but with conspiracist thinking. (Muhammad, legal practitioner)

In this regard, it may be that the approach that the government adopted towards both people seeking asylum and the lawyers who support them is best understood as a form of stochastic terrorism (Amman and Meloy, 2024; Angrove, 2024). That is to say that, by continually reiterating the narrative that these groups constitute a threat to society, there is, in effect, a rendering of these groups as far more likely recipients of violence. Indeed, recent far-right riots outside of hotels accommodating people seeking asylum and the repeated treatment of lawyers as akin to their clients suggest that the real-world manifestations of the discourses and forms of othering enacted by particular political actors are increasing manifesting towards acts of physical violence.

As an example of this, during one week in August 2024, the UK saw a surge in far-right activity across the United Kingdom, but particularly within England (Bancroft, 2024). This included rioters attempting to set fire to a hotel which they believed to be housing asylum seekers (Sinmaz, 2024). The riots followed the circulation of misinformation suggesting that the perpetrator of the Southport knife attack had been an asylum seeker who had entered the UK on a small boat (Quinn, 2024). Obviously, the government did not circulate this false narrative and relevant agencies acted quickly both to correct the misinformation and ensure legal accountability for those who had either spread it or participated in the violence. However, it is difficult not to draw links between the frequent allusions to those on 'small boats' being 'foreign national offenders' and the fact that this misinformation of this kind so successfully took hold (Oppenheim, 2024).

During this week of violence, a list was also shared on the social network Telegram. The list contained details of third sector organizations and legal officers working in the area of migration and asylum. This list purported to identify sites the far right would be targeting (Toth, 2024). Although, in most cases, the violence did not materialize, considerable anxiety was caused, particular among Muslim and ethnic minority communities in the UK (Simpson and McKee, 2024). Even if this incident was not caused by the narratives of government, a clear discursive link can be drawn between the way in which migration and asylum in the UK have been spoken about by government ministers and Members of Parliament and the framing of organizations which support refugees and migrants as legitimate targets for what were self-styled as 'pro-British' protests (Elliards, 2024). In this sense, as outlined earlier in this volume, the way in which legal representatives have been framed fits as a part of a broader meta-politics which has constructed lawyers as 'legitimate' targets for abuse and intimidation within a broader far-right colonization of political space.

It is, therefore, my argument that the narratives perpetuated by government have contributed to making legal representatives less safe and may well have played a role in legitimizing far-right violence, at least in the minds of those engaging in it.

A participant or a roadblock?

Aside from the stark concerns regarding personal safety, some participants also expressed a sense that both the public and the Home Office did not view them as participants in the legal process but rather as standing in the way of government goals and activities, which they seemed to prejudge as inherently legitimate and lawful. For example, Sophia said that 'I think in a lot of cases we are viewed as lefty do-gooders and possibly even people who aren't, who don't possibly have the expertise that we don't really know what we're talking about because obviously the Home Office would be the experts' (Sophia, legal practitioner).

Perhaps the most interesting point here is how this participant felt that the Home Office often viewed them as people who lacked expertise and felt that the hostility towards lawyers extended into the legal process itself. Here it is worth noting that the legal framework around asylum and other forms of protection in the UK is extremely complex and frequently changing.[7] As such, it requires significant expertise to properly advise people. Indeed, it is interesting here to note that, for Sophia, there was even a sense that the process itself – which often renders legal representatives into a very passive role at key moments such as the substantive interview – may contribute to a view of lawyers as lacking expertise. For example, even if a legal practitioner attends an interview with the person they are representing their capacity to intervene is extremely limited. The result of this is that Home Office decision-makers' actual experiences of legal representatives frame the representatives in a highly passive role observing proceedings, rather than as an active participant with a role in the process.

Asylum seekers' understanding of legal representatives

Issues over the role of the lawyer also extended to some people seeking asylum. In particular, participants reflect a concern that the passive role which the processes placed them into may have implications for their ability to build trust and rapport with the people they are supporting. For example, Sophia told me that '[m]aybe assumptions about the role of lawyers, the power of lawyers, that I see quite a lot, people unfortunately think that lawyers have a lot more power than we do. Ease of communication with the Home Office, I can't phone them up, there isn't a phone line unfortunately' (Sophia, legal practitioner).

This is interesting in the sense that those navigating the asylum system seemed to expect lawyers to have powers to directly intervene in order to address issues such as delays. The reality is that, with regard to getting responses from the Home Office, the opportunities for lawyers to take action are relatively limited. The experiences Sophia shared in this regard correspond to the time I have directly spent with asylum claimants, who can often become frustrated that legal representatives are not able to do things like address the delays around getting a substantive interview. Indeed, Damian outlined how 'we spend increasing amount of time just trying to deal with delays, chasing the Home Office, trying to get them to say what they are doing. … Obviously, the client is getting frustrated' (Damian, legal practitioner). Such frustrations may themselves be exacerbated by the way in which government has taken to talking about lawyers, often framing them as responsible for blocking or curtailing their agenda in the area of migration and asylum. Damian went on to tell me that

[7] The Law Commission, 'Simplification of the immigration rules', Law Com No 388 (House of Commons Library, 2020).

> with the delays they do start to think we are part of the delay as well. Because if we are not actively doing anything in their eyes … and there is nothing else we can do particularly and then we push the Home Office to do what they are supposed to do. (Damian, legal practitioner)

As this suggests, the delays within the process risk undermining trust between legal representatives and people seeking asylum.

In this regard, it is worth reflecting that the perceived power of lawyers by those navigating the asylum system may mean that they perceive a lack of assistance in response to issues such as delays as reflecting a lack of care and concern on the part of their representatives. This may, in turn, undermine their comfort in sharing elements of their narrative which could have implications for their ability to address the evidentiary issues outlined in section 4.1 of this chapter.

Sophia offered an example of how, in some cases, other organizations – such as those in the third sector – could also contribute to giving people seeking asylum a false conception of the powers and positionality of legal representatives. Specifically, they told me that

> [l]ast year there was a local LGBTQ organization on, I think they were looking specifically at accommodation and they said that lawyers were allocated by the Home Office and that was clearly taken, because they'd been interviewing people and this had come through and this had then gone to the organization doing the report, who hadn't themselves been a refugee organization. (Sophia, legal practitioner)

As noted previously, one of the most important things for a lawyer is to show the person that they are representing that they are on their side and that they, as a legal representative, are someone who can be trusted with the disclosure of information. This is particularly important because they need to support the claimant in getting to a place where they can narrate the kind of developed narrative of identity development that we have outlined earlier in this volume. It is, therefore, problematic for an asylum claimant to be left with a perception that their legal representative was appointed by the Home Office. This is because the Home Office is often viewed by asylum claimants as itself constituting a potential source of trauma. In this regard, overly associating one's own legal representative with the Home Office could undermine the ability of someone seeking asylum to properly take legal advice.

Linked to this, some participants reflected on a concern that their role effectively framed them as an extension of the Home Office in some contexts, even potentially legitimizing the system. For example, Amelia told me that

> [i]t's really tricky, it's a complex one, because sometimes I feel like I'm an extension of a system that is racist and homophobic, because I am explaining the way the system works and I can't change it for people, and I'm telling them how to navigate that system. For example in sexual identity claims, these are the types of questions you might be asked, or this is how you have to frame your journey. … So sometimes I wrestle with that, that am I just perpetuating this system. (Amelia, legal practitioner)

This reflection is interesting because, on the one hand, it reflects how limited the powers of lawyers are in this context. Lawyers can only work within the systemic confines and perimeters handed down to them by legal, social, institutional, cultural and political contexts. For example, as reflected across both the previous chapter and this one, lawyers operate in a system which requires highly stereotypical and deeply 'westernized' forms of evidence. This is due to the conceptual frameworks through which sexual diversities are understood and the fact that, while not themselves being a part of the law, these frameworks are a part of the 'emblematic knowledge' through which actors make sense of the world (Gary, 2004). However, in the pursuit of serving the best interests of their client, lawyers are often required to reproduce these logics in regard to the kinds of evidence which they advise claimants to compile. In a similar sense, lawyers could well be viewed as enacting a sort of gatekeeping role, at least in regard to the ways in which a claimant presents themselves to decision-makers. A similar anxiety was raised by Isabella:

> Sometimes I say oh we're just oiling the cogs of the Home Office, making it function. My colleagues tell me no, we fight them, but I'm like yeah we also facilitate like their system in some way. We are the link … to the client and to eliciting the evidence to enable the Home Office to make their important asylum decisions. So, we are very much yeah, facilitating to a degree. (Isabella, legal practitioner)

This duality of both facilitating the operation of the process but also holding the Home Office to account go to broader questions about whether it is better to work within institutions in order to reform them and seek to make them better, or if it is instead necessary to dismantle those same institutions (Bradley and De Noronha, 2022). Indeed, I know of several friends who have left legal practice because of exactly this sense that they were fundamentally enabling the continuation of an unjust system which ultimately harmed those they wished to help. Indeed, to link this back to Chapter 2, the approach taken to this could be seen to map relatively closely onto the gap between counter and anti-normative approaches in queer theory, or more broadly the gap between abolitionist and reformist approaches (Zanghellini, 2009).

Researchers in the French context have highlighted that this kind of dilemma over potential or perceived gatekeeping is one commonly faced by third sector organizations when deciding which claimants they will support (Giametta and Havkin, 2021). Indeed, Sophia's narrative reflects back on the arguments Bruce-Jones has made with regard to how the approach taken to one asylum claim may shift the expectations and norms that people trying to navigate the process in future are required to correspond with (Bruce-Jones, 2015). This duality was well put by Muhammad:

> So I think some clients think that I'm great and that I'm a real help and that I listen to them carefully and I'm empathetic and all that. I think some probably think I'm a pain in the arse, because I insist upon them providing all these documents that they don't think they ought to have to provide. (Muhammad, legal practitioner)

However, it is also pertinent to note that lawyers play a pivotal role in making an area of law, which the Law Commission has long recognized as being among the most complex, intelligible for those attempting to navigate the system.[8] This was something some participants directly recognized, contextualizing their complex feelings while acknowledging that the work they do to support individual clients is vital.

Indeed, far from the power some felt that the people they represented may associate with lawyers, Isabella recounted the need to reconceptualize what is viewed as an effective piece of work and how important it is to continue to centre the humanity of people in the asylum system. Specifically, they told me that,

> [i]f I think of the first appointment, I've achieved in an hour and a half if they've just smiled or looked at me, or I've sensed that they are trusting me, because they think I'm the Home Office, more often than not, when they first meet me. So, I have to be, really work hard to build that trust. (Isabella, legal practitioner)

Linking this to Isabella's broader narrative, the fundamental point here is that they have had to re-frame their own expectations around what can be achieved in the time that they have to accommodate the fact that it can sometimes take a very long time to show a person seeking asylum that you

8 The Law Commission, 'Simplification of the immigration rules', Law Com No 388 (House of Commons Library, 2020).

are someone they can trust. Obviously, this is problematic insofar as the need for this kind of time to build rapport and relationships is very much not funded under the current legal aid funding arrangements. But more broadly, it speaks to the complex role of legal representatives and the broader context within which this area of law operates, a context which requires the navigation of complex social relations as much as it does legal ones.

As with some of the narratives explored earlier, Isabella noted that many people navigating the asylum system initially struggle to differentiate between their own legal representative and the Home Office. Given this, they noted the importance of trying to build rapport and trust with the people that they are representing. It is important here to reflect on the difficult relationship between the availability of legal aid advice as highlighted earlier in this chapter and the time it takes to genuinely build a relationship with someone in the asylum system so that they feel comfortable to share their experiences with you (Bögner et al, 2010). The importance of the time and space necessary to build rapport is well noted within the academic literature (Dickson-Swift et al, 2007: 331–334) but is an equally pertinent consideration for legal representatives who need to build trust and honest communication in order to properly support the people they are representing.

Given the contradiction, it is worth further reflecting on how structural constraints impact the ability of legal representatives to give the people who they are representing the kind of support that navigating the asylum system would ideally entail. Nonetheless, despite these structural constraints, the narratives also help to clarify how fundamentally important it is to have legal representatives who are able to translate an extremely complex legal framework into an accessible format.

Home Office hostility

Perhaps reflecting this crucial role in making the process accessible for those seeking asylum, Ava reflected on the hostility which legal practitioners often face from the Home Office in the course of trying to do their job. Specifically, in outlining Home Office conceptions of a range of firms that they were not personally involved with they stated:

> Duncan Lewis they hate you. …They hate Wilsons as well I think, but they particularly hate Duncan Lewis. … I think they would regard me as an enemy. I think that would be my best guess. I did, years and years ago, I did some training at the Home Office and they were very hostile … they just basically got every immigration barrister they could find and we all went to train at the Home Office and it was crazy. … They did not like that and it was very hostile, very, very hostile. (Ava, legal practitioner)

The language deployed by Ava is striking here. The UK legal system is adversarial in nature. However, within the context of asylum, there is an expectation that, while it is clear that the burden of proof is on the claimant to prove that they are entitled to refugee status, the Home Office should work with them in order to discharge this burden.[9] Indeed, the framing of lawyers, who are fulfilling a fundamental right of the claimant in terms of entitlement to legal advice and representation, as the enemy is again of questionable consistency with the Basic Principles on the Role of Lawyers.[10] However, more broadly, the framing of lawyers as the enemy and seeming lack of good faith engagement with legal representatives raises real questions in regard to the commitment of the Home Office to working to achieve the right outcome, instead suggesting a prima facie conception of their actions as inherently legitimate and correct. Within a system governed by the rule of law, such a disposition should be regarded as at best unfortunate and at worst as a threat to the integrity of the system.

It is pertinent to note that Home Office staff are often not qualified legal practitioners. Whereas legal representatives in the immigration and asylum sector are expected to have specific qualifications in place before offering any form of immigration advice,[11] Home Office caseworkers often only have access to internal training provision and have frequently been recruited with education below the level of an undergraduate degree. It is, therefore, concerning to hear that when training was offered it was not engaged with.

In seeking to understand and contextualize the approach taken by Home Office staff towards legal representatives, it is worth reflecting that while their role is administrative they are ultimately working under the direction of the Secretary of State for the Home Department. In this sense, it is perhaps understandable that the staff working in the Home Office would be impacted by the broader rhetoric and narratives deployed by government ministers. Indeed, taking note of historic practices such as the awarding of a cake to the immigration officer who detained the highest number of 'illegal migrants', there is a clear foundation for the arguments and standpoints coming from

---

[9] See UK Visas and Immigration, *Assessing Credibility and Refugee Status in Asylum Claims Lodged on or after 28 June 2022* (Home Office, 28 September 2023), available at: https://www.gov.uk/government/publications/considering-asylum-claims-and-assessing-credibility-instruction/assessing-credibility-and-refugee-status-in-asylum-claims-lodged-on-or-after-28-june-2022-accessible (accessed 17 October 2024).

[10] United Nations Office of the High Commissioner for Human Rights, Basic Principles of the Role of Lawyers Adopted by the Eighth United Nations Congress on the Prevention and Treatment of Offenders, Havana, Cuba, Adopted 7 September 1990.

[11] Details of the requirements and nature of the role are set out on the Home Office jobsite, available at: https://www.homeofficejobs-sscl.co.uk/immigration-enforcement-role-overview (accessed 17 October 2024).

the government having a direct impact on the operation of the administrative state with regard to matters of migration and asylum (Wheaton, 2018). Thinking within a rule of law context, with a particular focus here on the importance of ensuring that decisions are taken because of the clear application of the stated legal framework, this would again be a cause for concern in regard to the compatibility of some elements of Home Office practice with fundamental norms of public law and public administration. It is noted here that legal realists or critical legal scholars would, of course, argue that legal decisions are never simply a case of applying the stated legal framework in a simple way, and I would agree (see Tushnet, 1990; Tamanaha, 2008). However, given the attention paid within mainstream representations of law to non-political application of legal frameworks, it is important to judge the extent to which the Home Office lives up to this orthodox accounting of the operation of law.

Indeed, Sophia made direct reference to the implications of overarching political narratives for the way in which decision-makers engage with legal representatives, telling me that,

> [i]t is very adversarial. I try not to, because if you are contacting a caseworker, you might sometimes contact quite a decent person and I'll jump on that person, I want to talk to them in a most nice way and we can just work together, but it's really tricky when the overarching like narrative of politicians is that we are helping like human traffickers, or leeches taking loads of legal aid money and all these people are gaming the system. (Sophia, legal practitioner).

If the narratives deployed by politicians are, as suggested by Sophia, playing a role in generating hostilities which make this facilitating role more difficult then this is an issue which requires further redress. Indeed, as I have argued elsewhere, there are very real reasons to be concerned about the standard and quality of decision-making at first instance (Powell, 2023a). Evidence of the issues with first instance decision-making can be seen in the fact that 48 per cent of refused claims were overturned on appeal in 2024 (Refugee Council, 2024).

In the next chapter, I will be looking at the role which third sector organizations play within the UK asylum system. Through doing this, I will seek to understand in greater depth how sexually diverse people experience the asylum process as well as how that process comes together in the context of such limited capacity for the provision of legal advice.

5

The Role of the Third Sector

Given the significant cuts to the legal aid regime, particularly in the context of the Legal Aid Punishment and Sentencing of Offenders Act 2012, the government has appeared to, at times, view the input of the third sector as an adequate substitute for the provision of legal aid support for people navigating the UK asylum system (see Sommerlad and Sanderson, 2013). This, among other factors, was a strong theme which came through in my discussions with both legal practitioners and representatives of third sector organizations. Given the significance of the third sector in this area, it is therefore important to devote critical attention to the role played by third sector organizations, which this chapter does. In particular, I look at how third sector organizations support sexually diverse people navigating the asylum system and the particular role third sector organizations adopt within the operations of the asylum system. I also look at the role of third sector organizations in shaping the conceptual frameworks which we have outlined across the preceding four chapters.

In asylum claims by sexually diverse people, there has been a notable role played by a range of third sector organizations and support groups set up with specific focuses on sexual diversity (Pullen and Franklin, 2024). These organizations have taken on surprisingly large roles supporting those navigating the asylum system across a complex range of issues from advice around the process of making an asylum claim, the authorship of letters attesting to the sexual diversity of the claimants, and issues around housing, education and employment. Further, the role of these organizations has, in places, blurred with that of legal representatives, with organizations providing information sessions covering the asylum process and the kinds of evidence that claimants will need (Findlay et al, 2007; Mayblin and James, 2019). In the context of the limited availability of legal aid support, this is often the only guidance asylum claimants have access to prior to formally commencing their asylum claim.

Within the interviews, almost all participants drew out the role played by Rainbow Migration both in the sense of actively offering support to individual claimants and in advocating for sexually diverse people seeking asylum within the institutional confines of the system, such as making representations to the Home Office on forthcoming legislative enactments. But many also made reference to the increasing number of organizations operating within this area and the significant support that these organizations provide to people navigating the asylum system.

5.1 The unknown party: the role of the third sector

The work undertaken by third sector organizations is relatively unknown, despite the fact that they play a crucial role in supporting claimants and engagement with them is frequently viewed as a key indication of a valid claim. Indeed, scholarship has documented how this relationship to expected evidence often results in organizations fulfilling a filtering role, deciding which claimants to support and when, and in doing so often playing a key role in which claims are ultimately successful (McGuirk, 2018; Ferreira, 2022).

In this section, I will look to the narratives of third sector representatives to explore the activities provided by third sector organizations, with a particular view to considering how these link with the services provided by legal representatives and how this impacts the experiences of sexually diverse people seeking asylum as well as the implications it has for the functioning of the UK asylum system.

The role of charities and third sector organizations in supporting people navigating the UK asylum system was noted by a number of participants. Indeed, some participants felt that the expected role of third sector organizations in this area extended significantly beyond that which we would have seen in other areas. Amelia told me:

> This has become something of a slightly weird thing with asylum and immigration … in that legal advice in asylum and immigration has been sort of considered to be a problem that the third sector can solve, in a way that legal advice isn't in any other sector, with the possible exception of housing. (Amelia, legal practitioner)

This is an interesting point, particularly when it is looked at alongside the legal aid related issues already noted in the previous chapter. On this view, the reduction in the availability of legal aid advice is being covered by the third sector. Certainly, it is clear that the role of the third sector organizations with whom I spoke during this study seemed to be broad in scope and included providing information regarding the law. For example, Rainbow Migration – as a third sector organization – was often viewed as the first point of contact for asylum seekers as opposed to legal representatives. In this regard, Ava[1] told me that

> Rainbow Migration has lots of different, many different facets and one is their advisory to their clients, so they have their monthly meetings ... but it's definitely the first port of call for people to find out information and then they have the support groups. ... If they actually have like have a decent amount of involvement with an individual like when they're involved it just makes it so much easier to win a case. So sometimes it can just be a letter, so they will give a letter to the people they know well. (Ava, legal practitioner)

As well as noting the extensive range of roles which Rainbow Migration plays on this account, and the range of different groups it supports, it is also notable that Ava notes that having Rainbow Migration involved in a case makes it much easier to win. Rainbow Migration provides a diverse range of services, including legal referrals and advice, casework around housing, mental health referrals, emotional support, support groups, and campaigning and advocacy. However, it is notable that Ava drew specific reference to providing a letter and the influence that this can have on the outcome of a case. This again corresponds to the narratives of refugees in Chapter 3 and the expectations around evidence that legal representatives raised during Chapter 4. This also corresponds to my previous work, which argued that engagement with particular kinds of spaces is often central to the way that decision-makers conceptualize sexual diversity (Powell, 2024a; see also Akin, 2017).

Rainbow Migration are providing not just health and social related services, but also directly stepping in to the gaps in legal guidance which have been left by the poor coverage of legal aid provision. However, Rainbow Migration are predominantly based in London. Although, their functions around advice operate across the UK save for the support groups. The geographical spread of services, provided by organizations such as Rainbow Migration, has significant implications for people who are dispersed to more rural areas (Karban and Sirriyeh, 2015). Indeed, Ava went on to express precisely this concern, telling me:

> Yeah, it's totally London, well not totally, but almost London-centric unfortunately. But they have the ear of the Home Office, I don't

[1] It should be noted that Rainbow Migration was known to all participants due to its significance in supporting LGBTIQA+ people seeking asylum and the mention of the organization in the narrative of any particular participant does not indicate their having any personal association with it.

> know any other organization that has the ear of the Home Office like they do. The Home Office they do come to them and they ask their opinion and they give their opinion, and you know loudly and clearly. (Ava, legal practitioner)

As Ava points out, while it is more difficult for Rainbow Migration to offer support for those are accommodated outside of London, they do also operate other functions around advocacy and consultation, including guiding other LGBTIQA+ refugee and asylum support groups. In this sense, the organization plays an important organizing and coordination role. For example, Rainbow Migration has frequently issued reports outlining the issues that sexually diverse asylum seekers face.[2] Indeed, at the time I was undertaking the doctoral study on which Chapter 3 of this volume is based, these reports formed perhaps the most complete set of primary data regarding how the system was operating. While these reports have now seemingly become less regular – likely due to the extreme pressure that third sector organizations find themselves under – Rainbow Migration and other organizations continue to submit evidence to parliamentary committees, including those looking into matters relating to the 'New Plan for Immigration'.[3] As such, their role extends beyond the direct provision of support to individual people seeking asylum to also encompass acting as a conduit for representing the needs of sexually diverse people to government.

As well as adopting this important role in advocacy around the implications of pending changes and a broader analysis of how the asylum and immigration system is working, some participants also outlined how changes within the availability of legal aid had led to Rainbow Migration playing an increasing role in offering direct legal support. Indeed, the interviews revealed that in places far away from London other organizations were also increasingly fulfilling a similar role. For example, Muhammad said:

> We had asylum briefing meetings, we would really say to people, you are not necessarily going to get the time from a lawyer to devote to this. So, this is what a narrative is, this is what a statement is, you may not even be literate, but this is what a statement is, it's telling your

[2] The full range of publications which Rainbow Migration have released can be found online. See https://www.rainbowmigration.org.uk/publications/ (accessed 17 October 2024).

[3] UK Visas and Immigration, *New Plan for Immigration: Legal Migration and Border Control* (Home Office, July 2022), available at: https://www.gov.uk/government/publications/new-plan-for-immigration-legal-migration-and-border-control-strategy/new-plan-for-immigration-legal-migration-and-border-control-accessible (accessed 17 October 2024).

> story from being born to now, in detail, your story. (Muhammad, legal practitioner)

As Muhammad makes clear, the asylum briefings offered an opportunity hear guidance regarding how the asylum system operates. In the contemporary context, with such limited availability of legal aid, this is crucial as it gives people a foundation to understand the asylum system even if they are presently left waiting for representation (Mayblin and James, 2019).

However, many third sector organizations do not have in-house legal representatives and some delivering these sessions may not be qualified to give immigration advice. In this sense, while they can deliver general guidance on the operation of the system, they would not be able to give support to people seeking asylum regarding elements of their own claim.

Legal support

Indeed, for some participants, the increasing need to provide legal guidance was a source of difficulty as it was difficult to navigate the line between helping people to understand the system that they were trying to navigate and crossing the line into the provision of legal advice. For example, Blair told me:

> We try to be really careful, especially in this recent case, but it's interesting, I mean we had a conversation with 'Right to Remain', from their worker and she said more is going to come your way, so be prepared, because nobody else is going to do it. ... So we were saying well look let's go through the 'Right to Remain' toolkit, let's go through the Rainbow Migration pages on LGBT evidence, let's think about what you might want to say in a substantive interview. ... But you know we keep on saying, we're not lawyers. (Blair, third sector worker)

In the context of greater difficulty accessing legal aid, those working within the third sector are likely to come under increasing pressure from the people they support to give advice about how to navigate the asylum process. However, the provision of immigration advice without accreditation with Office of the Immigration Serices Comissioner (OISC) is unlawful. The definition of legal advice for the purposes of immigration is set out at Section 82 of the Immigration and Asylum Act 1999. Specifically, this defines immigration advice as advice which:

> (a) relates to a particular individual;
> (b) is given in connection with one or more relevant matters;

> (c) is given by a person who knows that he is giving it in relation to a particular individual and in connection with one or more relevant matters; and
> (d) is not given in connection with representing an individual before a court in criminal proceedings or matters ancillary to criminal proceedings.

As this definition sets out, the scope of what might be considered to be immigration advice is broad. At its most simple, offering support such as explaining what claiming asylum entails does not fit within the definition of immigration advice. So, activities such as those mentioned by Blair, looking at the Right to Remain toolkit or exploring the pages Rainbow Migration offer around evidence, is likely safe ground. However, if the person you are supporting asks questions regarding their own asylum claim then answering could go past the scope of what is permitted and constitute offering immigration advice.

On the whole, most third sector participants did seem to be aware of the boundaries. For example, Mia told me that 'I always say we do everything but the legal bit. So, I'm not trained as a solicitor or OISC trained. So, I can't give legal advice, it's illegal' (Mia, third sector worker). However, this is significant for two reasons. First, it is significant because it requires very careful attention to detail in regard to the distinction between the general and the specific. This is because commenting on the general asylum system is safe ground, whereas commenting on the specific situation of the person you are supporting could fall within the definition of immigration advice, and thus be unlawful. Indeed, the slipperiness of this distinction can be seen in the fact that Right to Remain (2024) have put together guidance for those working in asylum support on how they can stay on the right side of this distinction.

Second, these restrictions can easily lead to tensions with claimants and a perception that those working for organizations are not willing to support them. This, in turn, can further fuel the sense of isolation and hostility that those navigating the asylum system experience as well as undermining attempts to build trust and a sense of psychological safety (Burgess et al, 2021). In this way, the current pressures on the legal aid system can be seen to undermine the ability of third sector organizations to fully support people navigating the asylum system by putting them into difficult situations such as those where distinctions between legal advice and legal support are tested and they are forced to operate in a space of tight legal distinctions which may well be difficult to communicate and explain.

Indeed, this need to build trust was explicitly noted by some participants. For example, Ash told me:

> We have to build trust with people. People have to, we have to be explicitly open about the fact that this is a safe space for LGBT people,

> because even if there was a flag in the corner, sometimes … people will know that this means this is a safe space for people. (Ash, third sector worker)

Building trust and a sense of safety is fundamental to offering effective support, as Mulé has documented in the Canadian context (2022). However, the blurred boundaries within the role of third sector organizations, combined with the issues many claimants have accessing legal advice, create conditions where the generation of trust and psychological safety is compromised by limitations around what help can be given, even where no other help is available. This, in turn, can result in claimants having more difficulty in terms of being forthcoming with the organizations working to support them, or at least feeling uncomfortable being open. Given that these organizations are often also one of the main sources of welfare support, this is concerning and could undermine the ability of third sector organizations to give support.

It could be argued that this problem has been exacerbated by the way in which government has sought to operate. In particular, through the creation of a number of funding streams which immigration and asylum charities can access, while concomitantly keeping legal aid funding frozen,with the net effect that the expansion of the third sector into areas which are ever closer to legal advice is effectively a facet of government policy. This was a particular concern raised by Sophia, who told me:

> We [a legal aid provider] cannot get funding as a charity, and so I've certainly noticed that there is an expectation from charity organizations that we would have similar sort of resources as they do, but actually they're often in a better position with that and they can have funding, whereas we are completely reliant upon the legal aid structure. So, an asylum claim that could go on for years, I could get 400 and something pounds for the firm. (Sophia, legal practitioner)

It is notable that the differential basis on which resourcing takes place could here be seen to put a strain on the relationship between third sector organizations and legal representatives. The growing devolution of roles which may previously have been undertaken by lawyers to charities and third sector organizations in a sense legitimizes the status quo. Because when new needs arise charities are often able to step in and step up, this means that the crisis of legal aid is potentially less apparent than it would otherwise be. Indeed, Sophia's narrative further reflected on this in the sense that they expressed a fear that the growing nature of the third sector meant that the crisis of legal aid in this area was not attracting public attention.

Expanding sources of third sector support

During the study, I engaged with a range of other organizations who offered various non-legal support services to sexually diverse people navigating the asylum process. This included organizations across a diverse range of cities including some in London, the Midlands, the North of England and Northern Ireland. These organizations were all either specifically aimed at sexually diverse people or were generalist organizations which had begun offering LGBTIQA+ specific services, usually in response to increasing levels of need. Other groups set up to support sexually diverse people seeking asylum are also evidenced through active webpages. Highlighting some of the work that was taking place within the Midlands, Blair told me:

> So in terms of what we actually do, sorry, in terms of what we do, we have a WhatsApp group, so when we've, usually we try and meet, if somebody has been, either people refer themselves or are referred to us, or they're friends of friends already in the group. We try as far as we can to keep it within the West Midlands, but if people are dispersed outside the West Midlands, we will try and keep a bit of contact. (Blair, third sector worker)

When compared to the range of services offered by Rainbow Migration, it might be reflected that the support offered by the Midlands group appears significantly more limited, focusing only on the social and support elements and not engaging with issues relating to law and advocacy. However, it should be reflected that, in light of the forms of evidence that were highlighted within Chapters 3 and 4, this kind of opportunity for socializing can often be reflective of some of the most fundamental types of evidence that people seeking refugee status need to have access to in regard to demonstrating the kinds of community engagement which the Home Office expects to see (Powell, 2024a).

Blair also noted the role that they had played in the offering of letters in support. Specifically, they told me:

> My approach [to a letter of support] is, I start off by saying who I am and how long I've been working with the group, what my professional life is and my sexuality and then I … [focus] on the actual individual and so that, the obvious thing we could do is say well we keep records, this person has been a regular member of the group and we would probably say something like, you know, our observation is that he is, he or she is actively involved. … So we talk about factual stuff and our observations of that. Then I mean if they've talked to us a bit about their story … [we can say] over a long period of time, they have been consistent, they sound authentic. (Blair, third sector worker)

The notes Blair makes regarding how they structure support letters is particularly interesting as it shows how such letters can help to establish that the claimant is, for example, gay, by drawing out the ways in which they are engaging with the community (Murray, 2016). As this suggests, engagement with such organizations can offer a very significant forum within which asylum claimants can put together and support their asylum claims.

Indeed, it is also interesting to note that many of the themes which Blair identifies as important to structuring letters of support mirror the way in which credibility assessments are made when a decision-maker is determining whether or not the claimant's evidence is credible and can be accepted within the context of an asylum claim (McGuirk, 2018; Giametta, 2020; Giametta and Havkin, 2021). This suggests that some of elements of the credibility determination framework are also being adopted by support providers when seeking to provide evidence in support of a claim.

Several other participants also noted the provision of letters as a key way in which they support asylum claimants. For example, Avery told me: 'We do provide people with letters to say that they've attended our events. We take photographs at all of our events and say look we send these to you, and you can send them to your solicitor' (Avery, third sector worker). Similarly, Ethan also noted the importance of providing letters to support the engagement of their regular attendees. Specifically, they told me:

> I do … supporting letters for clients' asylum claims in support of their identity basically. So saying from my professional experience I've worked with them for this much time and seen them this many times in the group and I believe their claims that they are LGBT. Yeah, but I have to have quite strict rules about who I give letters to and who I don't, so usually I have to have known someone for six months and they've had to come to at least 50 per cent of the group meetings in that time. (Ethan, third sector worker)

The importance of being able to show evidence of engagement with LGBTIQA+ organizations is highlighted frequently within the literature (Ferreira, 2022; García Rodríguez, 2023). It was also a point which came up within the context of the refugee narratives explored in Chapter 3 and the practitioner narratives which we explored in Chapter 4. In that sense, organizations providing this kind of space for people navigating the asylum system to be able to engage with other sexually diverse people and have evidence of that engagement can be seen as a core element of enabling people seeking sanctuary to provide narratives and evidence which is consistent with the conceptualizations of sexual diversity which decision-makers deploy. Further, the provision of letters is generally regarded as being an extremely strong and useful piece of evidence to support the claimant needing to show that they are actually a sexually diverse person, with an identity that corresponds to the way in which sexual diversity is commonly understood within the UK.

It is notable that Ethan makes a direct note of needing to apply careful rules around who they provide letters to. Indeed, other participants also mentioned concerns that they would undermine their own credibility if they provided letters too willingly or easily. In this sense, third sector organizations are not only acting as providers of support, but also, given that engagement with them and the letters and other forms of evidence which they can assist in providing is so pivotal, acting as a filtering device in terms of which claims are or are not accepted or validated as legitimate or truthful. Similar findings have been made in the French context (Giametta, 2020). A significant part of the concern likely relates to the potential that being seen to support unsuccessful claims may undermine the ability of the organization to provide support to others by undermining their legitimacy. However, the engagement of third sector organizations in this kind of filtering operation is interesting insofar as it speaks to how the conceptual framing and techniques of power deployed by the Home Office become diffused among other institutions, affecting how they play their own part within the refugee status determination process.

Note should be taken of the emphasis that participants such as Blair and Ethan put on how they seek to establish their own credibility within the context of writing witness letters and how, through doing so, they seek to bolster the credibility of the people they are supporting. What is of particular interest here is how the engagement with an organization over an extended period can help to give validation to the claimant's narrative. Having that longer engagement with a given organization or individual can give space for the claimant to showcase a longer-term iteration of that same narrative which is likely to significantly strengthen the chances that their lived realities will ultimately be seen as credible and providing adequate evidence to show that they are, for example, a lesbian.

It is also notable that both participants raised concerns about the prospect of undermining their own credibility by providing letters to claimants who they did not have extensive engagements with or by whose claims they were not convinced. This speaks not only to the filtering role noted earlier but may also show how the idea that there is a great risk of false claims getting through the system has spread to those working within support organizations. As Raj has documented, the asylum system is a site of deep-seated anxiety regarding the possibility of false claims getting through the system (Raj, 2017).

Considering this, it should be noted that one of the key functions which third sector organizations are playing in the asylum process is as themselves offering a form of evidence for the engagement with the LGBTIQA+

community that decision-makers exepect see in an asylum claim made on the basis of sexual diversity. Of course, access to these kinds of support organizations again interacts with other policies such as the dispersal system and the use of large-scale accommodation facilities, both of which may mean that people seeking asylum are accommodated in locations which are geographically remote from third-sector support organizations.

However, the study also noted a growth in support groups across UK cities. For example, Ezra outlined the role of his third sector organization in a UK city outside of England. Telling me that, :

> Most of our efforts and resources are dedicated towards mental health and wellbeing, through counselling support, through mental health advocates, Listening Ear etc. … But at the same time we also have housing support, hate crime support and my role sort of comes in with supporting a lot of asylum cases. A lot of like, sort of being a link between my colleague who is responsible for the hate crime advocacy and housing. (Ezra, third sector worker)

The organization that Ezra was involved put a lot of focus on support and healthcare and had less capacity to directly provide legal support for issues in relation to the asylum claim itself. This, of course, may reflect the fact that, as we have previously addressed, Northern Ireland does not have the same issues regarding the accessibility of legal aid, though a number of complexities remain for sexually diverse people seeking asylum (see McCloskey, 2020).

In the Northern Ireland context, they also noted that – particularly due to the role which religious organizations play in the provision of services (see Snyder, 2011) – they felt that there was a particular need to ensure that specific support was provided for sexually diverse people seeking asylum, instead of relying on the broader range of third sector immigration and asylum organizations. As Coyle has argued, the withdrawal of state support from a range of different areas can be seen to have made society less accessible for many LGBTIQA+ people, as religious organizations with whom LGBTIQA+ people may feel uncomfortable engaging have come to play a central role in the provision of services (Coyle, 2021). Given the specific Northern Irish context, these issues could be argued to be even more profound (O'Leary, 2009; Duggan, 2012). As such, the provision of specific services can be seen as particularly important.

The issue or concern was that a good deal of support was driven by churches and other religious institutions and there was, therefore, a worry that this might mean that accessing the support is not comfortable. It is also notable that all three of the Northern Ireland participants emphasized the limited extent of contact that they had with organizations based in Britain and the particularities of the situation in Northern Ireland. We made reference to some of these specificities within Chapter 4 in regard to matters around legal aid.

It is perhaps also notable that Ezra makes specific reference to the links between sexual diversity asylum and the need to ensure that hate crime provision was linked into this. This perhaps speaks to how the Home Office's expectations for asylum seekers to perform a kind of conspicuous, cosmopolitan, LGBTIQA+ identity are not only misaligned with the lived experiences of sexually diverse people seeking asylum, and not considerate of the material conditions within which people live, but also do not account for the ongoing difficulties which sexually diverse people continue to face in the UK (Lovelock, 2018; Walker, 2023). People who have previously experienced trauma on the basis of their sexual diversity may be more cautious if they are aware that hate crime and discrimination continue to be issues in the UK. In this regard, the links into hate crime services aptly draw attention to the multi-faceted ways in which sexual diversirty is experienced.

Looking elsewhere in the UK, one common theme arising with the third sector staff and volunteers who I spoke with was a sense of the rapidly growing levels of need among sexually diverse asylum seekers and refugees. For example, Blair told me: 'Yeah, 2014 it was about 12, now it's, I mean on our WhatsApp group we've actually got I think it's 220 people' (Blair, third sector worker). In a ten-year period, that is a more than 2,000 per cent increase in the numbers of the people involved in the WhatsApp group of this organization. While it is noted that this is partly due to not removing people who have secured leave to remain and are not in need of further support, it also reflects how often groups aimed at sexually diverse asylum claimants, once they have been formed, end up connecting with significant levels of unmet need. As mentioned previously, this need is particularly acute in light of the dispersal policy which can often result in people being accommodated in unfamiliar areas alongside significant numbers of people who they do not know (Fletcher, 2024). Indeed, in several cities, new support groups were starting up at the time that this project was taking place. As this shows, a lot of the support in this area is still scaling up its operations and this is likely reflective of more people presenting as requiring support over a broader geographical area than would previously have required it.

A number of other groups also referenced significant and rapid growth in the number of people they were supporting. This is less reflective of growing headline numbers of people seeking protection in the UK and relates more to the growing numbers of people being dispersed or housed in hotel accommodation within areas which historically had reasonably low numbers of asylum seekers accommodated within them (Glorius et al, 2016). In particular, in Oxfordshire, Nottingham and Belfast, new groups aimed at supporting LGBTIQA+ asylum claimants were set up within the year during which the research underlying this volume was undertaken.

Indeed, this growth of new organizations and support frameworks was directly referenced by Ethan, who described how the support they are involved in providing had effectively bubbled up in an organic manner from their being a sexually diverse member of staff at a migrant support organization. Specifically, they told me that:

> I would just speak to a couple of clients over the phone, kind of signpost them to services in … sexuality services, hate crime, all of the LGBT asylum and refugee charities that provide support to them and just do that. But then in the last, really since October last year that's when we've been starting like the lion's share of the work has been since then. Most of the referrals we've got has been since then. So I've started taking referrals for basically any LGBT asylum seeker or refugee that needs some advice. (Ethan, third sector worker)

Drawing on Ethan's narrative, it is interesting to reflect on the ad hoc nature of referrals into the service they were providing and how these essentially built up via word of mouth. This speaks to the positionality of the third sector in this area, without an official role but also acting as a fundamental provider of support for people navigating the asylum system.

Often these organizations would seek to fill gaps within existing service provision. Existing provision may be, for example, premised on therapeutic counselling support, but may lack any specific experience or knowledge to enable them to support sexually diverse claimants. An example of this can be seen in the narrative of Jessie, who told me when asked what role non-governmental organizations play:

> So there's therapeutic counselling at … and … does sort of, yeah advice, your general advice, filling forms, access to work, access to college, education, lots of different services. I used to work there, I don't anymore, but yeah doing quite a lot of holistic, oh foodbanks, walk-in, a warm place to have a free cup of tea and socialize. (Jessie, legal practitioner)

In this quote, I have withheld the names of the organizations to protect the anonymity of the participant. However, they are describing the operation and interlinking of third sector asylum organizations within a major UK city. As this suggests, the city – across its third sector organizations – had an extensive range of support services. Offering support ranging from counselling and food provision to advice on how to fill out forms and engage with educational opportunities. However, it was not until far more recently that any sort of specific and focused provision for sexually diverse people was introduced into that ecosystem. It is, in this sense, interesting to reflect again on the complex needs that sexually diverse asylum seekers have, as they will require all of the support noted in this quote in the same way as anyone else navigating the asylum system but may also have specific needs which are directly related to their sexual diversity. For example, a sexually diverse person seeking asylum may fall under the adults at risk policy and therefore also be entitled to be allocated more specific accommodation than the no choice basis initially offers.[4] Securing recognition that a given person fits under the adults at risk policy may, in turn, require an understanding of how sexually diverse people may be more at risk within accommodation.

Indeed, some of the participants I spoke to raised this. For example, when asked about how they deal with people who approach them from outside of their areas of operation, Blair said:

> Yeah so I mean that is one of the kind of dilemmas really. I mean we really try and refer people to either a local refugee support, who hopefully would be very open to LGBT issues, or we go down the LGBT route and say is there a kind of social group, or, I mean it's not always easy, because the gay world is not always without racism. … So it's really just in terms of our capacity, it's not ideal, but it's just what we can do really. (Blair, third sector worker)

It is interesting to note that Blair expressed as much concern about the potential that LGBIQA+ organizations and groups may not be inclusive of migrants and asylum seekers as they did about the possibility that local refugee support organizations may not be the best placed to support LGBTIQA+ people. This kind of concern is particularly pronounced in the context of the broader meta-politics which, as discussed in Chapter 2, frames both sexually diverse people and migrant communities as an external threat to the constructed conceptualization of 'the people'.

Putting aside concerns regarding hostility, the larger issue is likely to be a question over whether or not such organizations are well situated to be aware of the particular needs which a given group of refugees or asylum seekers has. For example, an organization which works on refugee housing may not be aware of issues sexually diverse people may face if housed with people from their country of nationality. This could lead to inappropriate forms of support being given. These issues are not unique to sexually

---

4 Written evidence submitted by Dr Alex Powell (Oxford Brookes University) and Dr Raawiyah Rifath (University of Exeter) (AAC0112).

diverse people, but sexual diversity may mean that these broader issues are experienced differently and require different forms of support.

Indeed, for the LGBTIQA+ specific organizations, one of the key roles was around signposting to other sources of support and supporting their service users with accessing that support. For example, Ezra told me that their role was often

> [j]ust like being there as you know a support person. Signposting, would be a big one, signposting them to organizations like, so having this initial like meeting with them, just understanding where they are at, and if it's someone who hasn't made a claim yet, making sure they're you know, they do it in the safest and best way possible and that would be because we don't have dedicated lawyers, or legal training as such, we'd be signposting them ... we would accompany them to like the Home Office, like making sure they are at the right place. (Ezra, third sector worker)

This role perhaps speaks the most clearly to the importance of specific provision for sexually diverse people, because this kind of support can help people to feel comfortable in engaging with broader elements of the support which is available, as well as ensuring that there is a point of contact for difficulties experienced within the asylum system. For example, if there is an organization which exists specifically to support sexually diverse people and they make a referral to housing support, then that same organization would be much better placed to pick up on any issues that the service user has when working with the housing provider. In this sense, specialist organizations may benefit people seeking asylum not just in regard to directly providing services, but also in terms of accessing other services.

5.2 Pulling in the same direction (claimants, practitioners and the third sector)

As the previous section has shown, third sector organizations play an increasing but often unrecognized role within the context of the UK asylum system (see Terry, 2017). This role has grown due to the changes to the UK's legal aid system with third sector organizations coming into contact with claimants, legal practitioners and the Home Office, and consequently having active engagements with all parts of the UK asylum system.

This raises questions over whether the component parts of the system are operating well together. Across the interviews with staff and volunteers working in third sector organizations, a number of reflections regarding engagements with other organizations and how these fit within the system more broadly were offered.

Some participants, such as Isabella, who had left the third sector after feeling that they were not able to offer the kind of support they wanted to within that setting, told me:

> All the root causes of a lot of mental health, homelessness, destitution lie in not having your papers. So I found myself in the charity sector putting a plaster on that and that wasn't enough, the root cause was representation, you know getting good legal representation and getting their papers. (Isabella, legal practitioner)

This reflection is interesting in the sense that it speaks to the one thing that most third sector organizations cannot do, provide legal representation. Although, note should be taken that other studies have suggested that housing is the pre-eminent issue facing people seeking asylum (Danisi et al, 2021). Nonetheless, Isabella's experiences in the third sector, and subsequent move into legal practice, perhaps speaks to the difficult positionality of third sector organizations. It is particularly notable that they describe their time working within the third sector as putting a plaster on the issues. Fundamentally, most of the issues facing asylum seekers do stem from legal restrictions placed upon them. For example, it is much more difficult to access safe and secure housing when you are offered a place to live on a 'no choice basis'[5] and prevented from undertaking employment.[6] Similarly, people who are given no means of earning their own income are significantly more likely to be reliant on diaspora or religious communities in ways which may undermine their ability to be open regarding non-normativities such as sexual diversity.

However, in the absence of securing leave to remain, these are conditions which will, generally speaking, continue to apply to people seeking asylum. In this sense, the law currently places a limit on the scope of the support which third sector organizations can provide. This speaks to some of the concerns expressed by Sophia that the third sector might be, in some ways, covering for the consequences of limited access to legal aid in a way which obscures the scale of the issues facing the sector.

---

[5] See UK Visas and Immigration, *Allocation of Asylum Accommodation Policy* (Home Office, 3 May 2024), available at: https://www.gov.uk/government/publications/asylum-accommodation-requests-policy/allocation-of-asylum-accommodation-policy-accessible (accessed 17 October 2024).

[6] See UK Visas and Immigration, *Permission to Work and Volunteering for Asylum Seekers* (Home Office, 9 October 2024), available at: https://www.gov.uk/government/publications/handling-applications-for-permission-to-take-employment-instruction/permission-to-work-and-volunteering-for-asylum-seekers-accessible (accessed 17 October 2024).

Referral and filtering

Many of the third sector organizations were aware of their own limitations in regard to providing legal support. For example, Jessie outlined a mutual referral system which they had with the one legal aid immigration and asylum law firm in their city. Specifically, they told me that

> [Name of firm], we have a referral system with them, so if someone finds them before they find us, [name of firm] will say no, in order to, well actually they're not taking any referrals at the moment, because they are so snowed under, but they will say if you want to come to us, you need to go through [name of third sector organization], because we help them with the registration process. (Jessie, third sector worker)

While this referral system exists it is notable here that the law firm currently did not have the capacity to take on further referrals and that, indeed, the third sector organization was acting more like a filter or triage centre than a referral mechanism, with the law firm asking claimants to work through them in terms of the registration process. This speaks both to how the third sector has become an integral part of the legal aid asylum system, but also to how the pressures on legal aid have created forms of filtering and triage that posit the third sector as a kind of stop-gap care while a claimant is awaiting legal support (Zetter et al, 2005; Mayblin and James, 2019). In this sense, the third sector can be seen as a kind of sticking plaster, exactly in the terms that Isabella articulated.

A similar concern was expressed by Blair who outlined how they were finding it increasingly difficult to pair the people who they support with solicitors and felt that they may have to start seeking legal support from other parts of the UK, such as from legal representatives in London. Specifically, they told me:

> There's a huge issue about lack of legal aid, so that means the number of solicitors offering immigration with legal aid is going down, so the list is getting smaller and smaller, month by month. So you have to work incredibly hard to get through to a solicitor. … I think we're going to have to contact people in London, there just isn't anybody around here. (Blair, third sector worker)

As we explored in Chapter 4, the difficulties with accessing legal aid representation are one of the most pressing issues facing people seeking asylum. In this regard it is also notable that helping people seeking asylum to find legal representatives seems to generate significant workload for third sector organizations. On one level, this shows the cohesiveness of the work between legal representatives and the third sector. However, it is also notable that the time spent trying to make contact with legal representatives is time that cannot be used to engage in other support activities. In this sense, and much as Isabella indicated, it seems that third sector organizations are providing a sticking plaster or stop-gap to cover the dysfunctionality of both legal representation and decision-making processes.

As this suggests, there are potential frustrations and stressors across the map of provision for asylum claimants. In this context, a further issue arises with regard to helping people seeking asylum to understand the different roles that the organizations who they are engaging with play within the system. This is important because not understanding which organization or person is responsible for what element of the asylum process could lead to frustration, disillusionment and a lack of trust in those seeking to offer support. For example, Ethan said:

> I think often when clients are going through a really difficult time, that's when those boundaries can get a bit blurred and they can just get frustrated really at any service. I mean there are parallels between a refugee charity and the Home Office and a solicitor, they are all organizations that are going to be somewhat bureaucratic, or you know that, they all kind of represent this kind of British culture, which can be frustrating to work with, I guess, if you're just being told no, all the time. If we're saying no to people, it's not because we want to, it's because we don't have any control in it usually, but hearing that from any organization is difficult. (Ethan, third sector worker)

As Ethan makes clear, their sense was that most claimants did understand the limitations within which they were operating. However, there were moments when things can get blurred. In this regard, it is notable that the UK operates what is now known as the 'Compliant Environment'.[7] This being the new name for the 'Hostile Environment' following on from the Windrush scandal (Goodfellow, 2019). As a result of this, those who are still in the asylum system or otherwise yet to regularize their status are met with a huge number of administrative barriers in day-to-day life. It is, therefore, unsurprising that it can become difficult to distinguish between which organizations are the ones putting up the barriers, and which are the ones advising you both of what those barriers are and the implications that they have, as well as attempting

[7] UK Visas and Immigration, *Impact Assessment: Compliant Environment: Overarching Equality Impact Assessment* (Home Office, 9 February 2023), available at: https://www.gov.uk/government/publications/compliant-environment-overarching-equality-impact-assessment/compliant-environment-overarching-equality-impact-assessment-accessible#:~:text=What%20is%20the%20aim%20of,from%20the%20risk%20of%20exploitation (accessed 17 October 2024).

to enable you to exist day-to-day within the context of those barriers. Indeed, as Ethan directly notes, the operation of third sector organizations and law firms is not wholly divorced from the Home Office as all of these organizations operate under regulatory frameworks which require significant amounts of bureaucracy (Borelli et al, 2023).

Delays, distress and role blurring

Other participants also noted this potential for the roles of different bodies to become blurred within the asylum process. For example, Blair told me:

> Yeah. I mean sometimes we have to explain that we're not employed by the Home Office. I was at a meeting with somebody and she said oh when I met you, a) I thought you were straight, and b) I thought you were employed by the Home Office. I thought God, how did we give that impression, so you know. So, there's all this thing about officialdom, or even volunteers, how they are perceived. (Blair, third sector worker)

This presents an interesting point as it shows the role of assumptions in structuring interactions. It is not only the assumption of the claimant that the third sector organization is affiliated to the Home Office, but also the assumption that the volunteer in question is heterosexual that may govern the comfort of the person seeking asylum in terms of engaging with the services (Powell, 2023b).

Of particular note here is the participant's reference to officialdom. Given that people seeking asylum are placed into a deeply bureaucratic setting, often being required to regularly report to Home Office staff and engage with lawyers and other legal processes, it is perhaps unsurprising that any meeting they are called into might carry an air of being official and professional. This, in turn, may have implications for the way in which people seeking asylum experience third sector organizations and whether they feel that they can be open and honest regarding both their sexual diversity and their needs (Held, 2023). In this context, it is likely to be difficult to generate the kind of trust that we discussed in the previous chapter as a result of the way that the 'official' nature of the relationships structures engagement.

The difficulty in regard to distinguishing between the different services and sources of support that an asylum claimant engages with can create problems around the building of relationships. This, in turn, speaks to the difficulties that arise for third sector organizations as they take on a larger role within the asylum process, as, in effect, they come to be seen as themselves a part of the process, which may limit their ability to create safe and trusted environments. Indeed, this issue is well documented within existing literature on legal consciousness within welfare systems and charities (Sarat, 2006; Headworth, 2020). As in that context, the way that organizations are made sense of within the broader context may interact with the ability of people within the system to feel that they can trust them as sources of support.

Detention support

One particular area of support where third sector organization are often the leading or only providers is in regard to support for those placed into administrative detention. The UK is notable for being one of a limited number of countries where there are no firm time limits on the use of administrative detention. Indeed, some people have been held for numerous years without ever being accused of any crime – other than migrating in and of itself – or facing any reasonable prospect of removal from the UK (Blanchard, 2018). Note should be taken that technically people should only be held in detention when there is a reasonable prospect of their removal.[8] However, given the issues which we have already noted with regard to legal aid, finding a legal representative to show that someone should not continue to be held in administrative detention can be extremely difficult. This means that significant numbers of people are at risk of harms arising from immigration detention (Turnbull, 2016).

As a result of this, one of the core activities that third sector organizations lead on is providing detention support. For example, Blair told me:

> The detention centre, if somebody had been for some reason put in detention we try and keep in contact with them and we had somebody who was being threatened deportation, we were able to sort of put the brakes on that, you know calling MPs and the great and the good, including the airline. (Blair, third sector worker)

As Blair articulates, keeping in contact with people who have been placed in detention is a particularly important role. Often people placed into detention may not yet have had a chance to make contact with a legal representative. As such, this is an important point where third sector organizations can do the linking work referenced earlier around seeking out legal representatives. This again speaks to third sector organizations playing a crucial and well integrated role within the asylum system.

As with large-scale accommodation or housing with other people from the person seeking asylum's county of nationality, detention facilities can

[8] See UK Visas and Immigration, *Detention: General Instructions* (Home Office, 28 September 2023), available at: https://assets.publishing.service.gov.uk/media/6509c3af22a783000d43e8cf/Detention+General+instructions.pdf (accessed 17 October 2024), p 9.

be difficult spaces for sexually diverse people. Within these spaces people may feel unable to publicly raise their reasons for claiming asylum (Fletcher, 2024). There are also numerous reports of homophobic incidents, including from those guarding the facility (see Wimark, 2021). This means that it is particularly important that people who are detained are in contact with supportive people and organizations. This is a role which third sector organizations are well placed to fulfil. This is important because, as mentioned previously, detention is technically intended as a precursor to imminent removal from the UK. For example, someone whose asylum claim has been determined to be inadmissible may find themselves placed into administrative detention pending their removal from the UK. Given this, fast action to contact legal representatives and lobby more broadly, such as by contacting MPs or other public figures, can be vital work. Particularly if it is taking place in the period before legal support has been identified and put in place.

Given that many people may not feel comfortable disclosing that they are sexually diverse, a part of the work here can also relate to identifying those who may need support as they may not have spoken publicly regarding their reason for seeking protection. People placed into detention can be seen as particularly vulnerable as they are held in large-scale facilities and will not have access to many of the sources of support that are accessible to people outside of detention facilities. In this sense, without people visiting detention facilities, there would be an increased risk that reasons for offering protection, or even just reasons to avoid removal, might be missed.

Concerns around the quality of legal representation

Alongside these occasions where the third sector works in tandem with other support facilities such as legal representatives, participants' narratives also drew attention to some moments where there were clashes. For example, Aisha referred to examples of occasions where they had concerns regarding the quality of the legal representation that people who they were supporting were receiving. Specifically, they said, '[t]he lawyers, this is a difficult one. Because very often by the time the women come to us they have already got a solicitor and often they are paying through the nose, borrowing, you know. I know solicitors are not necessarily very good' (Aisha, third sector worker). The reference to paying through the nose in this example makes it clear that they are referring to service users who are paying for private representation rather than those who are being represented by legal aid representatives. However, the concerns that they are drawing attention to are those that several people seeking asylum were detailed to have raised with third sector workers and volunteers. One particular theme among participants in this regard was a general sense that, partly due to the delays within the system, people seeking asylum were often keen to work with legal representatives promising fast turnaround times. This, in turn, often meant that those with individual means could be charged high prices for representatives who were not necessarily experts in the particular type of claim they were trying to make.

In a similar register, Avery told me about how some of the initial decisions which they had seen suggested to them that the people they were working with had received poor quality legal advice. Specifically, they told me:

> One of our group members showed me his refusal letter from the Home Office and he's bisexual, but there were times, he's from Ethiopia right, so there were times he'd use gay and bisexual interchangeably, because, we know that these are western labels. … We have Home Office staff who are making decisions, who are like this is L, this is G, this is B, you know and they kind of, they know what those particular boxes are and when they try to fit people into these boxes. … So it's really, really easy for people to trip up according to the Home Office rules and according to what we see as LGBT … when I read this guy's refusal letter, because I thought your solicitor hasn't prepared you, because it was full of credibility. I thought your solicitor hasn't prepared this with you at all. (Avery, third sector worker)

As noted in Chapter 4, there are some specifics to asylum claims by sexually diverse people – such as being able to help a claimant to articulate a developed conceptualization of their own sexuality – which require both experience on behalf of the legal representative and time and trust to help the claimant to build a narrative which will meet with the expectations of the Home Office. As such, it could be that the issues which Avery is picking up on here are caused by the constraints and workloads of the legal aid system rather than any individual failure or lack of care on the part of the legal representative. However, as with Aisha it is interesting to note Avery's sense that the quality of legal representation was problematic and that legal representatives – or at least a subset thereof – did not understand how to support sexually diverse claimants, nor how Home Office decision-making operates in this area.

In this sense, there was, for some participants, a somewhat difficult relationship between parts of the third sector and legal representatives. However, it could be said in this context that the third sector is offering a useful corrective in areas where legal practice is falling short. Such as by having more specific expertise around sexual diversity claims borne of the engagement with such a large number of people who are claiming asylum on this basis, which is a form of experience that few legal practitioners will easily have access to. So, this could also be viewed as an example of the sector working effectively together.

In regard to the differing roles of the players in the asylum system it is also interesting to note Avery's reflections on whether the third sector needed to be doing more to ensure that legal representatives were/are more fully aware of the particular issues within sexual diversity asylum claims. As this suggests, the relationship between legal representatives and the third sector is more multivariate and reciprocal than it might first seem. Rather than the third sector simply supporting claimants awaiting legal representation and helping with the matters that flow from either their reason for seeking sanctuary or the legal situations into which the UK places those who are seeking sanctuary, this example also shows how the third sector has played an active role in trying to shift how legal representatives engage with their profession and to raise awareness of the particularities of claims by sexually diverse people. This is important because, save for legal representatives who specialize in asylum claims made on the basis of sexual diversity, it is likely that third sector organizations set up to support LGBTIQA+ asylum claimants and refugees actually see far more of these claims than legal representatives and may therefore be better placed to provide advice and guidance. This is particularly likely to be the case for national level organizations such as Rainbow Migration who, as we will explore in what follows, play a significant role not just in engagement with the Home Office, but also in terms of supporting other third sector organizations.

Aisha went on to identify their concerns regarding quality very much do not apply to all legal representatives. Specifically, they went on to say:

> But on the other end of the spectrum, there's … [some] … who are absolutely brilliant. I mean a lot of solicitors won't talk to you, because they are going to charge you every time they do, so I might send a letter off to somebody's solicitor and never hear even if it got there. But … at least two of them know me personally and they might say to me, oh look, we've got this person come, who says she knows you, do you feel you could write a letter of support, because they know that that's helpful. So, I work quite closely with some of them. (Aisha, third sector worker)

Clearly, a part of the metric with reference to which Aisha was assessing whether or not the legal representation was effective was with reference to their willingness to discuss elements of the case with them. This draws direct attention to the role of the third sector as itself an active player within the UK asylum system, in the sense that rather than just offering complementary support they are acting as an active participant within a claimant's journey through the UK asylum system. It also shows how people seeking asylum may draw on the third sector as a means of support or intermediary guidance in their dealing with legal representatives or practitioners.

In this sense, the participants' narratives here show how the third sector has become a crucial player in the system, which, as Sophia had expressed, is now playing a significant role within the asylum system both in terms of the direct forms of support it is providing and in terms of mediating some of the engagements between asylum claimants and legal representatives.

5.3 Changing the narrative: re-conceptualizing the role of the third sector

As the previous section has outlined, the third sector is often covering over the gaps which result from the lack of state support and provision for those seeking sanctuary in the UK. In this section, I reflect on what the third sector could or, more aptly, should be doing (were proper state support to be implemented). Otherwise put, I look to what the role of the third sector would be if proper legal aid funding were restored, and decisions began being made in a timely manner.

Under the current UK legal framework, most asylum seekers are denied the right to work. Indeed, it is only under very tightly constrained circumstances that asylum seekers are permitted to access employment.[9] Many third sector organizations have run long-standing campaigns regarding the importance of being able to access paid employment.[10] This role around campaigning is generally common to many areas of third sector work across the UK (Royston, 2010; Duong, 2017). So, one area where we would likely see a role for the third sector, even in the context of proper state funding of legal representation, is within campaigning activities. This might be around examples such as the previously mentioned right to work. But it could also be in terms of things such as responding to consultations around proposed legal changes, as explored earlier.

Indeed, it is notable that a number of participants made reference to their organizations making submissions to parliamentary committees when the Nationality and Borders Act and Illegal Migration Act were passing through parliament.[11] Often, these organizations were the key players in outlining how the people who they support would be impacted by the

9 UK Visas and Immigration, *Permission to Work and Volunteering for Asylum Seekers* (Home Office, 9 October 2024), available at: https://www.gov.uk/government/publications/handling-applications-for-permission-to-take-employment-instruction/permission-to-work-and-volunteering-for-asylum-seekers-accessible (accessed 17 October 2024).

10 See, for example, Refugee Action, 'Lift the ban: Why giving people seeking asylum the right to work is common sense' (2020), available at: https://www.refugee-action.org.uk/wp-content/uploads/2020/07/Lift-The-Ban-Common-Sense.pdf (accessed 17 October 2024).

11 See Legislative Scrutiny: Nationality and Borders Bill, available at: https://committees.parliament.uk/work/1415/legislative-scrutiny-nationality-and-borders-bill/publications/ (accessed 18 May 2025).

proposed changes. In this sense, the campaigning role sits independently from support work. This also includes broader production of reports and studies into how the system is operating. Such reports, from organizations such as Rainbow Migration, were reasonably common until the mid-2010s. But their frequency has dropped off as the support needs of people seeking asylum have grown, alongside increasingly stringent demands on budgets and lesser levels of available state grants. As such, a properly funded system may actually allow organizations more capacity to focus in on broader systemically focused elements such as campaigning and research.

Alongside this consultative and campaigning role, the role third sector organizations have grown to play around creating support groups and offering forms of therapeutic and social support would likely also be maintained. It should be noted here that there would ideally be greater provision of state-funded/provided mental health case alongside these services (Egdell and Dutton, 2017). But, nonetheless, the importance of having provision which has experience around the specific needs of people seeking asylum means that there would likely be a need for support groups and other forms of counselling even if greater levels of state support were in place. Indeed, it is noted that a number of the organizations were offering tailored mental health support and counselling aimed specifically at people with lived experiences of forced displacement (see Morina et al, 2018; Puddifoot and Sandelind, 2024). This is, obviously, not something which the state could easily replicate and is therefore another core role that the third sector would likely continue to need to be involved in even if there were to be a profound change in the funding landscape.

The roles that would most likely change are those around the provision of legal guidance. In particular, it is argued that in the context of properly funded legal aid there would be less of a focus on the third sector providing briefing sessions for people seeking asylum as people seeking asylum would have access to a legal aid lawyer with relevant expertise. Although, there is a need for caution and nuance here, as some of the particularities of how asylum claims are made on the basis of sexual diversity mean that there would still likely be a role for third sector organizations in terms of joining people seeking asylum with relevant expert legal practitioners.

However, some of the issues we mentioned in section 5.1 of this chapter around how people working in the third sector are having to navigate a complex balance between providing people seeking asylum with information on the asylum processes while avoiding giving individual guidance, which could be interpreted as constituting legal advice, would be more easily avoided as there would be legal representatives on hand to direct asylum claimants to if they have questions relating to their specific situation. Of course, it is recognized that some third sector organizations have in-house legal representatives, but nonetheless this element of activity by third sector organizations adds complexity and the potential for misunderstanding to the system. As noted, this would also be useful in terms of avoiding issues such as undermining asylum seekers' trust by giving them the sense that third sector organizations are not helping.

The legal support role played by sexual diversity focused third sector organizations is likely to be a feature which separates sexual diversity asylum claims from other asylum claims, as the expertise of third sector organizations around this specific reason for claim is likely to be something which, due to its more specialized nature, would be more difficult to provide under the legal aid system for the number of claimants even if it were to be properly funded. In this sense, there may be a distinction between the sexual diversity asylum focused third sector here and the third sector in regard to asylum more broadly. Specifically, the particular expertise that arises in the context of asylum claims by sexually diverse people may be something which the third sector is better placed to provide than legal practitioners themselves, at least insofar as even a properly funded legal aid sector is unlikely to permit significant specialization towards asylum claims by sexually diverse people. This, of course, may well still come in a different form. For example, in a better funding scenario it may be that it would be more effective for briefing sessions around sexual diversity asylum claims to be provided for legal representatives rather than directly to people seeking asylum. This would give space for legal representatives to benefit from the significant expertise which third sector organizations have built in terms of understanding the operation of refugee status determination within claims made on the basis of sexual diversity.

In this register, while it could be seen as undesirable that the third sector has come to be required to play such a large role in the UK asylum system by necessity, they have also stepped into it in a manner which speaks to significant expertise which could not simply be replicated by means of increased legal aid funding. In this sense, it could be said that the third sector would continue to have an important role to play – particularly in regard to providing specialist support directed towards sexually diverse people seeking asylum – even if there is an increase in legal aid funding and that, far from being a sticking plaster as some participants suggested, it could be argued that the third sector has (whether by design or not) become a fundamental element of the broader UK asylum system, which, even in the context of faster and fairer decision-making and properly funded legal aid, would retain a highly important role to play both in terms of advocacy and in terms of offering support to people seeking asylum, but particularly to sexually diverse people whose claims contain specific complexities which are not always shared by other people seeking asylum.

6

The State of Play

During the period covered in this book, there has been a major shift in the state of play for asylum seekers arriving in the UK in search of refuge. The individualist system of refugee status determination that existed until 2022 has, taking account of the combined effects of the Nationality and Borders Act 2022 and the possible effects of the Illegal Migration Act 2023, been largely abolished (Powell, 2024b). Although this has subsequently been partially rowed back by the Labour government returned in July 2024, significant barriers to sanctuary have been retained. In the place of the individualist system imagined under the Refugee Convention, we are faced with a number of ad hoc visa frameworks that may permit those fleeing events which receive general recognition as a state of crisis to seek protection.

However, for those whose persecution is due to forms of non-normativity – the suppression of which is not generally regarded as in and of itself a form of crisis – these changes represent a significant risk of leaving no effective protection. Indeed, with some notable exceptions such as Afghanistan, the UK continues to enjoy very strong international relations with several states where sexually diverse people are subjected to treatment which can be argued to reach the threshold of persecution. Indeed, in the context of Donald Trump's second term and the sweeping curtailment of the rights of transgender people, it is also arguable that states such as the United States may fall into this category. There is a risk, therefore, that the changes brought about across the period of 2022–2024 may represent a significant curtailment of protection, with particularly pernicious implications for certain categories of sanctuary seeker, including women and sexually diverse people.

Even for those who are still able to claim, as the preceding chapters have noted, there exists a panoply of difficulties which must be circumnavigated before recognition as a refugee can be secured. Given this, this chapter explores the implications of contemporary politics and legal change both for those who are themselves navigating the asylum process and for those working to support them. These explorations cover not just concrete changes to the law, but also the impact of contemporary politics to understand how claimants have been impacted by the rhetoric engendered by politicians and the media. We then go on to explore how these intersections may further undermine the resilience of sexually diverse people navigating the UK asylum system before, finally, considering how we might challenge these difficulties within the framework of queer counter-normativity outlined earlier in this book.

6.1 Impact of contemporary politics and the new plan for immigration

During the period 2022–2024, issues relating to immigration and asylum formed a central focus of government activity. Not only were three pieces of legislation targeted at dealing with 'illegal' migration passed – the Nationality and Borders Act 2022, the Illegal Migration Act 2023 and the Safety of Rwanda (Asylum and Immigration) Act 2024 – but also issues relating to asylum formed a central focus of government campaigning. For sexually diverse people, this period was further complicated as politicians and public figures sparked controversies around gender identity, with a number of campaigns which focused on the perceived or constructed incompatibilities between the rights of trans people and women gaining prominence (Gupta and Pearce, 2024). This, in turn, led to some figures returning to discourses seen across the 1980s, with queer people being presented as a potential threat to children, young people and women (Davis and Kettrey, 2022; Lamble, 2023) within the context of a broader moral panic emerging out of the genus of the far-right anti-gender movement (Kovats, 2017; Lamble, 2024). In regard to both migration and issues around trans rights, the panics stoked by politicians, public figures and the media have often suffused with online movements promoting conspiracy theories (Sapountzis et al, 2023). This suffusion has intertwined with the broader meta-politics outlined in Chapter 2 to create a context where both migrants and people falling within non-normative categories, such as sexually diverse people, are presented as if they were an external threat to 'the people'.

At times, the focus of anti-migrant politics also strayed directly to the rights of sexually diverse people. For example, giving a speech in Washington, DC, Suella Braverman outlined her view that women and LGBTIQA+ people claiming asylum were conflating discrimination and persecution.[1] In this

[1] Suella Braverman, Keynote Address by UK Home Secretary Suella Braverman, 'UK-US security priorities for the 21st century' (American Enterprise Institute, 26 September 2023), transcript available at: https://www.aei.org/wp-content/uploads/2023/09/230926-Keynote-Address-by-UK-Home-Secretary-Suella-Braverman-Transcript.pdf?x91208 (accessed 9 February 2024).

context, participants outlined how a mixture of legal changes and political changes have had a deleterious effect on the UK's asylum system with some suggesting that this has, in effect, brought the system to the brink of collapse and others indicating a strong view that the words of political and media figures are being directly reflected within the practices of decision-makers. A suggestion which raises serious concerns in regard to the rule of law and the probity of decision-making.

Inadmissibility

One of the issues which caused the most concern to practitioners was the expansion of inadmissibility within the asylum system. Under Section 16 of the Nationality and Borders Act, Part 4A of the Nationality, Immigration and Asylum Act 2002 was amended to provide the Secretary of State for the Home Department with the power to declare the asylum claims of anyone who has a 'connection' to any third safe state inadmissible. The section also makes clear that a declaration of inadmissibility is not a refusal, and so does not attract a right of appeal. One of the main concerns around this has simply been that this has exacerbated anxieties and confusion within the system. For example, Elijah told me:

> For those who claim asylum after 28th June 2022, we are seeing very fast inadmissibility, so you could have claimed in a safe third country, why did you not, we're not even, we're just putting your claim on ice, we are not even processing it, until we decide whether we're going to grant it admissible, as well as notice of intents, to remove to Rwanda and these adults will not have had access to legal representatives. They will be getting these really frightening letters. (Elijah, legal practitioner)

We already discussed the issues with access to legal aid in Chapter 4 as well as how some other elements of current policy would exacerbate them. However, the point here is that in an effort to appear tough in order to 'deter' people from coming to the UK, a new barrier to even beginning the process of making an asylum claim has been created (Walsh and Sumption, 2024). As the UK does not currently have any workable return or transfer agreements in place, the reality of this is that claims are simply held in stasis, pending their being admitted into the refugee status determination system. Indeed, most of the claims initially declared inadmissible following the expansion of this policy were later admitted into the asylum system (Taylor, 2024). Despite this, the expansion of inadmissibility and the way in which it has been framed not only causes greater anxiety for people navigating the asylum system, but also further compromises the capacity of legal representatives and the third sector to provide support as they are now having to advise people about inadmissibility declarations in addition to the extensive range of other activities which they were already undertaking.

Concerns about the way in which inadmissibility operates, and the impact this would have on the asylum system more broadly, were noted by a number of participants. For example, Sophia told me:

> Obviously the inadmissibility is a huge issue and is, I think the LGBTQ population is going to be one that's particularly vulnerable of the various particularly vulnerable groups. … I think some of the most concern is, it is about, because those are the ones that might not, that have these, have sort of refusal rates are not well understood and at the other end may really, really find their position is very difficult and dangerous indeed. (Sophia, legal practitioner)

As this suggests, some participants felt that as well as the broad issues posed by inadmissibility, there were specific difficulties for particular kinds of claimant due to the broader ways in which society imposes vulnerability upon these groups. In particular, Sophia stressed that the effect of inadmissibility was to push key elements of the asylum claim to an earlier stage in the process. For example, if an asylum claimant wished to dispute the fact that their claim was inadmissible under the process set up under the Nationality and Borders Act then one way to do this would be to show that they had not passed through a third safe country. One modality in which this could be done would be to show both that the country which they passed through was not safe for sexually diverse people and that they themselves were a sexually diverse person. Otherwise put, the fundamental elements of a successful asylum claim on the basis of sexual diversity would now need to be proven at a far earlier stage, likely with less access to legal advice and less time to compile the evidence needed to support their claim to be sexually diverse, noting all of the issues which we have already identified in regard to this.

In terms of the implications of inadmissibility, Mia raised a concern that even temporary periods of inadmissibility at the outset of a claim were having significant welfare implications. Specifically, they said: 'This is, excuse my French, a fucking disaster waiting to happen. If you're going to make so many people inadmissible and no recourse to public funds, I can't find anywhere for people to go now. I've got several people on the streets currently, sleeping on buses' (Mia, third sector worker). As this suggests, the effects of inadmissibility are broad and go beyond just the question of refugee status, also posing urgent risks around access to support and accommodation. Indeed, as well as implications for individuals, situations such as these may also have an impact on third sector organizations in terms of taking up capacity and for a diverse range of services which need to provide the means for the person who has been declared inadmissible to subsist in a context where there has been a withdrawal of state support (see Saenz Perez, 2023).

Further, Riley identified that, for this reason, there were real risks that inadmissibility could lead to people being removed to unsafe countries. Specifically, they said:

> Let's say a person wants to make a claim on the basis of their sexual orientation and being returned to Afghanistan, arrived on a small boat. They don't know how the Illegal Migration Bill impacts them. … They're just put in a hotel, they have no access to legal advice there. … They probably don't know that if they arrived on, or after 7th March, it would be under the new Bill … which is … retrospective. They certainly I think wouldn't understand the complexities of the inadmissibility procedure and the impact that the Rwanda Court of Appeal judgement may or may not have on them. … But more importantly they, so many of, you know even if they managed to get hold of the Refugee Convention, to be like I'm a refugee, okay let me read and figure out what Article 1 of the Refugee Convention says, that wouldn't be the end of it, they would need to go to the Nationality and Borders Act and read the Home Secretary's interpretation of the Refugee Convention. … I think the reality is that most people don't understand … which parts of the law applied to them. I doubt they would be looking at the immigration rules, because it would be quite odd that the immigration rule would contain rules that were relevant to an asylum claim. (Riley, legal practitioner)

As this suggests, one of the problems with changes such as the expansion of inadmissibility, and the concomitant idea of fast removal to a country such as Rwanda – noting that at time of writing the Rwanda plan has now been scrapped[2] – is that it effectively exacerbates the existing issues around legal aid and support that we discussed during Chapter 4 and places further pressure on a system that is already not able to cope. This could be understood as an example of the phenomenon Hambly and Gill (2020) have referred to as Legal Quickening. Indeed, as Amelia expressed, this is likely to cause particular problems for those people seeking protection on the basis of their sexual diversity. Specifically, they said:

[2] United Nations Office of the High Commissioner for Human Rights, 'Experts welcome announcement to end UK-Rwanda asylum partnership' (United Nations, 10 July 2024), available at: https://www.ohchr.org/en/press-releases/2024/07/experts-welcome-announcement-end-uk-rwanda-asylum-partnership (accessed 18 October 2024).

> I mean that is going to affect LGBT claimants ... if removals go ahead to Rwanda, I can see that someone who has a sexuality-based claim would be trying to, would want to say that's unlawful to be removed to Rwanda, because they may be persecuted for it. ... I think generally it's just moving things to an earlier stage, people have less time to prepare their cases and to respond to things. (Amelia, legal practitioner)

The problem here is less that there are specific issues that make the laws and policies proposed between 2022 and 2024 have more significant impacts on sexually diverse people – although note should be taken that the question of what is or is not a safe country may well be more complicated in such cases – but rather that the shifts in the process mean that elements of the claim that would previously have been decided at the final stage of that asylum claim are instead pushed to a stage earlier in the process. In this way, the issues identified earlier in this book in relation to accessing appropriate legal advice with relevant expertise or presenting evidence of sexual diversity in a form that the decision-maker will be able to comprehend, are exacerbated.

This is demonstrative of a broader pattern within which policies have a more significant detrimental impact on people who, due to their social positionality, are vulnerabilized by society. In this case, the vulnerabilization stems not from the way in which sexual identities are conceptualized, but rather from how a simplistic duality between safe and unsafe is drawn. This is despite the fact that, as is clear on the face of the Refugee Convention, the question for the purposes of refugee status has never been whether a given country is or is not safe in general terms. But, rather, whether the country in question is safe for the particular person seeking recognition as a refugee. In this sense, one of the key reflections to draw forward is the need to challenge the over-simplified approach to conceptualizing safety by countering the norms through which safety is established.

Shifting workloads: inadmissibility and removal notices

Amelia outlined this further, describing how the changes brought about between 2022 and 2024 resulted in shifting the burden of the work to earlier in the process and outlining how this would result in the system becoming even more unworkable. Specifically, they told me that

> [b]ecause of the demand and the legal aid desert of not being, not having enough firms, you are removing the bulk of the work from later down the line, to right at the start. So where you've got an influx of 50 people that need work immediately, the instructions that I'm taking are completely different. I need to know what countries you've been to, was it reasonable for you to claim asylum in any of

> those places, why did you not, were you trafficked, were there any mental health reasons that you didn't claim asylum in those countries. (Amelia, legal practitioner)

As this suggests, the impact of recent changes cannot be understood in isolation. But, rather, it needs to be understood within the context of the broader issues that we have explored during this book, such as the extreme capacity constraints of contemporary legal aid. Further, as Graffin (2019) has documented, these concerns need to be framed within a context of significant practitioner burnout and high workloads. Within this context, the changes present significant challenges on the capacity of an already overstretched system. As we have outlined, when capacity is challenged, it is often those whose protection claims are 'complex' who will have the greatest difficulty in securing appropriate support with their asylum claim.

Other participants expressed concern regarding how this interacted with other elements of asylum policy. For example, Sophia was concerned that the changes introduced across 2022 to 2024 were having very problematic interactions with dispersal and putting claimants into hotel accommodation where there was a real risk of people facing removal before they had been able to access legal advice (see Burridge and Gill, 2017). As they put it:

> So you get a hotel in a village and there's three camping shops and a pub and that's what there is. … Now that's just insane, not only are there no services, there's insufficient legal advice … there are no lawyers. … So, if you're replicating that in other sort of rural, or non-sort of standard places, the number … that will slip through the net is immense … [people will be] detained to be put on the plane. It's a lottery about getting legal advice, we know that. (Sophia, legal practitioner)

In essence, the issue here is a simple one: moving everything to an earlier stage in the process and creating even more compressed timelines increases the risk of people being removed from the UK without having had the opportunity to consult legal advice. Given the complexity of the legal framework, and the fact that many people are not aware that being a sexually diverse person provides grounds for an asylum claim, there is an increased risk of people who should have access to protection under the UK legal framework being removed. These issues are further exacerbated due to the dispersal policy which may well lead to people being housed in areas where there is extremely little available legal support. This was well expressed by Ava, who said:

> But I think it's really going to be the same as before, which is if you lump LGBT queer refugees in with all other refugees … it will be

> disproportionate affects, so not being able to prepare a case properly and you know being a risk within the system itself, things like that. But kind of general things. (Ava, legal practitioner)

As this shows, and as addressed earlier, the issues arising from these changes is not that they have a direct effect which makes them more harmful to sexually diverse people. Rather, the issue is that sexually diverse people, and others who sit on one axis or another outside of the cluster of norms through which the category of human itself is conceived – note here that Judith Butler argues that the category of human should be considered as a differential grid that is given and retracted depending on compliance with a cluster of norms (Butler, 2009: 1–15) – are placed at additional risk by general policies such as these which add pressure to an already deeply constrained and dysfunctional process.

Anxiety, fear and government policy

Even for those people seeking asylum who were already in the system prior to the granting of royal assent for the Nationality and Borders Act and who, therefore, were entitled to be processed under the legal framework as it existed prior to June 2022, the frequent pronouncements by government ministers, and associated media attention paid to changes in relation to asylum, formed a significant source of anxiety, which itself had mental health implications for people seeking asylum and generated significant workload implications for those working to support them (Morgan et al, 2017; Wells et al, 2024). For example, Jessie said:

> We've had people running away from hotels, because they are scared and they haven't had a Rwanda letter, they're just scared. I mean I've had, the family I told you about whose, the women who arrived with the twins, her brother when she left the room at one point, he was in tears saying you have to tell me, you have to tell me is she going to be sent to Rwanda. I said okay, there's very few times I can categorically say something, but I can categorically tell you neither she nor the children will be sent to Rwanda. (Jessie, third sector worker)

The issue of anxiety and panic arising from the way in which policies have been spoken about was brought up by a number of other participants. For example, Elijah not only spoke of the fear that the Rwanda policy evoked for some claimants already in the UK, but also linked government rhetoric around asylum to broader concerns such as far-right attacks and protests in and around hotels accommodating asylum seekers. Specifically, they said:

> So that, the Rwanda policy was very impactful on people's fear. This week I interviewed a young person and [he had experienced a far-right incident][3] as soon as I said the word Home Office, he started crying, his experience of that public moment, I don't know if he will ever truly feel safe in this country, because that was his experience. … But it's an example of you know these, the media rhetoric, which led to that extremist terrorist doing that and then how it impacts on those personal experiences. … So yeah, it does all impact people greatly. (Elijah, legal practitioner)

Here it is interesting to note that, as we discussed in Chapter 4 with regard to legal practitioners, there was a real fear emanating from asylum claimants that the way in which government ministers spoke about them had incited far-right violence and placed them at risk (Wodak, 2020). Subsequent events such as the August 2024 attacks on asylum hotels in Rotherham and Tamworth and the targeting of asylum and immigration advice and support services across the UK via far-right social media networks and platforms speaks to how asylum and migrant support have become touchstone issues for far-right organizing (Bancroft, 2024). Such incidents also speak to how, in the context of far-right interest, actions of physical violence have become seen as increasingly acceptable by some figures. Indeed, it is notable that in the aftermath of the far-right riots, some figures adopted them into a framework of 'pro-British' protests (Brawn, 2024) while others sought to legitimize the actions by linking them to a sense of frustration, abandonment and the idea that some British people are governed and ruled in a different way to others (Keate, 2024). These framings should be seen as a net component of the broader meta-politics that we discussed during Chapter 2, themselves contributing to how conceptual frames such as migrants, asylum seekers and refugees are conceptualized within both discourse and action and, in so doing, shaping the extent to which the people fitting within these categories are viewed as humans whose lives call for mourning and protection (Butler, 2004a; 2009; Butler and Worms, 2023).

This, of course, significantly impacts the welfare of people seeking asylum who see the same news and read the same statements of government policy as anyone else in the UK and, in the absence of clear advice, are highly likely to worry about such announcements in both policy terms as well as in terms of their potential to further exacerbate hostility towards migrant communities and refugees. While the link to government policy and discourse is not direct, it is notable that those attacking hotels in Rotherham were heard

[3] The details of the incident have been withheld to protect anonymity.

shouting 'Stop the Boats' (Toth, 2024), the same slogan popularized by Rishi Sunak's Conservative government who made reducing the number of people coming to the UK to seek sanctuary one of the core pillars of its central policy platform.

Given this context, where those attempting to actively engage in criminal activity aimed at harming migrants are chanting one of the government's declared policy positions, it is hard to avoid the conclusion that the narratives set in motion by government have contributed to hostility aimed at people seeking sanctuary. At a theoretical level, we might understand this as a form of discursive politics which functions to remove asylum seekers from the schema of grievable life and instead position them as a threat to the majority (Butler, 2004a; 2004b: 18–39). That is to say, migrants are positioned not as human beings deserving of grieving, mourning and protection from violence, but instead as a threat to the UK and the people living within it. In this sense, the use of meta-politics by government fits with forms of populist and nationalist argumentation which operate by seeking to distinguish between friends and enemies in such a way as to direct blame for shortcomings at perceived external threats.

Of particular note in regard to the implications of this is that – as a signatory of the Refugee Convention and its 1967 Protocol – the UK has undertaken to recognize as refugees and give protection to everyone who meets the definition of a Refugee under Article 1A(2) of those instruments. However, as a consequence of the hostility that people navigating the asylum system often feel from both the Home Office itself and parts of the UK community, for some claimants the mere mention of the Home Office evokes fear and trauma. Remembering that an asylum claim is contingent on the claimant presenting the Home Office with a coherent and plausible narrative, often by means of an interview which takes place over multiple hours, it is concerning that the organization charged with taking this evidence is often associated with trauma on the part of people seeking asylum. In this regard, consideration should be taken of how the policy narratives deployed by ministers might undermine the ability of the Home Office to fulfil its functions in processing claims for asylum, not only by impacting how decision-makers approach the process but also by impacting the comfort that claimants have in openly sharing their experiences and narratives.

Politics over law

For some participants, there was a real sense that the politics of the situation had been prioritized over and above the legal workability of the framework ministers were creating. As noted earlier, this is significant not just in terms of its impact on people seeking asylum, but also in terms of its undermining the rule of law, which is generally argued to be a foundational element of liberal accounts of jurisprudence and state building (Bingham, 2011). For example, Muhammad said:

> Whichever government's been, including New Labour, you have this tension between speaking to the gallery, which requires the sort of demonization of refugees and also increasingly those who work with refugees. So that's the kind of Suella Braverman invasion rhetoric, but also like New Labour was very, very busy in terms of legislating like mad around making it more difficult for people to succeed with appeals and claim asylum and so on, despite you know spouting protection and human rights. … So now you have the kind of Braverman and Rwanda thing fits into this, the Rwanda Scheme. It's a kind of, it's paper tiger politics, it's creating easy targets and doing things that look like you are doing something, because that is supposedly the narrative that gets you the votes, whilst at the same time having to sort of navigate pragmatically what you've really got in your hand. (Muhammad, legal practitioner)

Here, particular note might be taken of the fact that the Illegal Migration Act 2023, as originally conceived, placed a bar on granting those who entered the UK unlawfully any form of leave to remain.[4] However, given that there was not any effective and legally defensible returns or transfer agreement in place, the legal effects would have resulted in the creation of a permanent backlog of hundreds of thousands of people who could neither be removed for the UK, nor granted any sort of permanent status (IPPR, 2024). It perhaps speaks to this issue that the government returned at the July 2024 general election acted within just two weeks, by means of Statutory Instrument, to undo this barrier on granting leave to remain, at least until Section 2 of the Illegal Migration Act is commenced.[5] The creation of a permanent backlog would have hugely exacerbated the costs of the asylum system (IPPR, 2024). In this sense, apart from the kind of paper tiger politics referenced by Muhammad, it is difficult to conceive of why a government would undertake to follow such a policy, given that its effects would hugely exacerbate the costs and, as already discussed, there are major doubts regarding the effectiveness of policies founded in deterrence (Mayblin, 2016; 2019). In this sense, it can be argued that the perceived political salience of migration and asylum has often been put before any sense of creating a functioning and workable asylum system (Boswell, 2015). This, of course, imposes significant harms on the claimants forced to rely on

---

[4] Illegal Migration Act 2023, s5.

[5] Illegal Migration Act 2023 (Amendment) Regulations 2024.

that unworkable system for protection, as well as contributing to the kind of meta-politics of grievability that we have outlined in this text.

Indeed, Zadia outlined how the Illegal Migration Act would mean that 'people who are deemed inadmissible are going to be stuck here, there is no plan to remove them. … So, I don't think the Illegal Migration Act is going to speed anything up' (Zadia, legal practitioner). As this suggests, it seems that the performative politics of being seen to be 'doing something' has often been prioritized ahead of creating a workable legal system with legal duties being given to the Home Secretary that they have no reasonable prospect of complying with and which will likely exacerbate the backlogs. Indeed, Zadia went on to express that 'it is only the politics that is in the way of resolving this [the backlog of claimants awaiting a decision]' (Zadia, legal practitioner). As this suggests, for some actors within the system, the political focus on asylum and migration was one of the central barriers to making the system work. Indeed, the declarations made by government might best be understood as a form of performative cruelty. Such a concept draws on Austin's sense of the phrase performative, in terms of being a statement which is itself an action in order to connote how the main force of law-making in this area lies not in making anything remotely resembling a viable change to the legal system, but instead in declaring, signposting and amplifying the cruelty of government policy (Austin, 1979: chapter 10).

It speaks to some of the issues with prioritizing politics over law that some of the main issues that early participants, interviewed early in 2023, raised with the Nationality and Borders Act 2022 were also repealed/undone before effects could be analysed. For example, Isabella told me of their concern arising out of the differential treatment provisions provided under the Nationality and Borders Act 2022. Specifically, when asked about the implications of recent legislation, such as the Nationality and Borders Act 2022, they said:

> I mean Group 1 and Group 2, so you know, they are, anyone who doesn't arrive regularly off an aeroplane with a visa, which is like 99 per cent of my clients, will at this rate be given Group 2 refugee, in temporary refugee permission, if they get through the process successfully and that is only for 30 months. Then the Home Office are going to have to renew it, and then up to ten years, so then every 2.5 years a renewal. So the Home Office's backlog is, what is it 100 and something thousand. So now they are going to quadruple the workload for themselves. (Isabella, legal practitioner)

As this suggests, during the debates around the Nationality and Borders Act the differential treatment of people based on mode of entry was viewed as being the most significant part of the legislation. Similarly, while the Act was being debated in parliament, I joined with a group of lawyers, academics and representatives of third sector organizations to discuss its implications. Within this group, we found essentially unanimous agreement that the stratification of asylum seekers into either Group 1 or Group 2 was going to be one of the most salient and significant implications of the raft of changes brought about by that legislation.[6] The reality, of course, was that shortly after the passing of the Nationality and Borders Act 2022, planning and discussions began around the Illegal Migration Act 2023. With this legislation placing a barrier on granting leave to remain for anyone who had entered the UK unlawfully via a 'third safe country', anyone who would have been a part of Group 2 was effectively prohibited from claiming asylum in the UK. In this sense, further evidence of the politicization could be seen in the fact that the government scrapped a policy in favour of a more punitive one before even allowing any real-world test of the implications of that policy. This suggests that the focus was not on creating effective policy, but rather on showing that the government was 'doing something' and, in so doing, enacting performative cruelty as a mode of showing how 'tough' and active the government was around the issue of 'illegal migration'. This chimes with criminological research, which has drawn attention to what is termed 'punitive populism' where punitive approaches are met with politically positive receptions irrespective of whether or not they are effective in terms of the stated goals of the criminal justice system (Garland, 2022).

Despite this, as Isabella's quote suggests, there was at the time that the Nationality and Borders Act 2022 was passed, prominent concern across both the third sector and among legal practitioners regarding the implications of this change and how it might interact with broader issues, such as how the shorter timeframes would work alongside the problems with legal aid capacity. As the Law Commission set out in their 'Simplification of the Immigration Rules' report, one of the biggest issues in the area of immigration and asylum law has been the immense complexity of the system and the frequent changes to which it is subject (Law Commission, 2020). In this sense, even though the distinction between Group 1 and Group 2 – like the later absolute bar on any grant of leave to remain – had reasonably limited actual legal effects, attention should also be paid to the implications that these enactments, and the public pronouncement around them, has had on the capacity of organizations who work to support refugees and asylum seekers.

This point was well made by Ezra, who told me about the volume of time which had been taken up with attempting to understand the changes to the

[6] Reimaging the New Plan for Immigration, Institute of Advanced Legal Studies, University of London, Tuesday, 3 May 2022.

system and the practical implications which these would have. Specifically, they said:

> Yeah the past few months have really been just trying to work out, what this means, what does the Nationality and Border Act mean for our work, how is that going to be impacting the clients, you know asylum seekers etc. So it's like, there's been a lot of like, okay like what do we do with this, how can we clarify this just from a legal point of view and day-to-day work point of view. (Ezra, legal practitioner)

In this regard, it is pertinent to note that one effect of the hugely politicized law-making in the field of asylum and migration between 2022 and 2024 is that, depending on when an asylum claimant entered the UK and began their asylum claim, their claim may sit under three reasonably distinctive legal frameworks. While lawyers and support organizations are familiar with working in a highly complex legal area, the need to be familiar with differing legal provisions in this way has significant implications for the capacity of those supporting asylum claimants and will, therefore, impact upon the availability of frontline legal advice, guidance and support.

Indeed, this capacity limitation applies not only to people working to support refugees and asylum seekers, but also to decision-makers within the Home Office itself. For example, Isabella expressed concerns:

> I think they [the Home Office] will struggle [with interpreting and applying new legislation]. Already we are seeing, I'm sure you've been exposed to reasons for refusal letters, but often they are just complete nonsense. So we've even had the wrong nationality, the wrong gender, yeah, so they are copy and paste jobs, so they are already pretty weak. So then to start to engage with the new changes, it might take time and yeah and expertise. So I think they will, generally there's such a massive seismic shift when you've already got a dysfunctional system that's just extending the work for the Home Office, it's madness really. (Isabella, legal practitioner)

Given that Home Office decision-makers – and even Home Office Presenting Officers who often represent the Home Office within the tribunal – are not required to have a law degree or formal legal qualifications, there is arguably a significant risk that such rapid changes to the legal framework will further undermine the quality of decision-making. As I have argued elsewhere, poor decision-making at first instance can result in serious delays and hugely undermine the welfare of asylum claimants (Powell, 2023a). Given the broader concerns around wider policies such as dispersal and the use of large-scale accommodation facilities, as well as the greater complexity of asylum claims made on the basis of sexual diversity, these issues carry the potential to lead to disproportionate impacts and harms for particular communities of sanctuary seekers, including those who are making claims on the basis of sexual diversity.

This concern for capacity on the part of both those supporting refugees and asylum seekers and the Home Office was also expressed by Riley, who said:

> One of the headline points is ... the onslaught of changes to law and policy. It used to be the case I think some years back that we would have a piece of immigration legislation every 20, 30, ten, five years. ...We've had the Nationality and Borders Bill, back to back with the Illegal Migration Bill, for example in just this parliamentary session and that's really, it's a tumultuous time in the legal landscape and that is something that asylum lawyers will have had to keep themselves apprised of. So the changing legal landscape makes their job all the more complex. (Riley, legal practitioner)

Riley's remarks here raise two matters of concern, the first is around the capacity implications of the frequent changes. We have addressed these earlier, but it is perhaps pertinent to note that there has recently been a huge increase in the volume of legislation – and statutory instruments – pertaining to immigration and asylum. This increased volume presents a difficulty for all participants in the legal process, as they will need to ensure that they familiarize themselves with the shifting picture. As such, the concern is not just for the capacity of solicitors who support asylum claimants, but also for other elements of the refugee status determination system including the third sector and even the Home Office, who will need to be in a position to support people in a diverse range of legal situations.

In this sense, an adequate understanding of the functioning of the UK asylum system cannot be gained without reference to the impact of the policy announcements and changes on the capacity of the actors within the system as well as on the actual legal framework. When the broader context is considered, the number of legal changes which took place over the period 2022 and 2024 should be seen as a serious impediment to the effective functioning of the asylum system, and, as such, something which actively undermined the ability of the system to provide authoritative and reasoned decisions on asylum claims. But, for legal practitioners, there is also the second consideration that if the system is tightened this may mean that they are more frequently called upon to give bad news, which can, in turn, have implications for the emotional welfare and capacity of both legal representatives and the people who they are working to support (Graffin, 2019; Jones and Graffin, 2020).

For some participants, it was important to remain clear that civil servants, including decision-makers within the Home Office, are simply doing their best to carry out their role in line with the policy of the elected government. For example, Lucas stated:

> I think some of the civil servants have terrible jobs implementing ridiculous political decisions. I have to say, I'm trying to think of the past, because it's come to a standstill, this whole system has come to a standstill. I don't think they really engage. I have to say they did more in the past. There used to be senior members in the asylum system, when I did a lot more asylum, who would be quite good. But I feel that the asylum system is quite faceless. (Lucas, legal practitioner)

Civil servants are required to be politically independent.[7] It would not be the place of decision-makers or other civil servants to block or undermine government policy. But, it is equally important to bear in mind that in a system such as the asylum system, implementation of policy is dependent on those policies corresponding to the reality of the system (Niklasson et al, 2020). Where the policy is not consistent with reality – such as policy premised on removals which not only will not, but cannot, happen – this causes significant harms to the people seeking to navigate their way through that system.

Political rhetoric and administrative decision-making

Beyond this, it is also striking to consider the number of participants who identified a sense that political rhetoric was directly impacting decisions or at least feeding into how decision-makers conducted themselves. For example, Amelia said:

> I feel that that rhetoric impacts decision making, because if you're working for the Home Office and you're buying into that idea you can sometimes feel those threads of thought coming through in refusal letters. It's kind of replicating the idea that you are actually just an economic migrant or something like that in a refusal letter. I think that's gone past the point of someone's claim and that's speculating on their actual purpose for claiming asylum, based on nothing. (Amelia, legal practitioner)

---

[7] See Civil Service UK, *The Civil Service Code* (16 March 2015), available at: https://www.gov.uk/government/publications/civil-service-code/the-civil-service-code (accessed 18 October 2024).

On one level, it is perhaps unsurprising that decision-makers would reflect and be impacted by political rhetoric. They are, after all, people who exist within the same political context as everyone else. As such, the ideas which they bring to their engagements with asylum claimants are shaped by the same discourses and narratives as any other person, this is to say that the conceptual categories through which they make sense of the world are shaped by the meta-politics they encounter from a range of sources which inform their day-to-day lives. From this perspective, it is to be expected that the narratives deployed by politicians would shape the views of actors within the asylum system, even if their role is designated as administrative in nature.

However, we should also note that while broad asylum policy is a political matter under the remit of the Secretary of State for the Home Department, one of the most senior ministerial positions in the UK government, decisions on individual cases are supposed to be objective decisions which apply the factual scenario of the claimant to the stated legal and regulatory framework in order to reach an outcome. In this sense, the idea that political resonances are entering into individual asylum decisions should be a source of real concern and, if substantiated, would speak to a fundamental defect within the current operations of the UK asylum system, as well as the operation of the UK's liberal legal system more broadly.

Similar concerns regarding the implications of contemporary politics were also raised by other participants. For example, Ava said:

> There's no question, you can just see the cynicism in some of them and it's not always like that, it's not always like that, you do get, so we don't see it of course, well I don't see really the grants, because they don't come my way the grants normally, they only happen with the refusals … but it definitely is politically motivated, there's no question. (Ava, legal practitioner)

While Ava acknowledges that they see more refusals than grants, and are therefore likely seeing an unrepresentative sample of poor decision-making practice, it is significant that they so clearly express the view that decision-making is being impacted by politics, stating that there is 'no question' that this is happening. As stated earlier, this should not be the case as the decisions should simply be an application of the framework to the claimant's particular scenario, and political narratives should not have a bearing on the rendering of individual asylum decisions.

Turning away from decision-makers directly, Muhammad expressed concerns regarding how both the media and politicians conceptualize and construct human rights claims within the broader discourse:

> They'll use that kind of language and the *Daily Mail* and the *Sun* and all the rest of it have a field day with all of that and nobody really pays much attention to the very boring human rights cases that win, which are really just about people who have overstayed in the UK, who might have come in illegally, who have got a partner here, or they have a child with somebody, or whatever, just ordinary stories. The foreign national criminal story is making the, is constructing the sort of narrative around all of that and it seems to me that it. ... There's an old phrase, bad cases make bad law, and that it does feel to me and again there are people whose practices are all about foreign national prisoners and I completely believe those people have the right to run their cases and run them really, really well. But it ends up really distorting what's really, what human rights is really about I think. (Muhammad, legal practitioner)

The reference to the use of language such as 'foreign national criminal' or foreign national offenders is notable as the fear of foreign offenders being able to stay in the UK is often used as a talking point to bolster anti-migrant narratives (De Noronha, 2018). Indeed, it is arguable that – through the Illegal Migration Act 2023 – the government of the UK actively encouraged a conceptual slippage between people seeking asylum and foreign national offenders, insofar as they sought to focus attention on the idea that the entry to the UK is 'illegal', therefore creating a conceptual link between entering the UK outside of formal and structured approaches and the commission of criminal offences (Griffiths, 2017). This can be seen in the multitude of references to criminality within the statements of Suella Braverman during her period as Secretary of State for the Home Department as documented throughout this volume. However, as Muhammad is outlining, such situations are not the norm. In stating this, it should be borne in mind first that there are, for people of many nationalities, no safe and legal routes through which the UK can be entered and that the Refugee Convention explicitly prohibits penalization on the basis of the mode by which someone seeking asylum enters the sanctuary country.[8]

Taking all of this together, then, it is clear that the recent period is notable not only for the nature of the laws passed and their legal effects on the rights of people seeking sanctuary in the UK, but also for how the surrounding political context has impacted the ability of the asylum system to function. In short, the cut and thrust of the highly politicized field of asylum and immigration in the UK has undermined the ability of all sides to undertake what should be an essentially administrative process in terms of determining

[8] Convention Relating to the Status of Refugees, 28 July 1951, 189 UNTS 137, A31.

whether or not a given claimant meets the definition set out in the Refugee Convention. The knock-on implications of this can and should be viewed as a threat to not only the rights of people seeking asylum but also to the safety of migrants and ethnic minority communities, arguably playing a role in the stoking of the violence witnessed in August 2024, which included active attempts to set fire to a hotel known to be housing people seeking asylum.

Indeed, as with gender and sexuality, this is where a counter-normative approach rooted in queer and other critical theories can offer significant headway. Specifically, it is important to recognize that any administrative framework would likely result in the enacting of violence against some people seeking asylum. However, from a counter-normative perspective, we can begin to identify how the meta-politics deployed within political and media domains has shifted the conceptual frames through which much asylum decision-making is approached for the worse and can, accordingly, recognize that the first step to creating a more functional system likely lies in a conceptual re-imagining of human rights and asylum in the terms suggested by Muhammad. Specifically, in a conceptual return to the role of human rights and their centrality to everyday lives (Chase, 2012).

6.2 Sexual diversity in asylum claims

Some of the difficulties outlined earlier can also have problematic interactions with other political discourses such as those around gender identity and LGBTIQA+ rights more broadly. The result of this can be to add further complexity to the difficulties I have examined throughout this volume.

Since around 2020, various strands of thought ranging from 'gender critical feminists' (see McLean, 2021; Thurlow, 2024) to religious groups (Żuk and Żuk, 2020) and political figures widely viewed as being on the right of the political spectrum (Makwana et al, 2018) have sought to argue that the granting of rights such as the right to self-identify in one's lived gender constitute a threat to the safety of others. Some scholars have linked these arguments to discourses of white supremacy and associated the positions with the political far right (Clarke, 2024). The identities of those disseminating such views have been diverse. Ranging from famous children's authors such as J.K. Rowling (Gwenffrewi, 2022) to government ministers such as Kemi Badenoch (Elgot, 2024).

The political salience of the issue can perhaps be exemplified in the fact that the idea that the leader of the opposition 'did not know what a woman is' was frequently viewed as a useful attack line during exchanges at Prime Minister's Questions.[9] During this period, libraries also became sites of

[9] HC Deb, 24 January 2024, Vol 744, Col 290.

protest with groups organizing to oppose children's stories being read by drag queens (Perry, 2022). Indeed, turning to the online ecosystem, there were several incidents of public figures accusing LGBTIQA+ people of being groomers or paedophiles, some of which went on to lead to legal actions for defamation (Addle, 2024).

The period between 2022 and 2023 saw a sharp rise in hate crimes committed against transgender people.[10] The period has also seen a series of controversies over the provision of gender-affirming care to young people, with the government responding by limiting access to treatments such as puberty blockers.[11] Indeed, unlike the proposed plans to send people seeking asylum to Rwanda, plans to ban young people from accessing puberty blockers were not abandoned by the Labour government returned in July 2024, but made permanent.[12] As this suggests, contestations in regard to the rights of LGBTIQA+ people seem likely to remain politically salient moving forward, with the way in which LGBTIQA+ identities – but particularly trans identities – are conceptualized being increasingly connected to ideas of risk, danger and social contagion in a manner familiar to narratives of the 1980s (Epstein, 1988; Filip-Crawford and Neuberg, 2015).

The link between this and issues relating to asylum arises from both being constituent strands in what has often been described as a 'culture war' (Anthony, 2021) or a 'war on woke' (Davies and MacRae, 2023). Within this context, both migrants and people of diverse genders and sexualities have been framed as a potential threat to an imagined British way of life. A series of moral panics have emerged that seek to cast particular groups as a threat to the majority which must be contained. As addressed in Chapter 1, the war on woke bears striking resemblance to earlier controversies in relation to the idea of 'political correctness gone mad' (Hall, 1995: 166).

The same moves, combining fears about migration with fears about shifting conceptions of gender and sexual subjectivity as a part of a broader movement around and within cultural norms can be traced in countries as diverse as Hungary (Kovats and Peto, 2017; Scott, 2020), the United States (Brightman et al, 2024), Brazil (Da Costa Santos, 2021) and the UK (Thurlow, 2024). In the context of gender, Judith Butler has usefully traced

---

[10] Home Office, *Hate Crime, England and Wales, 2022 to 2023*, second edition (2 November 2023), available at: https://www.gov.uk/government/statistics/hate-crime-england-and-wales-2022-to-2023/hate-crime-england-and-wales-2022-to-2023 (accessed 9 July 2024).

[11] See The Medicines (Gondaotrophin-Releasing Hormone Analogues) (Emergency Prohibition) (England, Wales and Scotland) Order 2024.

[12] The Medicines (Gondaotrophin-Releasing Hormone Analogues) (Emergency Prohibition) (Extension) Order 2024.

the contours of the phenomenon, drawing attention to its particular links with other conspiratorial patterns of thinking (Butler, 2024). Similar patterns to those which they identify can be argued to arise within the context of contemporary anxieties over migration.

While it is easy to dismiss such disputes as detached from day-to-day concerns, Stuart Hall has explained their function as a kind of meta-politics, which shape how we understand and conceptualize subjectivities (Hall, 1995). This can be seen, to some extent, in the attempt of political figures to focus attention on the idea of foreign national offenders, thus constructing 'illegal migrants', who may have come to the UK seeking asylum, as potentially dangerous. This kind of movement can be viewed as an attempt to shift subjectivities and thus limit the grievability and legibility of asylum seekers as legitimate receipts of empathy and understanding (Butler, 2009: 3; 2004a; 2004b: 18–39). I argue that this process is similarly being carried out with regard to transgender people, and particularly transgender women, with attempts to characterize them as dangerous men rather than people who are simply seeking respect and equal treatment in the gender with which they identify. In this sense, rather than understanding these movements on the basis of their substantive arguments, we might better understand them as discursive enactments of meta-politics, intended to shift public understanding of the groups in question from a grounding that humanizes and generates empathy to a grounding that centres the idea that they are dangerous and both dehumanizes and de-personalizes trans people and migrants as a threat to the broader community which must be stemmed and cauterized.

Supporting sexually diverse asylum seekers in the culture war

The significance of these two intertwined issues was something which participants raised as affecting their work in terms of supporting sexually diverse refugees and asylum seekers. For example, some participants such as Ethan reflected that people had come to their premises to protest or preach. Specifically, they said:

> We've had people coming, well we've had one person coming to the [name of centre] and like preaching outside and saying that we're turning men into women and like all these things and they were specifically attacking like the women that work here, the Muslim women that work here and telling them that they're you know traitors to their religion and things like that. … I think that has increased over the past few years, the kind of heat of that has just kind of got worse, as the government, the media are pushing this kind of narrative of asylum seekers. (Ethan, third sector worker)

As this suggests, the narratives around trans people here intersected with religious narratives, leading to staff within the centre being approached and heckled in a manner that questions their religious fidelity. This fits broader conceptualizations of religion and sexuality as being mutually incompatible (Akachar, 2015). It is further of note here that Ethan felt that the frequency of incidents such as this had increased as a direct result of the narratives and discourses deployed by the government and the media.

Indeed, Ethan went on to express a sense that trans people and asylum seekers specifically, as well as migrants in general, were groups that people felt like they could get away with harassing. Specifically, Ethan said:

> It's part of the culture wars isn't it at the moment, so it seems like those two issues are what they're pushing. Refugee asylum seekers, migrants in general and trans people, it seems like, it's probably the two groups of people that they think they can get away with harassing, or addressing, because like other rights are a bit more well established in the UK and a bit more mainstream … but um, yeah it does feel like these two groups have kind of been targeted. (Ethan, third sector worker)

It is interesting to see Ethan express the idea that the discourses on migration and trans rights might be linked, at least in regard to being people for whom the kind of mistreatment is viewed as acceptable. As this positing of a link suggests, people seeking asylum on the basis of being a sexually diverse person find themselves at the intersection of two discourses which both focus on casting them as an external threat to the imagined homogeneity of British society. Of course, further note should be taken that a component part of the anti-migration discourse involves a kind of homonationalism which posits admitting people of certain religions, or who happen to be from particular countries or cultures, as itself a threat to the rights of women, lesbians and gay men (Sifaki et al, 2022). It is, in this sense, interesting to see an attempt to tie together both narratives fundamentally founded on hostility towards people who are sexually or gender diverse with a proclaimed concern that people from other cultures coming to the UK will undermine the rights of sexually diverse people.

The idea that the culture war in regard to gender was a source of negative impact for sexually diverse refugees and migrants was also expressed by other participants. For example, Muhammad, who expressed a sense that the culture war battle meant that the lived experiences of sexually diverse people were being marginalized and ignored. Specifically, they said:

> I think you could see probably the same thing with trans people that people might not even be able to get their head round, you know, my Nigerian trans male client, and that's part of the problem with

> the whole thing around gender identity and sexuality is actually is the whole bloody culture war is being fought over people's heads and nobody is really listening to kind of ordinary trans people, or ordinary. … Do you know what I mean, it's like kind of, it's all this kind of ideological warfare, but not really basing it in, in the experience of what people's lives are. It just becomes about the extremes. (Muahammad, legal practitioner)

This idea of basing things in the extremes links back to the earlier point about framing the subjectivities of people who are actually migrants or trans. Fringe cases such as individual acts of violence are misrepresented as if they are representative of the whole. This is not only an act of meta-politics, but also a common feature of forms of prejudice and bigotry. When this kind of reasoning is deployed in regard to characteristics such as race, most can identify that it stems from a kind of prejudice and does not represent any sound basis for policy making. However, there seems to be a cognitive barrier to recognizing the absence of probative or evidential value in individual incidents in relation to both migrants and gender diverse people. Indeed, much as Butler has argued with regard to the anti-gender movement, it can be seen that individual stories are viewed through a phantasm, a modality of thought that refracts in a way that constructs a conception of them as representative of a given condition (Butler, 2024). Indeed, one could go further and point out the extent to which this approach to reasoning and evidence map on to other forms of conspiratorial thinking (Linders, 2023). But, in essence, the issue here is that this kind of construction of whole groups as a threat or source of harm on the basis of anecdotal evidence has material effects and causes harm to the communities framed in these terms by shifting the conceptual terms on which people understand one another.

Even where there had not yet been any kind of specific events related to the rhetoric around both migration and trans rights, other participants expressed a concern that their status as sexually diverse presented a specific or exacerbated risk as a result of contemporary turns in policy and discourse. For example, Blair said:

> Yeah everybody's anxieties have shot up, including ours. So there's a lot of you know, is it true that they're going to send me to Rwanda next week, and we've sort of taken the line, well at the moment, there were various cases and hopefully working with [name withheld] if somebody is LGBT there's a particular reason for them not going to Rwanda. (Blair, third sector worker)

Here the anxieties are not related to the broader culture wars or issues around trans rights, but rather to how the stated policies of the government – such as the plan to send those entering the UK unlawfully via a third safe country on to Rwanda to have their asylum claims decided – might potentially have disproportionate impacts for sexually diverse people. In this regard, the concern is that Rwanda is a country from which sexually diverse people have recently been granted asylum in the UK (Rainbow Migration, 2022).

The unifying theme across the issues of culture war and the extra vulnerability to elements of the Rwanda plan is that the experiences of sexually diverse people seeking asylum are impacted by multifarious forms of law, policy and discourse, which mean that we can only understand the experiences of people navigating the asylum system on this basis through an intersectional lens that accounts for the complex social categories they occupy and the different social responses and enactments to and around these complex social positionalities. Indeed, it is in this sense that a counter-normative approach of the kind outlined in the early chapters of this book shows its utility. Specifically, queer theory and counter-normativity provide us with the tools to recognize how narratives shape subjectivities and how, concomitantly, those subjectivities can be unmade by counter-discourses.

As such, if we seek to look at asylum in an isolated way, without an equal contextual understanding of the operation of discourses on sexually diverse people, then we miss many elements of the complexity around this group. The result of this is that we are stopped from fully appreciating the experiences they are likely to have and the difficulties they are likely to have to navigate. Indeed, looking more broadly, we should also be aware of how the stigma directed towards refugees and asylum seekers is something that may inhibit the ability of people navigating the asylum system to form relationships with members of the LGBTIQA+ community in the UK. In this regard, note should be taken of the significant levels of stigma directed at refugees in the UK more broadly, and how this may impact on abilities to integrate and form relationships (York, 2022: 57–100). We should also take note of the significant levels of racism existing within spaces designed at LGBTIQA+ in the UK (Hunter, 2010; Held, 2015). For these reasons, the subjectivities and relationships of sexually diverse refugees and asylum seekers are highly complex and not reducible to analysis either on the basis of only their being people seeking asylum and refugees or on the basis of their being sexually diverse people. Rather, it is only by approaching refugee status determination around sexual diversity across the diverse range of impinging factors, as I have in this book, that we can start to build a clear picture of how different subjectivities have become consolidated within the system and the social and political context within which that framework operates.

As this suggests, we cannot hope to understand the experiences of either sexually diverse asylum seekers or the people who work and volunteer to support them without looking at the broader implications of discourses and apparatuses and seeking to understand how they shape and re-shape subjectivities, and in turn, how this shapes precarity and our ability to empathize with and understand one another. It is not just politics that we need to be attuned to and take account of, but also the forms of meta-politics engaged and (re-)articulated within legal and political processes.

6.3 Theory and practice

Some of the conceptual frameworks we have used across this volume may seem theoretically dense and potentially disconnected from the day-to-day operations of law. Words like precarity (Butler, 2004a; 2004b 18–39), grievability (Butler, 2009: 3), apparatus (Agamben, 2009: 3) and discourse can be useful in that they enable us to, with precision, consider the implications of language for lives and the operation of the legal framework. However, they often also leave us talking about matters that are hard to grasp and from which it can be particularly difficult to draw concrete implications.

For example, across Chapters 3 and 4, our discussion of the forms of evidence deployed by decision-makers in order to determine whether a given claimant is a sexually diverse person extensively focused on the constructed nature of sexual categories and the meanings which we attach to them. This is important, insofar as the conceptual tools we have used enable us to see how the concepts through which we understand and situate sexual diversity are deeply essentialized – produced in order to give a sense of control and conceptual clarity to what is an essentially inarticulable and intangible status – and do not readily map onto the lived experiences of those forced to navigate the asylum system. However, despite this, it is also the case that the current legal framework places the burden of proof onto the claimant, and it is therefore to some extent unavoidable that forms of essentialism – strategic or otherwise – will emerge within the asylum process. Put simply, the current function of the system means that, despite the conceptual issues raised, it remains necessary for some form of essentialism to be deployed within the system in order for it to be possible to navigate. In this sense, it is necessary here to put forward some concrete proposals to address the theoretical issues raised across this volume and seek to use the theoretical frameworks which we have deployed in order to improve practice and to begin to tie together how the issues raised across this book can be addressed within the bounds of the current legal framework.

In this regard, and building on the issues raised primarily in this chapter – but which have also sat implicitly behind each of the chapters we have addressed up until this point – the first and most urgent need in this area is for greater attention to be paid to the implications of language and discourse. Adopting the work of Butler, Foucualt, Heidegger, Gramsci and Hall means, first and foremost, abandoning the presuppositions of modernism – principally the idea that the individual is a stable unit and a collection of individuals make up a society – and instead positing the radical contingency of the subjectivities and subjects. This includes engaging with the mutability of the different classifications, categories and constructions into which any of us may be placed.

Language, grievability and subjectivity

In this sense, and much as Davis (2010: 10) argues in his characterization of Heidegger, we need to acknowledge that 'language demarcates the parameters of the real wherein humans can meaningfully dwell. Language domesticates being: it makes the world liveable for us … it is language that allows us to perceive and understand things as the things that they appear to us to be'. By acknowledging this, we are able to move from considering language as something that describes the world and instead understand it as something that shapes the world. The meta-politics within which meaning and value is ascribed, retracted and distributed. This poses particular considerations for law and politics, pointing to the importance of considering the implications of how people and groups are framed, and becoming more aware of the lineage associated with the frameworks which we deploy to make sense of and frame the world around us and those who inhabit it.

Adopting such an understanding moves us forward to the position articulated by Butler that rather than being a biological category, human being is a mutable status and that

> lives appear one way or the other only when viewed from specific historical perspectives; they acquire and lose value depending on the framework in which they are regarded, which is not to say that any given framework has the full power to decide the value of life. The differential ways in which the value of life is gauged are informed by tacit schemes of valuation according to which lives are deemed to be more or less grievable. (Butler, 2020: 73)

Following this, the discourses which we employ, and the apparatus which we deploy, are engaged in a continuous cycle of (re)production that constructs some lives as grievable and worthy of protection, mourning and violence, and others as surplus and dangerous, to be excised for the protection of 'the people'. It is these norms, around concepts, schemas and frameworks, that a counter-normative approach enables us to challenge.

The operation of this kind of discursive onto-power can be clearly seen in the events of 2 September 2015. On this day, a body washed onto a beach from the Mediterranean Sea. Deaths in the Mediterranean are by no means rare, and it is not uncommon to have numerous deaths reported without note of the names of those lost.[13] However, this was different. The body belonged to two-year-old Alan Kurdi (Walsh, 2015). While so many migrants who lost their lives went without names, Kurdi was given a name, a face and an individual identity. As El-Enany (2016: 13) asks, 'how did it come about that White Europeans were able, all of a sudden, to humanize the body of a refugee, least of all, the body of a Muslim?' It is striking that in sharp contrast to the many others[14] who died, the photo of Kurdi went viral, often accompanied by #CouldBeMyChild (Grierson et al, 2015).

Kurdi was like the many other migrants who attempt to cross the Mediterranean or English Channel irregularly. Someone arriving in the UK in his situation would – between the passing of the Illegal Migration Act and July 2024 – likely have faced a total bar on leave to remain and continuing threat of removal the second they turned 18. Further, immediately prior to his arrival, David Cameron – then UK prime minister – had referred to those seeking to reach Europe, including Alan Kurdi and his family, as a swarm (BBC News, 2015; Taylor, 2021: 468). While media figures such as Katie Hopkins, at the time legitimized through appearances on shows such as the BBC's *Question Time*, had referred to these same people as 'cockroaches' (Stone, 2015).

To draw this together as directly as possible, my argument is that Alan Kurdi was no different to those referred to as cockroaches. But some mix between his youth, his race and the specific horror of how his body came to lie on a Turkish beach allowed feelings of empathy to penetrate through the abstractions and cultivated ignorances which are required to sustain both Europe and the UK's militarized border regimes. Much as El-Enany argued, 'feelings of empathy are known to encourage cooperation and assistance between human-beings, while an absence of identification with the suffering of others can lead to violence and abuse' (El-Enany, 2016: 14). In this sense, something about Kurdi allowed empathy to penetrate through the situation and humanize him, restoring the epistemological capacity to apprehend his humanity to those who, by means of the dehumanizing discourses directed towards migrants, had lost this ability.

Dehumanization, abstraction and metaphor form a shield through which both empathy and the humanity of others such as migrants is foreclosed,

[13] The Missing Migrants Project charts the numbers of people disappearing or dying during journeys to an international migration destination and puts into stark relief the number of people killed during migratory journeys of this kind. See https://missingmigrants.iom.int/ (accessed 18 October 2024).

[14] Estimates put the number of people 'missing' at sea across the Mediterranean in the tens of thousands since 2015. See https://missingmigrants.iom.int/ (accessed 18 October 2024).

enabling us to be ignorant to the harms they experience. Butler has argued that, ultimately, 'the epistemological capacity to apprehend a life is partially dependent on that life being produced according to norms that qualify it as a life' (Butler, 2009: 3). Taken in this register, then, the language we have just seen discussed is not ephemeral or symbolic, but rather shapes our very ability to apprehend those seeking sanctuary as human beings. Politics and policies are not merely things that are enacted to and by human beings, but form a part of the apparatus through which our conceptions of the human being – who is deserving of empathy, respect and mutuality – are shaped. The meta-politics outlined earlier is, therefore, not symbolic or secondary but rather has implications for our capacity to apprehend humanity and should be a paramount consideration.

Taken in this register, the use of the language of 'small boats' (Townsend, 2023), the framing of all irregular entry as 'illegal migration'[15] and the use of language such as 'invasion' (Hubbard, 2022) operates to reify and (re)produce those seeking sanctuary as objects who pose a threat to 'the people' of the UK. This, in turn, inures us to the concrete (and extremely violent) implications of policies and inhibits our capacity to empathize. Turning towards practical implications, there is a clear and urgent need for greater attention to be paid to how language produces subjectivities and to reflect this in the way in which policy and laws are framed, formulated and applied. This need applies not just to the political context and the way in which migrants and transgender people are addressed, but also to the way that sexual diversity is conceptualized within procedures such as refugee status determination.

Such a call is not particularly new. UK law already recognizes the way in which subjectivities can be (re)produced through its criminalization of offences such as stirring up racial hatred.[16] Indeed, Holocaust scholars have long noted the role of dehumanization – which I would argue is best understood as relating to the re-production of subjectivities – in creating the conditions within which genocide occurs (Bauman, 2004; 2014; De Ruiter, 2023). However, such lessons are often missed in the languages deployed by political and media figures when discussing people seeking asylum.

In the immediate term, this posits an urgent need to address the discourses deployed by political figures and within the media towards migrants. Signals of just how dangerous this situation has become can be seen in the tacit endorsement of political violence by politicians such as the leader of the Reform UK Party, Nigel Farage (Dodd, 2024). To be clear, this is not in any

---

[15] The Illegal Migration Act 2023.

[16] Public Order Act 1986, S18.

sense an explicit endorsement. The actual violence was clearly condemned. However, it was also identified that those perpetrating the violence had 'legitimate concerns' and implied that the violence would continue if those 'concerns' were not addressed. Otherwise put, if the political agenda that Farage himself supported was not enacted, then there would be greater violence. Taking this example, it could be argued that some elements of anti-migrant discourse, such as the use of the language of invasion or suggestions of using weapons to 'stop the boats', could and should be viewed in the same register as active incitements to violence and might even be considered to be a form of stochastic terrorism (Angrove, 2024; Amman and Meloy, 2024). This is to say that we might consider the use of language such as 'stop the boats' and the engagement of frames such as 'invasion' to be direct enactments of political violence which, while allowing political figures the ability to deny accountability and, indeed, condemn specific acts of violence, nonetheless renders people at significantly greater vulnerability to acts of harm.

Turning to sexually diverse asylum seekers and refugees more specifically, across Chapters 3 and 4 critical attention was directed to how forms of evidence of being an LGBTIQA+ person are produced and understood within the process of refugee status determination. I explored how these forms of evidence are not representative of the lived realities of sexually diverse refugees and asylum seekers. For example, I explored how the expectations around how people will experience their identities and engage with the broader community are reflective of social and cultural norms prominent in the UK, rather than reflecting anything which is inherent within or of sexual diversities and how these evidential expectations are discordant not just with the way that people seeking asylum may make sense of their own sexual diversities, but also with the structural conditions in which the asylum system places people seeking asylum.

As with the example of anti-migrant politics, this book has deployed queer and critical theoretical frameworks to look at how the norms currently existing within the practices of the UK asylum system do not correspond to the lived realities of people seeking to navigate this system. Further, I have looked at how a series of practical issues undermine the ability of claimants to correspond to these expectations. However, it is acknowledged that – absent a fundamental transformation of the landscape, such the abolition of borders – asylum claimants, as well anyone else seeking to avoid removal from the UK due to their sexual or gender diversity, will need to offer some evidence to support this. Therefore, the next section problematizes the use of models and suggests that stepping back from reliance on them may help to address the recent trends and issues within sexual diversity asylum claims.

Sexual diversity asylum after models

Across participant narratives, significant critical attention has been paid to the use of models such as the Difference, Stigma, Shame, Harm (DSSH) model. While no explicit mention is made of the DSSH model (Dawson and Gerber, 2017) within the 2016 Asylum Policy Instruction: Sexual Orientation in the Asylum Claim,[17] it is clear from the topics within the policy that it draws significantly upon this model. As evidenced across Chapters 3 and 4 of this volume, the key themes within the model seem to have contributed to the creation of an overly identitarian approach to the issue of refugee status determination with decision-makers focusing on highly developed stories of emotional journeys and concrete engagement with the LGBTIQA+ community suggesting that – much as Dawson and Gerber feared it may – the model has resulted in the calcification of fixed expectations for what constitutes a genuine or credible sexual diversity (Dawson and Gerber, 2017). Indeed, as Åberg has argued in the Swedish and Dutch context, the nexus of shame and identity pursued by the policy could even be seen to frame internalized homophobia as being an implicit requirement for securing international protection as a sexually diverse person (Åberg, 2023). In this sense, the model should be understood as contributing to a highly essentialized conceptualization of sexually diverse identities. One that the findings of this book suggest an urgent need to depart from.

While the model does not focus overly on distinctive categories of difference, it can nonetheless be argued that it continues to posit an ontological or given conceptualization of sexual difference as a form of fixed status that fundamentally governs who someone 'is' (Dawson and Gerber, 2017: 293). Indeed, Chelvan, the author of the model, is aware of this, setting the model as a part of a broader push to assess the credibility of sexual and gender diversity in relation to identities rather than conduct (Chelvan, 2011: 60–62). Of course, in terms of context, note should be taken that the model was put together at a time where it formed a direct response to issues of overly sexualized questions being asked (Juss, 2015). But, as I have argued elsewhere, the risk here is that such models have now swung the pendulum too far the other way, resulting in expectations for highly developed narratives of identity development of the kind discussed in Chapters 3 and 4 (Powell, 2021a).

Of a particular concern here is that, as we have explored in the previous sections, identity is not a universal construction but rather is a production

[17] UK Visas and Immigration, 'Asylum Policy Instruction: Sexual Orientation in Asylum Claims' (Home Office, 2016), available at: https://assets.publishing.service.gov.uk/government/uploads/system/uploads/attachment_data/file/543882/Sexual-orientation-in-asylum-claims-v6.pdf (accessed 17 June 2024).

of specific cultural and historical conditions. As argued, it is only through and within these contingent conditions that we are constituted as subjects. In this sense, one concern is that models such as the DSSH model may privilege those who experience their sexual diversities in a manner that is consistent with how such phenomena are deployed, displayed and situated within Europe, while simultaneously providing a range of characteristics and expectations which generate additional incredulity for those who do not experience their sexual diversity in a manner that accords with the performances of sexual difference commonly seen in the UK.

In effect, the focus on difference, and particularly the idea of claimants explaining their emotional responses to realizing their difference, becomes another modality within which decision-makers seek essentially fixed conceptions of sexuality that align with the kinds of sexual difference and narratives of identity development commonly seen in the UK.

It is certainly the case that, for some claimants, the DSSH model can provide a positive model that gives a road map for the demonstration of a credible and well evidenced sexual diversity. However, given the extremely well-documented cultures of disbelief within the Home Office as an institution, it is important to maintain an awareness that introducing a model such as this may itself mean that those who do not fit with the model find that their claim is, in fact, made more difficult. In this sense, note should be taken that Rainbow Migration and other organizations have noted real issues with expectations around claimants articulating a deeply developed and thought-out narrative of difference (Rainbow Migration, 2018). This, in the very language of the DSSH, speaks to the risks associated with models, that those whose experiences are not well mapped onto the model are then faced with reified expectations around what it is to be LGBTIQA+.

Given this, there is an urgent need for greater caution around the use of models. I note here that I have only really explored one model in detail, but this is presently one of the most well-known and frequently applied models, particularly in the UK system. It has also been given status within the United Nations High Commissioner for Refugee's 'Guidelines on international protection'[18] and has been adopted by numerous other asylum systems as a central pillar of their approach to asylum claims by sexually diverse people (Åberg, 2023). As such, it is an important site of analysis with regard to thinking through the issues that sexually diverse people face when trying to navigate asylum systems. While models can be helpful, note should be

[18] UNHCR, 'Guidelines on international protection no 9: Claims to refugee status based on sexual orientation and/or gender identity within the context of Article 1A(2) of the 1951 Convention and/or its 1967 Protocol Relating to the Status of Refugees', HCR/12/09, paras 62–63.

taken that they necessarily essentialize the lived realities of human beings and can just as easily offer a reason for refusal as they can a mode of verification. Further, given that the deployment of a form of argument within one asylum claim can have implications for future claimants by constructing and consolidating how decision-makers conceptualize and make sense of sexual diversity (Bruce-Jones, 2015), it is argued that continuing to use such models places a real risk of marginalizing the most vulnerable claimants.

This critique around models, in essence, applies to all models for determining whether or not someone is or would be perceived as a sexually diverse person. This is because any model which is applied, over time, runs the risk of becoming calcified as a kind of checklist through which the question of whether or not someone is a sexually diverse person can allegedly be answered. Concerns over precisely this were expressed by a number of legal representatives who were worried that by utilizing models they may be cementing fixed expectations into the minds of decision-makers.

The primary issue here is that models rely on simplification (Mayblin, 2019). In seeking to offer prescriptions on which decision-makers can base their judgments, they fix particular ideas of what it means to be a sexually diverse person. This inherently carries a risk of giving reasons for refusal in exactly the same way that it carries the potential of providing a way of proving that a given claimant is a sexually diverse person. Given the narratives of both refugees and legal practitioners, I argue that the use of models has, in this case, become a central reason for refusal in many cases and should therefore be abandoned. More specifically, decision-makers should focus on standard refugee law tests, as outlined in *HJ (Iran)* and *HT (Cameroon)*,[19] rather than seeking to use models like DSSH as a tool through which to undertake refugee status determination for sexually diverse claimants. In stating this, note should be taken that I have also problematized the test for creating the conditions for an overt focus on discrete sexual identity (Powell, 2025). However, returning to the fundamentals of refugee law will at least decentre the idea of claimants offering developed accounts of identity development, narratives of difference and stories of shame.

Given this, the core policy recommendation arising from this book is the urgent need to cease the use of models for sexual diversity asylum claims within the UK asylum system. Instead, policy and decision-maker practice should return to looking for the fundamental elements required under refugee law: a well-founded fear of persecution for a Convention reason. This will generally be either a particular social group or political opinion in regard to sexual diversity. Indeed, one more positive approach which should

[19] *HJ (Iran) and HT (Cameroon) v Secretary of State for the Home Department* [2010] UKSC 31, [2011] 1 AC 596 [82–83].

be given greater consideration is whether sexual diversity asylum claims might better be understood in regard to the violation of social norms, than in regard to belonging to a particular group. A focus on the violation of social norms may entail looking at the political opinion ground as the basis for international protection in regard to sexual diversity, rather than a focus on membership of a particular social group. It is possible that many of the issues around an overreliance on identity and the expectation that claimants will have formulated complex narratives of difference could be avoided if the focus was instead on the violation or perceived violation of social and political norms within the country of origin. This is an example of how a counter-normative approach can lead us in looking to alternative norms which may perpetuate less harmful conceptualizations of subjectivities that – without the need for fundamental reform – allow legal and administrative frameworks to operate in a manner that better aligns with the lived experiences of people navigating that system.

6.4 Conclusion

The UK asylum system is dysfunctional, haunted by hostility and political rhetoric, which, combined with extensive delays and significant issues around access to legal aid, present significant difficulties for those coming to the UK to seek sanctuary. As outlined across this book, these issues affect all asylum seekers. However, there are various factors which make sexually diverse people seeking asylum more vulnerable to their implications.

These factors are multi-faceted, ranging from the complex intersections of sexual diversities and borders to the incorporation of overly simplified models which have led to fixed and calcified expectations on the part of decision-makers. All of which is exacerbated by the hostile rhetoric emanating from government and the media and the range of performative policies designed to give the appearance of a government that is 'doing something' to tackle 'illegal migration'. These policies, like the models used within the refugee status determination system, contribute to the production of particular subjectivities which enact epistemological injustice and violence on those who are understood through them.

Taken together, what I have explored is a broad range of systemic failures which cause real harm to sexually diverse people navigating the UK asylum system. In terms of solutions, this book has limited answers. However, as has been argued, a recognition of the value of meta-politics and an understanding of how political narratives re-shape subjectivities is urgently needed to avoid further harm. While, within the asylum system itself, a move away from models such as the DSSH model, which, far from its original goal to act as a useful tool for decision-makers, has resulted in difficulties for claimants not fitting a very particular narrative, would help to return us to the fundamental questions which refugee status determination is intended to address. In short, for positive change to come, it is at the level of conception, subjectivity and meta-politics that reform is needed.

Sexual diversity, like all human phenomena, is complex and messy, and it may be that it is only by abandoning the idea of simple answers that we can provide decision-makers with relevant training and support to start addressing asylum claims in a fair, ethical and sustainable way.

References

Åberg, K. 2023. A requirement of shame: On the evolution of the protection of LGB refugees. *International Journal of Refugee Law*, 35(1), 37–57.

Abes, E. and Kasch, D. 2007. Using queer theory to explore lesbian college students multiple dimensions of identity. *Journal of College Student Development*, 48(6), 619–636.

Addle, E. 2024. I'll be drinking the bar dry: Crystal on Laurence Fox libel victory and death threats. *The Guardian*, 30 January. Available at: https://www.theguardian.com/culture/2024/jan/30/ill-be-drinking-the-bar-dry-crystal-on-libel-victory-and-death-threats (accessed 18 October 2024).

Adler, L. 2018. *Gay Priori: A Queer Critical Legal Studies Approach to Law Reform*. Duke University Press.

Adler, L. 2020. Life at the corner of poverty and sexual abjection: lewdness, indecency, and LGBTQ youth. In Ashford, C. and Maine, A. (eds) *Research Handbook on Gender, Sexuality and the Law*. Edward Elgar. 76–90.

Affolter, L. 2022. Trained to disbelieve: The normalisation of suspicion in a Swiss asylum administration office. *Geopolitics*, 27(4), 1069–1092.

Agamben, G. 1998. *Homo Sacer: Sovereign Power and Bare Life*. Stanford University Press.

Agamben, G. 2009. *What is an Apparatus? And Other Essays*. Stanford University Press.

Ahmed, S. 2006. *Queer Phenomenology: Orientations, Objects, Others*. Duke University Press.

Akachar, S. 2015. Stuck between Islamophobia and homophobia: Applying intersectionality to understand the position of gay Muslim identities in the Netherlands. *DiGeSt. Journal of Diversity and Gender Studies*, 2(1–2), 173–187.

Akin, D. 2017. Queer asylum seekers: Translating sexuality in Norway. *Journal of Ethnic and Migration Studies*, 43(3), 458–474.

Albury, K. and Byron, P. 2014. Queering sexting and sexualisation. *Media International Australia*, 153(1), 138–147.

Alessi, E.J., Alexander, L., Lee, Y.G., Fletcher, C., Aziz, A. and Zadeh, L. 2024. How do legal aid cuts in England and Wales impact LGBTQ+ people seeking asylum? Perspectives from providers and directly affected people. *Sexuality Research and Social Policy*, 1–16.

Ali, S. 2025. Changes in 'good character' policy for citizenship applications will affect many with refugee leave. *Bindmands LLP Blog*, 13 February. Available at: https://www.bindmans.com/news-insights/blogs/changes-in-good-character-policy-for-citizenship-applications-will-affect-those-with-refugee-leave/ (accessed 19 April 2024).

Allouche, S. 2020. Different normativity and strategic 'nomadic' marriages: Area studies and queer theory. *Middle East Critique*, 29(1), 9–27.

Amadiume, I. 2015. *Male Daughters, Female Husbands: Gender and Sex in an African Society*. Zen Books.

Amman, M. and Meloy, R. 2024. Incitement to violence and stochastic terrorism: Legal, academic, and practical parameters for researchers and investigators. *Terrorism and Political Violence*, 36(2), 234–245.

Angove, J. 2024. Stochastic terrorism: Critical reflections on an emerging concept. *Critical Studies on Terrorism*, 17(1), 21–43.

Anthony, A. 2021. Everything you wanted to know about the culture wars – but were afraid to ask. *The Guardian*, 13 June. Available at: https://www.theguardian.com/world/2021/jun/13/everything-you-wanted-to-know-about-the-culture-wars-but-were-afraid-to-ask (accessed 10 October 2024).

Ashford, C., Morris, M. and Powell, A. 2020. Bareback sex in the age of preventative medication: Rethinking the 'harms' of HIV transmission. *The Journal of Criminal Law*, 84(6), 596–614.

Atkins, J. and Finlayson, A. 2013. 'A 40-year-old black man made the point to me': Everyday knowledge and the performance of leadership in contemporary British politics. *Political Studies*, 61(1), 161–177.

Attwood, F. 2006. Sexed up: Theorizing the sexualisation of culture. *Sexualities*, 9(1), 77–94.

Austin, J. 1979. *Philosophical Papers*. Clarendon Press.

Baars, G. 2019. Queer cases unmake gendered law, or, fucking law's gendering function. *Australian Feminist Law Journal*, 45(1), 15–62.

Bancroft, H. 2024. Asylum seekers 'glad to be alive' after Rotherham hotel attack, says activist who guarded entrance. *The Independent*, 5 August. Available at: https://www.independent.co.uk/news/uk/home-news/uk-riots-rotherham-hotel-asylum-seekers-b2591548.html (accessed 11 May 2025).

Banerjee, P. 2015. The subaltern: Political subject or protagonist of history. *South Asia: Journal of South Asian Studies*, 38(1), 39–49.

Barrett, D. and Bartlett, C. 2020. Labour, lawyers and luvvies block bid to deport rapists: Murderer and sex criminals were among 23 crooks spared from boarding flight to Jamaica at the last minute. *Daily Mail*, 2 December. Available at: https://www.dailymail.co.uk/news/article-9011775/Labour-lawyers-luvvies-block-bid-deport-rapists.html (accessed 17 October 2024).

Bates, T. 1975. Gramsci and the theory of hegemony. *Journal of the History of Ideas*, 36(2), 351–366.

Bauman, Z. 2004. Categorical murder, or: how to remember the Holocaust. In Lentin, R. (ed) *Re-Preseting the Shoah for the 21st Century*. Berghahn Books. 25–40.

Bauman, Z. 2014. Sociology after the Holocaust. In Jamieson, R. (ed) *The Criminology of War*. Routledge. 183–211.

BBC News. 2015. David Cameron criticised over migrant swarm language. *BBC News*, 30 July. Available at: https://www.bbc.co.uk/news/uk-politics-33716501 (accessed 10 October 2024).

BBC News. 2022. Sir David Amess murder: Ali Harbi Ali given whole-life sentence. *BBC News*, 13 April. Available at: https://www.bbc.co.uk/news/uk-england-61094059 (accessed 17 October 2024).

BBC News. 2023. Suella Braverman to target 'crooked' immigration lawyers. *BBC News*, 8 August. Available at: https://www.bbc.co.uk/news/uk-politics-66437588 (accessed 17 October 2024).

Bentham, J. 1970. *Of Laws in General*. Edited by Hart, H.L.A. Athlone Press.

Berlant, L. 1998. Collegiality, crisis, and cultural studies. *Profession*, 105–116.

Bingham, T. 2011. *The Rule of Law*. Penguin.

Birks, M.J., Chapman, Y. and Francis, K. 2007. Breaching the wall: Interviewing people from other cultures. *Journal of Transcultural Nursing*, 18(2), 150–156.

Black, C., Gustafsson, B., Larsson, I.B. and Bertero, C. 2011. Managing the legal proceedings: An interpretive phenomenological analysis of sexually abused children's experience with the legal process. *Child Abuse & Neglect*, 35(1), 50–57.

Blanchard, C. 2018. Never truly free: The humanitarian impact of the UK immigration detention system. *The British Red Cross*. Available at: file:///C:/Users/p0090716/Downloads/Never-Truly-Free-March-2018.pdf (accessed 17 October 2024).

Bögner, D., Brewin, C. and Herlihy, J. 2010. Refugees' experiences of Home Office interviews: A qualitative study on the disclosure of sensitive personal information. *Journal of Ethnic and Migration Studies*, 36(3), 519–535.

Bonansinga, B. and Forrest, C. 2025. 'Stop the boats': Populist contagion and migration policymaking in the UK. *Ethic and Racial Studies*, 1–19.

Borelli, C., Poy, A. and Rué, A. 2023. Governing asylum without 'being there': Ghost bureaucracy, outsourcing, and the unreachability of the state. *Social Sciences*, 12(3), 169–187.

Boswell, C. 2015. The double life of targets in public policy: Disciplining and signalling in UK asylum policy. *Public Administration*, 93(2), 490–505.

Bouchet-Mayer, C. and Ferez, S. 2024. Cross-effects of cultural and gay capitals in access to refugee status on the grounds of SOGI in France: Study of the formal and informal preparations of West African men for asylum trials. *Journal of Refugee Studies*, 37(3), 734–749.

Bourdieu, P. 1992. *The Logic of Practice*. Polity.

Bowden, B. 2007. Civilization and savagery in the crucible of war. *Global Change, Peace & Security*, 19(1), 3–16.

Bradley, G.M. and De Noronha, L. 2022. *Against Borders: The Case for Abolition*. Verso.

Brawn, S. 2024. BBC slated for framing of English riots as 'pro-British'. *The National*, 5 August. Available at: https://www.thenational.scot/news/24497438.bbc-slated-framing-english-riots-pro-british/ (accessed 18 May 2025).

Brickell, C. 2001. Whose 'special treatment? Heterosexism and the problems with liberalism. *Sexualities*, 4(2), 211–235.

Brightman, S., Lenning, E., Lurie, K.J. and DeJong, C., 2024. Anti-transgender ideology, laws, and homicide: An analysis of the trifecta of violence. *Homicide Studies*, 28(3), 251–269.

Brown, K., Mondon, A. and Winter, A. 2021. The far right, the mainstream and mainstreaming: Towards a heuristic framework. *Journal of Political Ideologies*, 28(2), 162–179.

Brown, W. 2004. 'The most we can hope for ...': Human rights and the politics of fatalism. *The South Atlantic Quarterly*, 103(2), 451–463.

Bruce-Jones, E. 2015. Death zones, comfort zones: Queering the refugee question. *International Journal on Minority and Group Rights*, 22(1), 101–127.

Buchowski, M. 2006. The specter of orientalism in Europe: From exotic other to stigmatized brother. *Anthropological Quarterly*, 79(3), 463–482.

Burgess, A., Potocky, M. and Alessi, E.J. 2021. A preliminary framework for understanding suicide risk in LGBTQ refugees and asylum seekers. *Intervention Journal of Mental Health and Psychosocial Support in Conflict Affected Areas*, 19(2), 187–196.

Burridge, A. and Gill, N. 2017. Conveyor-belt justice: Precarity, access to justice, and uneven geographies of legal aid in UK asylum appeals. *Antipode*, 49(1), 23–42.

Butler, J. 1999. *Gender Trouble: Feminism and the Subversion of Identity*. Routledge.

Butler, J. 2004a. *Precarious Life: The Powers of Mourning and Violence*. Verso.

Butler, J. 2004b. *Undoing Gender*. Routledge.

Butler, J. 2008. Sexual politics, torture, and secular time. *British Journal of Sociology*, 59(1), 1–23.

Butler, J. 2009. *Frames of War: When is Life Grievable?* Verso.

Butler, J. 2020. *The Force of Nonviolence*. Verso.

Butler, J. 2024. *Who's Afraid of Gender?* Allen Lane.

Butler, J. and Worms, F. 2023. *The Liveable and the Unliveable: A Conversation Initiated by Arto Charpentier and Laure Barillas*. Fordham University Press.

Cammaerts, B. 2022. The abnormalisation of social justice: The 'anti-woke culture war' discourse in the UK. *Discourse and Society*, 33(6), 730–743.

Caplan, P. 1989. *The Cultural Construction of Sexuality*. Routledge.

Chase, A.T. 2012. Legitimizing human rights: Beyond mythical foundations and into everyday resonances. *Journal of Human Rights*, 11(4), 505–525.

Chelvan, S. 2011. Put your hands up (if you feel love). *Immigration, Asylum and Nationality Law*, 25(1), 56–66.

Chelvan, S. 2018. LGBTI asylum claims: The difference, stigma, shame, harm model (legal updates). Available at: http://www.righttoremain.org.uk/legal/lgbti-asylum-claims-the-difference-shame-stigma- harm-model/ (accessed 3 May 2025).

Chelvan, S. 2020 The DSSH Model and the Voice of the silenced: Aderonke Apata-The Queer Refugee:"I Am a Lesbian". In Raj, S. and Dunne, P. (eds) *The Queer Outside in Law: Recognising LGBTIQ People in the United Kingdom*. Springer International, 79–105.

Clarke, H. 2024. (Re) producing sex/gender normativities: LGB alliance, political whiteness and heteroactivism. *Journal of Gender Studies*, 1–12.

Clements, B. and Field, C. 2014. Public opinion towards homosexuality and gay rights in Great Britain. *Public Opinion Quarterly*, 78(2), 523–547.

Cobain, I. and Taylor, M. 2016. Far-right terrorist Thomas Mair jailed for life for Jo Cox murder. *The Guardian*, 23 November. Available at: https://www.theguardian.com/uk-news/2016/nov/23/thomas-mair-found-guilty-of-jo-cox-murder (accessed 17 October 2024).

Cohen, C. 2020. Punks, bulldaggers, and welfare queens: The radical potential of queer politics. In McCann, C., Kim, S.K. and Ergun, E. (eds) *Feminist Theory Reader: Local and Global Perspectives*. Routledge.

Cohen, S. 2011. *Folk Devils and Moral Panics*. Routledge.

Coleman, L.M. 2024. *Struggles for the Human: Legality and the Politics of Rights*. Duke University Press.

Colpani, G. and Habed, A. 2014. 'In Europe it's different': Homonationalism and peripheral desires for Europe. In Ayoub, P. and Patternotte, D. (eds) *LGBT Activism and the Making of Europe: A Rainbow Europe*. Palgrave Macmillan. 73–93.

Cook, M. 2016. London, Aids and the 1980s. In Graham, K. and Avery, S. (eds) *Sex, Time and Place: Queer Histories of London C.1850 to the Present* . Bloomsbury Academic. 49–65.

Coyle, S. 2021. The queer, the cross and the closet: Religious exceptions in equality law as state-sponsored homophobia. *Laws*, 10(4), 83–100.

Crace, J. 2023. Rishi never said he would stop the boats – it was all that lectern's doing. *The Guardian*, 19 December. Available at: https://www.theguardian.com/politics/2023/dec/19/rish-never-said-he-would-stop-the-boats-it-was-all-that-lecterns-doing (accessed 10 October 2024).

Crawley, H. 2000. Gender, persecution and the concept of politics in the asylum determination process. *Forced Migration Review*, 9(1), 17–20.

Curry, T. 2018. Killing boogeymen: Phallicism and the misandric mischaracterizations of black males in theory. *Res Philosophica*, 95(2), 235–272.

Da Costa Santos, G.G. 2021. Anti-gender politics and the authoritarian turn in Brazil. *Brasiliana: Journal for Brazilian Studies*, 10(1), 96–125.

Danisi, C., Dustin, M., Ferreira, N. and Held, N. 2021. *Queering Asylum in Europe: Legal and Social Experiences of Seeking International Protection on Grounds of Sexual Orientation and Gender Identity*. Springer Nature.

Davies, H.C. and MacRae, S.E. 2023. An anatomy of the British war on woke. *Race & Class*, 65(2), 3–54.

Davis, A.J. and Kettrey, H.H. 2022. Clear and omnipresent danger: Digital age culture wars and reactions to drag queen story hour across diverse subreddit communities. *Social Currents*, 9(1), 25–44.

Davis, B. 2010. *Martin Heidegger: Key Concepts*. Routledge.

Dawson, J. and Gerber, P. 2017. Assessing the refugee claims of LGBTI people: Is the DSSH model useful for determining claims by women for asylum based on sexual orientation? *International Journal of Refugee Law*, 29(2), 292–322.

Dean, T. 2018. Foreword: I keep my treasure in my arse. In Meili, M., *Towards a Gay Communism: Elements of a Homosexual Critique*. Pluto Press. vi–xv.

De Hart, B. 2017. Sexuality, race and masculinity in Europe's refugee crisis. In Grütters, C., Mantu, S. and Minderhoud, P. (eds) *Migration on the Move: Essays on the Dynamics of Migration*. Brill Nijhoff.

D'Emilio, J. 2012. *Sexual Politics, Sexual Communities: The Making of a Homosexual Minority in the United States, 1940–1970*. University of Chicago Press.

De Noronha, L. 2018. The figure of the 'foreign criminal': Race, gender and the FNP. In Bhatia, M., Poynting, S. and Tufail, W. (eds) *Media, Crime and Racism*. Palgrave Macmillan. 337–358.

Derry, C. 2020. *Lesbianism and the Criminal Law: Three Centuries of Regulation in England and Wales*. Palgrave Macmillan.

Dershowitz, A.M. 2024. *War on Woke: Why the New Mccarthyism Is More Dangerous Than the Old*. Hot Books.

De Ruiter, A. 2023. To be or not to be human: Resolving the paradox of dehumanisation. *European Journal of Political Theory*, 22(1), 73–95.

Dhoest, A. 2019. Learning to be gay: LGBTQ forced migrant identities and narratives in Belgium. *Journal of Ethnic and Migration Studies*, 45(7), 1075–1089.

Diamond, L.M. 2000. Sexual identity, attractions, and behavior among young sexual-minority women over a 2-year period. *Developmental Psychology*, 36(2), 241–250.

Diamond, L.M. 2005. A new view of lesbian subtypes: Stable versus fluid identity trajectories over an 8-year period. *Psychology of Women Quarterly*, 29(2), 119–128.

Diamond, L. 2008. *Sexual Fluidity: Understanding Women's Love and Desire*. Harvard University Press.

Dickson-Swift, V., James, E.L., Kippen, S. and Liamputtong, P. 2007. Doing sensitive research: What challenges do qualitative researchers face? *Qualitative Research*, 7(3), 327–353.

Dodd, V., Quinn, B. and Mason, R. 2024. Former counter-terror chief accuses Farage of inciting Southport violence. *The Guardian*, 31 July. Available at: https://www.theguardian.com/uk-news/article/2024/jul/31/farage-accused-of-inciting-southport-violence-by-former-counter-terror-chief (accessed 18 October 2024).

Draz, M. 2017. Born this way? Time and the coloniality of gender. *JSP:Journal of Speculative Philosophy*, 31(3), 372–384.

Duggan, L. 2002. The new homonormativity: The sexual politics of neo-liberalism. In Castronovo, R. and Nelson, D. (eds) *Materializing Democracy: Towards a Revitalized Cultural Politics*. Duke University Press. 175–194.

Duggan, M. 2012. *Queering Conflict: Experiences of Homophobia in Northern Ireland*. Routledge.

Duong, H.T. 2017. Fourth generation NGOs: Communication strategies in social campaigning and resource mobilization. *Journal of Nonprofit & Public Sector Marketing*, 29(2), 119–147.

Dustin, M. and Ferreira, N. 2021. Improving SOGI asylum adjudication: Putting persecution ahead of identity. *Refugee Survey Quarterly*, 40(3), 315–347.

Dustin, M. and Held, N. 2021. 'They sent me to the mountain': The role space, religion and support groups play for LGBTIQ+ asylum claimants. In Mole, R.C. (ed) *Queer Migration and Asylum in Europe*. UCL Press. 184–215.

Egdell, V. and Dutton, M. 2017. Third sector independence: Relations with the state in an age of austerity. *Voluntary Sector Review*, 8(1), 25–40.

Ekman, M. 2022. The great replacement: Strategic mainstreaming of far-right conspiracy claims. *Convergence*, 28(4), 1127–1143.

Elam, G. and Fenton, K.A. 2003. Researching sensitive issues and ethnicity: Lessons from sexual health. *Ethnicity and Health*, 8(1), 15–27.

El-Enany, N. 2016. Aylan Kurdi: The human refugee. *Law and Critique*, 27, 13–15.

Elgot, J. 2024. Tories will allow bars on trans women, says Kemi Badenoch. *The Guardian*, 2 June. Available at: https://www.theguardian.com/society/article/2024/jun/02/tories-will-allow-bars-on-trans-women-says-kemi-badenoch (accessed 18 October 2024).

Elliards, X. 2024. Hundreds complain to BBC after English riot labelled 'pro-British'. *The National*, 16 August. Available at: https://www.thenational.scot/news/24522924.hundreds-complain-bbc-english-riot-lebelled-pro-british/ (accessed 17 October 2024).

Engelmann, L. 2016. Photographing AIDS: on capturing a disease in pictures of people with AIDS. *Bulletin of the History of Medicine*, 90(2), 250–278.

Epstein, S. 1988. Moral contagion and the medicalizing of gay identity: AIDS in historical perspective. *Research in Law, Deviance and Social Control*, 9, 3–36.

Fausto-Sterling, A. 2000. *Sexing the Body: Gender Politics and the Construction of Sexuality*. Basic Books.

Ferreira, N. 2022. Utterly unbelievable: The discourse of 'fake' SOGI asylum claims as a form of epistemic injustice. *International Journal of Refugee Law*, 34(3–4), 303–326.

Fetner, T. 2001. Working Anita Bryant: The impact of Christian anti-gay activism on lesbian and gay movement claims. *Social Problems*, 48(3), 411–428.

Filip-Crawford, G. and Neuberg, S. 2015. Homosexuality and pro-gay ideology as pathogens? Implications of a disease-spread lay model for understanding anti-gay behaviours. *Personality and Social Psychology*, 20(4), 332–364.

Findlay, A., Fyfe, N. and Stewart, E. 2007. Changing places: Voluntary sector work with refugees and asylum seekers in core and peripheral regions of the UK. *International Journal on Multicultural Societies*, 9(1), 54–74.

Fletcher, C. 2024. Heteronormative accommodations: Strategies of in/visibility for LGBTIQI+ people in asylum accommodation. *Journal of Immigration, Asylum and Nationality Law*, 38(1), 32–49.

Fobear, K. 2015. 'I thought we had no rights': Challenges in listening, storytelling, and representation of LGBT refugees. *Studies in Social Justice*, 9(1), 102–117.

Foss, R.J. 1994. The demise of the homosexual exclusion: New possibilities for gay and lesbian immigration. *Civil Liberties Law Review*, 29, 439–475.

Foucault, M. 1971. *The Archaeology of Knowledge and the Discourse on Language*. Pantheon Books.

Foucault, M. 1976. *The History of Sexuality Volume 1: The Will to Knowledge*. Translated by Hurley, R. Penguin.

Foucault, M. 1986. *The History of Sexuality: The Care of the Self*. Translated by Hurley, R. Pantheon Books.

Foucault, M. 1990. *The History of Sexuality: The Use of Pleasure*. Translated by Hurley, R. Vintage Books.

Foucault, M. 2000. Truth and juridical forms. In Faubion, J. (ed) *Foucault, Power*. New Press. 31–45.

Foucault, M. 2001. *The Order of Things: An Archaeology of the Human Sciences*. Routledge.

Foucault, M. 2019. *Discipline and Punish: The Birth of the Prison*. Translated by Alan Sheridan. Penguin Books.

Foucault, M. 2021. *The History of Sexuality: Confessions of the Flesh*. Edited by Gros, F. and translated by Hurley, R. Pantheon Books.

Freedom From Torture. 2019. Lessons not learned: The failures of asylum decision-making in the UK. *Freedom From Torture*. Available at: https://www.freedomfromtorture.org/sites/default/files/2019-09/FFT_LessonsNotLearned_Report_A4_FINAL_LOWRES_1.pdf (accessed 13 October 2024).

García Rodríguez, D. 2023. Critiquing trends and identifying gaps in the literature on LGBTQ refugees and asylum-seekers. *Refugee Survey Quarterly*, 42(4), 518–541.

Garland, D. 2022. What is penal populism? Public opinion, expert knowledge, and penal policy-formation in democratic societies. In Liebling, A., Shapland, J., Sparks, R. and Tankebe, J. (eds) *Crime, Justice and Social Order: Essays in Honour of A.E. Bottoms*. Oxford University Press. 249–272.

Gary, E. 2004. Judging facts: Managing expert knowledges in legal decision-making. In Edmond, G. (ed) *Expertise in Regulation and Law*. Routledge.

Gentleman, A. 2017. 'I can't eat or sleep': The woman threatened with deportation after 50 years in Britain. *The Guardian*, 28 November. Available at: https://www.theguardian.com/uk-news/2017/nov/28/i-cant-eat-or-sleep-the-grandmother-threatened-with-deportation-after-50-years-in-britain (accessed 10 October 2024).

Gentleman, A. 2020. *The Windrush Betrayal: Exposing the Hostile Environment*. Guardian Faber Publishing.

Giametta, C. 2017. *The Sexual Politics of Asylum: Sexual Orientation and Gender Identity in the UK Asylum System*. Routledge.

Giametta, C. 2020. New asylum protection categories and elusive filtering devices: The case of 'queer asylum'in France and the UK. *Journal of Ethnic and Migration Studies*, 46(1), 142–157.

Giametta, C. and Havkin, S. 2021. Mapping homo/transphobia: The valorization of the lgbt protection category in the refugee-granting system. *ACME: An International Journal for Critical Geographies*, 20(1), 99–119.

Gibson, S. 2013. Testimony in a culture of disbelief: Asylum hearings and the impossibility of bearing witness. *Journal for Cultural Research*, 17(1), 1–20.

Gleeson, K. 2007. Discipline, punishment and the homosexual in law. *Liverpool Law Review*, 28, 327–347.

Glorius, B., Doomernik, J. and Darling, J. 2016. Asylum in austere times: Instability, privatization and experimentation within the UK asylum dispersal system. *Journal of Refugee Studies*, 29(4), 483–505.

Goodfellow, M. 2019. *Hostile Environment: How Immigrants Became Scapegoats*. Verso.

Gordon, C. 2020. Introduction. In Faubion, J. (ed) *Michel Foucault: Power. Essential Works of Foucault 1954–1984: Volume Three*. Penguin Books. xi–xiii.

Grabham, E. 2008. Intersectionality: Traumatic impressions. In Grabham, E., Cooper, D., Krishnadas, J. and Herman, D. (eds) *Intersectionality and Beyond: Law, Power and the Politics of Location*. Routledge. 183–203.

Graffin, N. 2019. The emotional impacts of working as an asylum lawyer. *Refugee Survey Quarterly*, 38(1), 30–54.

Gramsci, A. 1998. *Selections from the Prison Notebook*. Lawrence & Wishart.

Grierson, J., Bonomolo, A. and Travis, A. 2015. Migrant deaths: Funerals held as EU leaders meet for crisis summit. *The Guardian*, 23 April. Available at: https://www.theguardian.com/world/2015/apr/23/migrant-deaths-funerals-held-after-mediterranean-disaster (accessed 18 May 2025).

Griffiths, M. 2017. Foreign, criminal: A doubly damned modern British folk-devil. *Citizenship Studies*, 21(5), 527–546.

Griffiths, M. and Yeo, C. 2021. The UK's hostile environment: Deputising immigration control. *Critical Social Policy*, 41(4), 521–544.

Gupta, K. and Pearce, R. 2024. From conflict to collaboration: Solidarity and compromise in trans and women's movements. In Connaughton, S. and Pukallus, S. (eds) *The Routledge Handbook of Conflict and Peace Communication*. Routledge. Chapter 18.

Gwenffrewi, G. 2022. JK Rowling and the echo chamber of secrets. *Transgender Studies Quarterly*, 9(3), 507–516.

Hambly, J. and Gill, N. 2020. Law and speed: Asylum appeals and the techniques and consequences of legal quickening. *Journal of Law and Society*, 47(1), 3–28.

Halberstam, J. 1998. *Female Masculinity*. Duke University Press.

Hall, S. 1995. Some 'politically incorrect' pathways through PC. In Dunant, S. (ed) *The War of Words: Politically Correct Debate*. Virago. 164–185.

Hardy, C. 2003. Refugee determination: Power and resistance in systems of Foucauldian power. *Administration & Society*, 35(4), 462–488.

Hart, H. 1961. *The Concept of Law*. Oxford University Press.

Hassan, L. 2000. Deterrence measures and the preservation of asylum in the United Kingdom and United States. *Journal of Refugee Studies*, 13(2), 184–204.

Headworth, S. 2020. The power of second-order legal consciousness: Authorities' perceptions of 'street policy' and welfare fraud enforcement. *Law & Society Review*, 54(2), 320–353.

Held, N. 2015. Comfortable and safe spaces? Gender, sexuality and 'race' in night-time leisure spaces. *Emotion, Space and Society*, 14, 33–42.

Held, N. 2017. 'They look at you like an insect that wants to be squashed': An ethnographic account of the racialized sexual spaces of Manchester's Gay Village. *Sexualities*, 20(5–6), 535–557.

Held, N. 2023. 'As queer refugees, we are out of category, we do not belong to one, or the other': LGBTIQ+ refugees' experiences in 'ambivalent' queer spaces. *Ethnic and Racial Studies*, 46(9), 1898–1918.

Herlihy, J., Scragg, P. and Turner, S. 2002. Discrepancies in autobiographical memories: Implications for the assessment of asylum seekers: Repeated interviews study. *BMJ*, 324(7333), 324–327.

Hilton-Morrow, W. and Battles, K. 2015. *Sexual Identities and the Media: An Introduction*. Routledge.

Hooke, A.E. 1987. II. The order of others: Is Foucault's antihumanism against human action? *Political Theory*, 15(1), 38–60.

Hopgood, S. 2000. Reading the small print in global civil society: The inexorable hegemony of the liberal self. *Millennium*, 29(1), 1–25.

Hubbard, P. 2022. Suella Braverman's talk of a refugee 'invasion' is a dangerous political gambit gone wrong. *The Conversation*, 22 November. Available at: https://theconversation.com/suella-bravermans-talk-of-a-refugee-invasion-is-a-dangerous-political-gambit-gone-wrong-193638 (accessed 18 October 2024).

Hubbard, P., Gorman-Murray, A. and Nash, C. 2015. Cities and sexualities. In DeLamater, J. and Plante, R. (eds) *Handbook of the Sociology of Sexualities*. Springer. 287–305.

Hunter, M.A. 2010. All the gays are White and all the Blacks are straight: Black gay men, identity, and community. *Sexuality Research and Social Policy*, 7, 81–92.

IPPR. 2024. Home Office 'chaos' leaves up to 55,500 asylum seekers stuck in perma-backlog. *IPPR*, 28 February. Available at: https://www.ippr.org/media-office/home-office-chaos-leaves-up-to-55-500-asylum-seekers-stuck-in-perma-backlog (accessed 18 October 2024).

Jansen, S. 2019. 'Pride or shame?': Assessing LGBTI asylum applications in the Netherlands following the XYZ and ABC judgements. *COC Netherlands*. Available at: https://www.sogica.org/wp-content/uploads/2019/02/Jansen_Pride-or-Shame-LGBTI-asylum-in-the-Netherlands_2019.pdf (accessed 15 October 2024).

Johnston, T.R. 2015. Beyond 'Born this Way'. *PhiloSOPHIA*, 5(1), 140–144.

Jones, E. and Graffin, N. 2020. *Mental Health and Wellbeing in the Legal Profession*. Policy Press.

Jubany, O. 2011. Constructing truths in a culture of disbelief: Understanding asylum screening from within. *International Sociology*, 26(1), 74–94.

Juss, S. 2015. Sexual orientation and the sexualisation of refugee law. *International Journal on Minority and Group Rights*, 22(1), 128–153.

Karban, K. and Sirriyeh, A. 2015. LGBT asylum seekers and health inequalities in the UK. In Fish, J. and Karban, K. (eds) *Lesbian, Gay, Bisexual and Trans Health Inequalities*. Policy Press. 187–204.

Kassisieh, G. 2008. From lives of fear to lives of freedom: A review of Australian refugee decisions on the basis of sexual orientation. *Gay & Lesbian Rights Lobby*.

Keate, N. 2024. Farage says slow police response stoke UK's far-right riots. *Politico*, 6 August. Available at: https://www.politico.eu/article/nigel-farage-keir-starmer-uk-riots-far-right-killing-southport-police-socials/ (accessed 18 May 2025).

Kirby, P. 2024. French left celebrates as far right faces surprise defeat. *BBC News*, 7 July. Available at: https://www.bbc.co.uk/news/articles/c0478d1zrldo (accessed 12 April 2025).

Kovats, E. 2017. The emergence of powerful anti-gender movements in Europe and the criss of liberal democracy. In Kottig, M., Bitzan, R. and Peto, A. (eds) *Gender and Far Right Politics in Europe*. Springer International. 175–189.

Kovats, E. and Peto, A. 2017. Anti-gender discourse in Hungary: A discourse without a movement. In Patternote, D. and Kuhar, A. (eds) *Anti Gender-Campaigns in Europe: Mobilizing Against Equality*. Rowman & Littlefield. 117–129.

Koven, M. 2014. Interviewing: Practice, ideology, genre, and intertextuality. *Annual Review of Anthropology*, 43(1), 499–520.

Lalor, K. and Browne, K. 2018. Here versus there: Creating British sexual politics elsewhere. *Feminist Legal Studies*, 26(2), 205–213.

Lamble, S. 2023. Sexual peril and dangerous others: The moral economies of the trans prisoner policy debates in England and Wales. *Sexualities*, 28(2), 492–513.

Lamble, S. 2024. Confronting complex alliances: Situating Britain's gender critical politics within the wider transnational anti-gender movement. *Journal of Lesbian Studies*, 28(3), 504–517.

Latham, R. 1995. Liberalism's order/liberalism's other: A genealogy of threat. *Alternatives*, 20(1), 111–146.

LaViolette, N. 2013. Overcoming problems with sexual minority refugee claims: Is LGBT cultural competency training the solution? In Spijkerboer, T. (ed) *Fleeing Homophobia*. Routledge.

Law Commission. 2020. Simplification of the immigration rules. Law Com No 388: House of Commons Library.

Law Society. 2024. Riots and attacks on lawyers. *The Law Society*, 5 August. Available at: https://www.lawsociety.org.uk/contact-or-visit-us/press-office/press-releases/riots-and-attacks-on-lawyers (accessed 20 May 2025).

Lenegan, S. 2022. The reality of Priti Patel's 'bespoke' humanitarian routes. Free Movement, 22 March. Available at: https://freemovement.org.uk/the-reality-of-priti-patels-bespoke-humanitarian-routes/ (accessed 9 February 2024).

Lewis, R.A. 2014. 'Gay? Prove it': The politics of queer anti-deportation activism. *Sexualities*, 17(8), 958–975.

Linders, N. 2023. Mainstreaming the great replacement: The role of centrist discourses in the mainstreaming of a far-right conspiracy theory. In Bracke, S. and Aguilar, L.M.H. (eds) *The Politics of Replacement: Demographic Fears, Conspiracy Theories and Race Wars* Routledge. 162–179.

Lipsky, M. 2010. *Street-level Bureaucracy: Dilemmas of the Individual in Public Service*. Russell Sage Foundation.

Loizidou, E. 2007. *Judith Butler: Ethnics, Law, Politics*. Routledge.

Lopes Heimer, R.D.V. 2020. Homonationalist/Orientalist negotiations: The UK approach to queer asylum claims. *Sexuality & Culture*, 24(1), 174–196.

Lovelock, M. 2018. Sex, death and austerity: Resurgent homophobia in the British tabloid press. *Critical Studies in Media Communication*, 35(3), 225–239.

Luibhéid, E. 2023. Sexual citizenship, pride parades, and queer migrant im/mobilities. *Ethnic and Racial Studies*, 46(9), 1877–1897.

Luibheid, L. 2002. *Entry Denied: Controlling Sexuality at the Border*. University of Minnesota Press.

Makwana, A.P., Dhont, K., De keersmaecker, J., Akhlaghi-Ghaffarokh, P., Masure, M. and Roets, A. 2018. The motivated cognitive basis of transphobia: The roles of right-wing ideologies and gender role beliefs. *Sex Roles*, 79, 206–217.

Malterud, K., Siersma, V.D. and Guassora, A.D. 2016. Sample size in qualitative interview studies: Guided by information power. *Qualitative Health Research*, 26(13), 1753–1760.

Mant, J., Newman, D. and Cooke, E. 2024. Lived realities of legal aid: Austerity, the pandemic and beyond. *International Journal of the Legal Profession*, 1–22.

Mars-Jones, A. 2017. Thc Wildeblood scandal: The trail that rocked 1950s Britain- and changed gay rights *The Guardian*, 14 July. Available at: https://www.theguardian.com/books/2017/jul/14/against-the-law-the-wildeblood-scandal-the-case-that-rocked-1950s-britain-and-changed-gay-rights#:~:text=The%20Wildeblood%20case%20was%20less,imprisonment%20in%201895%20was%20then (accessed 3 May 2025).

Massad, J. 2002. The Gay International and the arab world. *Public Culture*, 14(2), 361–385.

Mason, R. 2023. 'An activist blob': Tory Party attacks on lawyers a timeline. *The Guardian*, 16 August. Available at: https://www.theguardian.com/politics/2023/aug/16/tory-party-criticisms-legal-professionals-timeline (accessed 10 October 2024).

Matthews, J. 2002. An ambiguous juncture: Racism and the formation of Asian femininity. *Australian Feminist Studies*, 17(38), 207–219.

Mayblin, L. 2016. Complexity reduction and policy consensus: Asylum seekers, the right to work, and the 'pull factor' thesis in the UK context. *The British Journal of Politics and International Relations*, 18(4), 812–828.

Mayblin, L. 2019. Imagining asylum, governing asylum seekers: Complexity reduction and policy making in the UK Home Office. *Migration Studies*, 7(1), 1–20.

Mayblin, L. and James, P. 2019. Asylum and refugee support in the UK: Civil society filling the gaps? *Journal of Ethnic and Migration Studies*, 45(3), 375–394.

McCloskey, J. 2020. Effective access to justice: Myth or reality? *Northern Ireland Legal Quarterly*, 71(1), 73–80.

McGlynn, N. 2018. Slippery geographies of the urban and the rural: Public sector LGBT equalities work in the shadow of the 'Gay Capital'. *Journal of Rural Studies*, 57, 65–77.

McGuirk, S. 2018. (In) credible subjects: NGOs, attorneys, and permissible LGBT asylum seeker identities. *PoLAR: Political and Legal Anthropology Review*, 41(S1), 4–18.

McLean, C. 2021. The growth of the anti-transgender movement in the United Kingdom: The silent radicalization of the British electorate. *International Journal of Sociology*, 51(6), 473–482.

Mhaoileoin, N. 2019. The ironic gay spectator: The impacts of centring western subjects in international LGBT rights campaigns. *Sexualities*, 22(1–2), 148–164.

Mignolo, W.D. 2009. Who speaks for the 'human' in human rights? *Hispanic Issues Online*, 5(1), 7–25.

Millbank, J. 2009. 'The ring of truth': A case study of credibility assessment in particular social group refugee determinations. *International Journal of Refugee Law*, 21(1), 1–33.

Millbank, J. 2010. From discretion to disbelief: Recent trends in refugee determinations on the basis of sexual orientation in Australia and the United Kingdom. In Chan, P. (ed) *Protection of Sexual Minorities Since Stonewall: Progress and Stalemate in Developed and Developing Countries*. Routledge. 257–281.

Morgan, G., Melluish, S. and Welham, A. 2017. Exploring the relationship between postmigratory stressors and mental health for asylum seekers and refused asylum seekers in the UK. *Transcultural Psychiatry*, 54(5–6), 653–674.

Morgensen, S.L. 2012. Theorising gender, sexuality and settler colonialism: An introduction. *Settler Colonial Studies*, 2(2), 2–22.

Morina, N., Akhtar, A., Barth, J. and Schnyder, U. 2018. Psychiatric disorders in refugees and internally displaced persons after forced displacement: A systematic review. *Frontiers in Psychiatry*, 9, 433–448.

Morris, M. 2018. 'Gay capital' in gay student friendship networks: An intersectional analysis of class, masculinity, and decreased homophobia. *Journal of Social and Personal Relationships*, 35(9), 1183–1204.

Morris, M. 2021. The politics of testing positive: An autoethnography of media (mis) representations at the 'start' and 'end' of different pandemics. *Culture, Health & Sexuality*, 23(11), 1485–1499.

Mowlabocus, S. 2010. *Gaydar Culture, Gay Men, Technology and Embodiment in the Digital Age*. Routledge.

Mulé, N.J. 2022. Mental health issues and needs of LGBTQ+ asylum seekers, refugee claimants and refugees in Toronto, Canada. *Psychology & Sexuality*, 13(5), 1168–1178.

Murray, D.A. 2016. Queer forms: Producing documentation in sexual orientation refugee cases. *Anthropological Quarterly*, 89(2), 465–484.

Nasser-Eddin, N., Abu-Assab, N. and Greatrick, A. 2018. Reconceptualising and contextualising sexual rights in the MENA region: Beyond LGBTQI categories. *Gender & Development*, 26(1), 173–189.

Nelken, D. 2006. Getting at law's boundaries. *Social & Legal Studies*, 15(4), 598–604.

Newman, D. and Robins, J. 2021. 'The demise of legal aid'? Access to justice and social welfare law after austerity. *Amicus Curiae*, 3(2), 418–441.

Niklasson, B., Christiansen, P.M. and Öhberg, P. 2020. Speaking truth to power: Political advisers' and civil servants' responses to perceived harmful policy proposals. *Journal of Public Policy*, 40(3), 492–512.

Nilsson, E. 2014. The 'refugee' and the 'nexus' requirement: The relation between subject and persecution in the United Nations Refugee Convention. *Women's Studies International Forum*, 46, 123–132.

Nussbaum, M. 1999. The professor of parody: The hip defeatism of Judith Butler. *The New Republic*, 22 February. Available at: https://newrepublic.com/article/150687/professor-parody (accessed 3 May 2025).

O'Leary, R. 2009. Christians and gays in Northern Ireland: How the ethno-religious context has shaped Christian anti-gay and pro-gay activism. In Hunt, S. (ed) *Contemporary Christianity and LGBT Sexualities*. Routledge. 123–139.

O'Murray, S. and Roscoe, W. 1998. Diversity and identity: The challenge of African homosexaulities. In O'Murray, S. and Roscoe, W. (eds) *Boy-Wives and Female Husbands: Studies of African Homosexualities*. Macmillan. 267–279.

Oppenheim, M. 2024. Tory peer accepts party's stop the boats slogan fuelled far right riots. *The Independent*, 14 September. Available at: https://www.independent.co.uk/news/uk/politics/timothy-kirkhope-sunak-conservative-stop-the-boats-b2612780.html (accessed 17 October 2024).

Parker, J. 2025. AfD embraces mass deportation of migrants as German election nears. *BBC News*, 13 January. Available at: https://www.bbc.co.uk/news/articles/c62q937y029o (accessed 12 April 2025).

Perry, S. 2022. Oxford library forced to limit access during drag event protest. *Oxford Mail*, 23 August. Available at: https://www.oxfordmail.co.uk/news/20714533.oxford-library-forced-limit-access-drag-event-protest/ (accessed 18 October 2024).

Pickett, B.L. 2000. Foucaultian rights? *The Social Science Journal*, 37(3), 403–421.

Pidd, H. 2019. Home Office gives man asylum after accepting people can be gay and single. *The Guardian*, 23 December. Available at: https://www.theguardian.com/uk-news/2019/dec/23/home-office-gives-man-asylum-after-accepting-people-can-be-gay-and-single#:~:text=A%20man%20accused%20of%20pretending,outdated%20stereotypes%20about%20gay%20people (accessed 13 April 2024).

Powell, A. 2020. Normative understandings: Sexual identity, stereotypes, and asylum seeking. In Ashford, C. and Maine, A. (eds) *Research Handbook on Gender, Sexuality and the Law*. Edward Elgar.

Powell, A. 2021a. 'Sexuality' through the kaleidoscope: Sexual orientation, identity, and behaviour in asylum claims in the United Kingdom. *Laws*, 10(4), 90–110.

Powell, A. 2021b. Queering refugee law: A study of sexual diversity in asylum policy and practice in the United Kingdom. Doctoral dissertation, City, University of London.

Powell, A. 2023a. Administrative violence: First-instance decision making in sexual diversity asylum claims. In Wheatle, S. and O'Loughlin, E. (eds) *Diverse Voices in Public Law*. Bristol University Press. 223–243.

Powell, A. 2023b. Developed: Administrative violence in sexual diversity asylum claims at the UK Home Office. In Smith, A. and Dalton, D. (eds) *Gender, Sexuality and the UN's SDGs: A Multidisciplinary Approach*. Palgrave Macmillan. 41–63.

Powell, A. 2024a. The place where only gays go: Constructions of queer space in the narratives of sexually diverse refugees. *Journal of Place Management and Development*, 17(2), 171–185.

Powell, A. 2024b. The UK's new plan for immigration: Normativity, crisis, and a 'bespoke' rationale for humanitarian/refugee protection. *Journal of Immigration, Asylum and Nationality Law*, 38(1), 66–82.

Powell, A. 2025. HJ (Iran) & HT (Cameroon) (United Kingdom): Queer reflections on a landmark case on the rights of LGBT+ refugees. In Ferreira, N., Moscati, M. and Raj, S. (eds) *Queer Judgments*. Counterpress. 477–495.

Powell, A. and Rifath, R. 2023. Sexual diversity and the Nationality and Borders Act 2022. *Legal Studies*, 43(4), 757–761.

Pruitt, L.J. 2019. Closed due to 'flooding'? UK media representations of refugees and migrants in 2015–2016: Creating a crisis of borders. *The British Journal of Politics and International Relations*, 21(2), 383–402.

Puar, J.K. 2006. Mapping US homonormativities. *Gender, Place & Culture*, 13(1), 67–88.

Puar, J. 2012. *Terrorist Assemblages: Homonationalism in Queer Times*. Duke University Press.

Puar, J. 2013. Rethinking homonationalism. *International Journal of Middle East Studies*, 45(2), 336–339.

Puddifoot, K. and Sandelind, C. 2024. Knowing your past: Trauma, stress, and mnemonic epistemic injustice. *Journal of Social Philosophy*, 56(2) 261–281.

Pullen, C. and Franklin, I. 2024. 'Were in this together': NGO advocacy and LGBTQ+ asylum claimants: Intimate/care citizenship as co-presence and imagined equality. *Sexualities*, 28(4), 1586–1607.

Quinn, B. 2024. Misinformation about Southport attack suspects spreads on social media. *The Guardian*, 30 July. Available at: https://www.theguardian.com/uk-news/article/2024/jul/30/misinformation-southport-attack-suspect-social-media-conspiracy-theories (acccessed 17 October 2024).

Rainbow Migration. 2013. *Missing the Mark: Decision Making on Lesbian, Gay (Bisexual, Trans and Intersex) Asylum Claims*. Unison.

Rainbow Migration. 2018. *Still Falling Short: The Standard of Home Office Decision-Making in Asylum Claims Based on Sexual Orientation and Gender Identity*. Available at: https://uklgig.org.uk/?page_id=1225 (accessed 3 May 2025).

Rainbow Migration. 2022. I fled Rwanda due to homophobia – I fear for gay refugees being sent there. *Rainbow Migration*, 19 July. Available at: https://www.rainbowmigration.org.uk/news/i-fled-rwanda-due-to-homophobia-i-fear-for-gay-refugees-being-sent-there/ (accessed 18 October 2024).

Raj, S. 2017. A/effective adjudications: Queer refugees and the law. *Journal of Intercultural Studies*, 38(4), 453–468.

Rancière, J. 2004. Who is the subject of the rights of man? *South Atlantic Quarterly*, 103(2/3), 297–310.

Rao, R. 2015. Re-membering Mwanga: Same-sex intimacy, memory and belonging in postcolonial Uganda. *Journal of Eastern African Studies*, 9(1), 1–19.

Refugee Council. 2024. Top facts from the latest statistics on refugees and people seeking asylum. *Refugee Council*. Available at: https://www.refugeecouncil.org.uk/information/refugee-asylum-facts/top-10-facts-about-refugees-and-people-seeking-asylum/#:~:text=5.,from%2029%25%20in%202010 (accessed 17 October 2024).

Rehaag, S. 2008. Patrolling the borders of sexual orientation: Bisexual refugee claims in Canada. *McGill LJ*, 53, 59–101.

Right to Remain. 2023. Group 2 refugee classification to be scrapped. *Right to Remain*, 9 June. Available at: https://righttoremain.org.uk/group-2-refugee-classification-to-be- (accessed 11 May 2025).

Right to Remain. 2024. Legal support (taking action without giving legal advice). *Right to Remain*, 20 August. Available at: https://righttoremain.org.uk/toolkit/legal-support/ (accessed 17 October 2024).

Roulston, K. and Choi, M. 2018. Qualitative interviews. In Flick, U. (ed) *The SAGE Handbook of Qualitative Data Collection*. SAGE.

Royston, S.P. 2010. Third sector campaigning strategies: A study of third sector organisations campaigning for the reform of UK child poverty policy. Doctoral dissertation, University of York.

Rubin, G. 2006. Thinking sex: Notes for a radical theory of the politics of sexuality. In Parker, R. and Aggleton, P. (eds). Palgrave Macmillan. 143–179.

Rubin, G. and Butler, J. 2012. Sexual traffic: Interview with Gayle Rubin by Judith Butler. In Rubin, G. (ed) *Deviations: A Gayle Rubin Reader*. Duke University Press. 276–310.

Ruez, D. 2017. 'I never felt targeted as an Asian … until I went to a gay pub': Sexual racism and the aesthetic geographies of the bad encounter. *Environment and Planning A*, 49(4), 83–910.

Saenz Perez, C. 2023. The securitization of asylum: A review of UK asylum laws post-Brexit. *International Journal of Refugee Law*, 35(3), 304–321.

Salamanca, O.J. 2016. Assembling the fabric of life: When settler colonialism becomes development. *Journal of Palestine Studies*, 45(4), 64–80.

Sapountzis, A., Figgou, L. and Michos, I. 2023. Conspiracy theories in online deliberation on gender identity legislation: Dilemmas of prejudice and political partisanship and implications for LGBTQI+ claims. *Feminism & Psychology*, 33(2), 197–214.

Sarat, A. 1990. 'The law is all over': Power, resistance and the legal consciousness of the welfare poor. *Journal of Law and the Humanities*, 2, 343–379.

Sarat, A. 2006. 'The law is all over': Power, resistance and the legal consciousness of the welfare poor. In Ewick, P. (ed) *Consciousness and Ideology*. Routledge. 347–385.

Savin-Williams, R. 2005. *The New Gay Teenager*. Harvard University Press.

Savin-Williams, R.C. 2006. Who's gay? Does it matter? *Current Directions in Psychological Science*, 15(1), 40–44.

Savin-Williams, R. 2017. *Mostly Straight: Sexual Fluidity Among Men*. Harvard University Press.

Schmitt, C. 2008. *The Concept of the Political*. Translated by Schwab, G. University of Chicago Press.

Schotten, C.H. 2016. Homonationalism: From critique to diagnosis, or, we are all homonational now. *International Feminist Journal of Politics*, 18(3), 351–370.

Schuster, L. 2020. Fatal flaws in the UK asylum decision-making system: An analysis of Home Office refusal letters. *Journal of Ethnic and Migration Studies*, 46(7), 1371–1387.

Scott, J. 2023. Net migration: The history of turmoil within the Tories since Cameron's 'tens of thousands' pledge. *Sky News*, 25 May. Available at: https://news.sky.com/story/net-migration-the-history-of-turmoil-within-the-tories-since-camerons-tens-of-thousands-pledge-12882189 (accessed 23 October 2024).

Scott, J.W. 2020. Hungarian border politics as an anti-politics of the European Union. *Geopolitics*, 25(3), 658–677.

Sedgwick, E.K. 2008. *Epistemology of the Closet*. University of California Press.

Sen, P., Crowley, G., Arnell, P., Katona, C., Pillay, M., Waterman, L.Z., et al. 2022. The UK's exportation of asylum obligations to Rwanda: A challenge to mental health, ethics and the law. *Medicine, Science and the Law*, 62(3), 165–167.

Shaw, A. and Verghese, N. 2022. LGBTQI+ refugees and asylum seekers. *Williams Institute*, June. Available at: https://williamsinstitute.law.ucla.edu/publications/lgbtqi-refugees-asylum-seekers/

Shidlo, A. and Ahola, J. 2013. Mental health challenges of LGBT forced migrants. *Forced Migration Review*, 42, 9–11.

Sifaki, A., Quinan, C.L. and Lončarević, K. (eds). 2022. *Homonationalism, Femonationalism and Ablenationalism: Critical Pedagogies Contextualised.* Routledge.

Sigona, N. and Benson, M. 2024. Bespoke humanitarian visa schemes like those for Ukraine and Hong Kong can't replace the asylum system. *The Conversation*, 30 January. Available at: https://theconversation.com/bespoke-humanitarian-visa-schemes-like-those-for-ukraine-and-hong-kong-cant-replace-the-asylum-system-222086 (accessed 9 February 2024).

Silbey, S.S. 2005. After legal consciousness. *Annual Review of Law and Social Science*, 1(1), 323–368.

Simpson, M. and McKee, R. 2024. Violence has left us living in state of fear. *BBC News*, 7 August. Available at: https://www.bbc.co.uk/news/articles/cdjwexmpxn1o (accessed 17 October 2024).

Sinmaz, E. 2024. Rioters try to torch Rotherham asylum seeker hotel amid far-right violence. *The Guardian*, 4 August. Available at: https://www.theguardian.com/uk-news/article/2024/aug/04/rioters-try-to-torch-rotherham-asylum-seeker-hotel-amid-far-right-violence (accessed 11 May 2025).

Slack, J. 2016. Enemies of the people: Fury over 'out of touch' judges who have 'declared war on democracy' by defying 17.4m Brexit voters and who could triger constitutional crisis. *Daily Mail*, 3 November. Available at: https://www.dailymail.co.uk/news/article-3903436/Enemies-people-Fury-touch-judges-defied-17-4m-Brexit-voters-trigger-constitutional-crisis.html (accessed 17 October 2024).

Smith, E. 2023. From the Aliens Act to the hostile environment. In Le Louvier, K. and Hough, K. (eds) *UK Borderscapes: Sites of Enforcement and Resistance*. Routledge. 21–37.

Snyder, S. 2011. Un/settling angels: Faith-based organizations and asylum-seeking in the UK. *Journal of Refugee Studies*, 24(3), 565–585.

Sommerlad, H. and Sanderson, P. 2013. Social justice on the margins: The future of the not for profit sector as providers of legal advice in England and Wales. *Journal of Social Welfare and Family Law*, 35(3), 305–327.

Sontag, S. 1989. *Aids and Its Metaphors*. Farrar Straus and Giroux.

Spade, D. 2015. *Normal Life: Administrative Violence, Critical Trans Politics, and the Limits of Law*. Duke University Press.

Sparke, M. 2016. Health and the embodiment of neoliberalism: Pathologies of political economy from climate change and austerity to personal responsibility. In Springer, S., Birch, K. and MacLeavy, J. (eds) *Handbook of Neoliberalism*. Routledge. 237–252.

Spijkerboer, T. 2013. Sexual identity, normativity and asylum. In Spijkerboer, T. (ed) *Fleeing Homophobia: Sexual Orientation, Gender, Identity and Asylum*. Routledge. 253–270.

Spijkerboer, T. 2018. Gender, sexuality, asylum and European human rights. *Law and Critique*, 29(2), 221–239.

Spivak, G. 1985. Criticism, feminism and the institution. *Thesis Eleven*, 10–11(1), 175–187.

Spivak, G. 2004. *Can the Subaltern Speak?* Routledge.

Stone, J. 2015. Katie Hopkins' migrant 'cockroaches' column resembles pro-genocide propaganda, says the UN. *The Independent*, 24 April. Available at: https://www.independent.co.uk/news/uk/politics/katie-hopkins-migrant-cockroaches-column-resembles-progenocide-propaganda-says-the-un-10201959.html (accessed 18 October 2024).

Stychin, C.F. 2003. Same-sex sexualities and the globalization of human rights discourse. *McGill LJ*, 49, 951–268.

Stychin, C.F. 2005. Being gay. *Government & Opposition*, 40(1), 90–109.

Sullivan, A. 1996. *Virtually Normal: An Argument About Homosexuality*. Picador.

Sweeney, J.A. 2009. Credibility, proof and refugee law. *International Journal of Refugee Law*, 21(4), 700–726.

Syal, R. 2023. Target of Tory 'lefty lawyer' dossier forced to review security after email. *The Guardian*, 8 August. Available at: https://www.theguardian.com/politics/2023/aug/08/target-of-tory-lefty-lawyer-dossier-forced-to-review-security-after-email (accessed 11 May 2025).

Tamale, S. 2011. Researching and theorising sexualities. In Tamale, S. (ed) *African Sexualities: A Reader*. Pambuzuka Press.

Tamanaha, B.Z. 2008. Understanding legal realism. *Texas Law Review*, 87, 731.

Tatchell, P. 2017. 1967, the myth of gay decriminalisation: Anti-gay laws remained on the statute book, arrests rocketed. *Peter Tatchell Foundation*, 23 May. Available at: https://www.petertatchellfoundation.org/1967-the-myth-of-gay-decriminalisation/ (accessed 13 October 2024).

Taylor, C. 2021. Metaphors of migration over time. *Discourse & Society*, 32(4), 463–481.

Taylor, D. 2024. Home Office will decide asylum claims of thousands stuck in Rwanda scheme limbo. *The Guardian*, 19 July. Available at: https://www.theguardian.com/uk-news/article/2024/jul/19/home-office-will-decide-asylum-claims-of-thousands-stuck-in-rwanda-scheme-limbo (accessed 18 May 2025).

Terry, V.L. 2017. Organisational responses in challenging times: A case study of asylum seeker and refugee third sector organisations. Doctoral dissertation, University of Birmingham.

Thurlow, C. 2024. From TERF to gender critical: A telling genealogy? *Sexualities*, 27(4), 962–978.

Tomlinson, J. 2022. Bureaucratic warfare: Administrative justice and the crisis of the 'new bespokism'. *Journal of Immigration, Asylum and Nationality Law*, 36(3), 178–201.

Topel, K.D. 2016. So, what should I ask him to prove that he's gay: How sincerity, and not stereotype, should dictate the outcome of an LGB asylum claim in the United States. *Iowa Law Review*, 102(2), 2357–2384.

Toth, A. 2024. Revealed: Inside the far-right Telegraph messaging channels where UK rioters organise. *The Independent*, 12 August. Available at: https://www.independent.co.uk/news/uk/home-news/riots-uk-far-right-telegram-app-terrorgram-b2592513.html (accessed 17 October 2024).

Townsend, M. 2023. How the 'small boats week' unravelled. *The Observer*, 13 August. Available at: https://www.theguardian.com/uk-news/2023/aug/13/how-the-small-boats-week-unravelled (accessed 10 October 2024).

Tschantret, J. 2018. Cleansing the caliphate: Insurgent violence against sexual minorities. *International Studies Quarterly*, 62(2), 260–273.

Turnbull, S. 2016. 'Stuck in the middle': Waiting and uncertainty in immigration detention. *Time & Society*, 25(1), 61–79.

Tushnet, M. 1990. Critical legal studies: A political history. *Yale Law Journal*, 100, 1515—1544.

Tushnet, M. 1992. Political correctness, the law, and the legal academy. *Yale Journal of Law and the Humanities*, 4, 127–164.

Valentine, G. 1997. (Hetero)sexing space: Lesbian perceptions and experiences of everyday spaces. In McDowell, L. and Sharp, J. (eds) *Space, Gender, Knowledge: Feminist Readings*. Routledge. 284–300.

Vogler, S. 2016. Legally queer: The construction of sexuality in LGBQ asylum claims. *Law & Society Review*, 50(4), 856–889.

Walker, A. 2023. Transphobic discourse and moral panic convergence: A content analysis of my hate mail. *Criminology*, 61(4), 994–1021.

Walker, P. 2024. Sunak pressures Lords to pass Rwanda Bill and denies Tory split on issue. *The Guardian*, 18 January. Available at: https://www.theguardian.com/uk-news/2024/jan/18/rishi-sunak-rwanda-bill-tory-fractures-house-of-lords (accessed 16 June 2024).

Walsh, B. 2015. Alan Kurdi's story: Behind the most heart-breaking photo. *Time Magazine*, 29 December. Available at: https://time.com/4162306/alan-kurdi-syria-drowned-boy-refugee-crisis/ (accessed 19 October 2024).

Walsh, P. and Sumption, M. 2024. UK policies to deter people from claiming asylum. *The Migration Observatory at the University of Oxford*, 23 January. Available at: https://migrationobservatory.ox.ac.uk/resources/commentaries/uk-policies-to-deter-people-from-claiming-asylum/#:~:text=2024 The%20key%20provisions%20designed%20to,any%20other%20safe%20third%20country (accessed 18 October 2024).

Weeks, J. 2012. Queer (y) ing the 'modern homosexual'. *Journal of British Studies*, 51(3), 523–539.

Weeks, J. 2015. Beyond the categories. *Archive of Sexual Behaviour*, 44(5), 1091–1097.
Weeks, J. 2016. *Coming Out: The Emergence of LGBT Identities in Britain from the 19th Century to the Present*. Quartet Books.
Wells, M., Glennan, C.E. and Seage, C.H. 2024. 'It's a difficult situation to be an asylum seeker in the UK. It's not easy at all': An exploration of the social and psychological impact of seeking asylum in Wales. *Journal of Health Psychology*, 29(14), 1629–1639.
Wemyss, G. 2018. 'Compliant environment': Turning ordinary people into border guards should concern everyone in the UK. *The Conversation*. Available at: https://theconversation.com/compliant-environment-turning-ordinary-people-into-border-guards-should-concern-everyone-in-the-uk-107066 (accessed 19 July 2023).
Wessels, J. 2012. HJ (Iran) and HT (Cameroon): Reflections on a new test for sexuality-based asylum claims in Britain. *International Journal of Refugee Law*, 24(4), 815–839.
Wessels, J. 2013. Discretion in sexuality-based asylum cases: An adaptive phenomenon. In Spijkerboer, T. (ed) *Fleeing Homophobia: Sexual Orientation, Gender Identity and Asylum*. Routledge. 78–106.
Wessels, J. 2023. *Concealment Controversy: Sexual Orientation, Discretion Reasoning and the Scope of Refugee Protection*. Cambridge University Press.
Weststrate, N.M. and McLean, K.C. 2010. The rise and fall of gay: A cultural-historical approach to gay identity development. *Memory*, 18(2), 225–240.
Wheaton, O. 2018. Immigration officers 'rewarded with cake for arresting most illegal immigrants', trade union claims. *The Independent*, 15 June. Available at: https://www.independent.co.uk/news/uk/home-news/cake-reward-ice-immigration-officers-arrest-most-illegal-immigrants-a8400256.html (accessed 17 October 2024).
White, S.K. 1999. As the world turns: Ontology and politics in Judith Butler. *Polity*, 32(2), 155–177.
Wilding, J. 2021. *The Legal Aid Market: Challenges for Publicly Funded Immigration and Asylum Legal Representation*. Policy Press.
Williams, A., Cloke, P. and Thomas, S. 2012. Co-constituting neoliberalism: Faith-based organisations, co-option, and resistance in the UK. *Environment and Planning A*, 44(6), 1479–1501.
Wimark, T. 2021. Housing policy with violent outcomes: The domestication of queer asylum seekers in a heteronormative society. *Journal of Ethnic and Migration Studies*, 47(3), 703–722.
Winter, A. 2019. Online hate: From the far-right to the 'alt-right' and from the margins to the mainstream. In Lumsden, K. and Harmer, E. (eds) *Online Othering: Exploring Digital Violence and Discrimination on the Web*. Palgrave Macmillan. 39–65.

Wodak, R. 2020. *The Politics of Fear: The Shameless Normalization of Far-right Discourse*. SAGE.

Worth, O. 2023. The great moving Boris show: Brexit and the mainstreaming of the far right in Britain. *Globalizations*, 20(5), 814–828.

York, S. 2022. *The Impact of UK Immigration Law: Declining Standards of Public Administration, Legal Probity and Democratic Accountability*. Springer.

Yoshino, K. 2000. The epistemic contracts of bisexual erasure. *Stanford Law Review*, 52(2), 353–461.

Yuval-Davis, N. 2000. Citizenship, territoriality and the gendered construction of difference. In Isin, E. (ed) *Democracy, Citizenship and the Global City*. Routledge. 171–189.

Zanghellini, A. 2009. Queer, antinormativity, counter-normativity and abjection. *Griffith Law Review*, 18(1), 1–16.

Zanghellini, A. 2020. Antihumanism in queer theory. *Sexualities*, 23(4), 530–548.

Zetter, R., Griffiths, D. and Sigona, N. 2005. Social capital or social exclusion? The impact of asylum-seeker dispersal on UK refugee community organizations. *Community Development Journal*, 40(2), 169–181.

Zisakou, S. 2024. Feeling queer, feeling real: affective economics of truth in queer asylum politics. *Ethnic and Racial Studies*, 1–22.

Zotti, A. 2021. The immigration policy of the United Kingdom: British exceptionalism and the renewed quest for control. In Ceccorulli, M., Fassi, E. and Lucarelli, S. (eds) *The EU Migration System of Governance: Justice on the Move*. Palgrave Macmillan. 57–89.

Zounlome, N.O., Wong, Y.J., Klann, E.M. and David, J.L. 2019. 'I'm already seen as a sexual predator from saying hello': Black men's perception of sexual violence. *Journal of Interpersonal Violence*, 36(19–20), 10809–10830.

Żuk, P. and Żuk, P. 2020. 'Murderers of the unborn' and 'sexual degenerates': Analysis of the 'anti-gender'discourse of the Catholic Church and the nationalist right in Poland. *Critical Discourse Studies* , 17(5), 566–588.

Index

References to notes show both the page number and the note number (231n3).